THE SYSTEM IS THE KEY AT ROULETTE

Other Books By The Author

Veterans Employment Preference Statutes: A State-by-State and Federal Government Handbook, McFarland & Co., Jefferson, NC (2001)

THE SYSTEM IS THE KEY AT ROULETTE

A Practical Guide To Interpreting Occult Patterns
And ***Winning*** At Casino Gaming

By V. I. Brown

iUniverse, Inc.
New York   Bloomington

The System Is The Key At Roulette
A Practical Guide To Interpreting Occult Patterns
And Winning At Casino Gaming

iUniverse books may be ordered through booksellers or by contacting:

iUniverse
1663 Liberty Drive
Bloomington, IN 47403
www.iuniverse.com
1-800-Authors (1-800-288-4677)

ISBN: 978-1-4401-3887-4 (sc)
ISBN: 978-1-4401-3886-7 (ebook)

Printed in the United States of America

iUniverse rev. date: 1/12/2010

BLESSED BET PUBLICATIONS
Website: www.blessedbetpubs.com

THE SYSTEM IS THE KEY AT ROULETTE

DISCLAIMER

The information contained herein is promulgated for information purposes only. No passage in this book should be construed as advocating gaming in any form, or of advocating a belief in occultism or its various forms. This information is meant for individuals who, when purchasing this book, already have an interest in the subject matter contained herein. Accordingly, this book is designed for the general public to augment the existing body of knowledge of the subject matter. The author and publisher thereby disclaims responsibility for any losses, financial or otherwise, which the purchaser may incur when partaking of gaming in any form as a result of having reviewed this information, or when attempting to make practical use of the enclosed theories concerning occultism. Accordingly, the author and publisher offers no warranty, express or implied, that the purchaser will profit from this book.

For my father and grandfather who both spawned and perpetuated a proud family tradition of successful gaming.

Contents

Introduction

The author has been a regular practitioner of roulette for nearly twenty-five years. As such, he has uncovered the fact that patterns will always materialize in this game. If one can see patterns in the numbers which occur, and thereby deduce approximately when a number or a group of numbers should occur, then one should indeed have an edge over the "house." Because of his insights the author is compelled to share these in order to augment the existing body of knowledge concerning the casino game of roulette. Better to inform the public of information of which it has heretofore likely been ignorant. In addition, the author desires to demonstrate to the gaming public that it can be as creative as the author in playing this game.

A collateral task upon which the author embarks here is to seek unification of seemingly diverse subject matter: (1) games of chance (2) number theory and (3) the occult. The author will demonstrate herein that there is a link among these three subjects because the standard theory of numbers, especially as it pertains to gaming in general, is hereby rendered obsolete. There is an element of the occult in roulette and in other games of chance. This occult element causes numbers which occur in these games to behave in ways which belie the established pattern, that is, according to theory.

In order to make his case that roulette numbers are not what they are purported to be, that is, always random, the author observed and documented his observations of numbers occurring on the wheels of one gaming casino. These will be discussed below and they have been documented in the Figures which are offered later in this book.

The author's credentials to examine and to explain this subject matter are quite informal. There is no school of which he is aware which formally trains an individual to play the game, aside from the training schools which gaming establishments offer to employees. He has never attended such. However, he has gamed at roulette in every gaming establishment, save one, in Atlantic City, NJ which is one of the three premier gaming cities of the United States, and indeed of the world. Other locales where he has played the game are in five of the six gaming establishments in metropolitan St. Louis, MO, and also in San Juan, P.R. and Port Au Prince, Haiti. It was in Atlantic City casinos that the author first recognized the patterns which he describes herein. It was in the casinos of metropolitan St. Louis where he began to document these.

Further, the author has also read many books on the game of roulette. He therefore knows that no individual has ever written a comprehensive book on the subject. The author hereby offers this work which is comprehensive in that it explores all aspects of the game, and certainly in greater detail than any other work heretofore available.

I. RECOLLECTIONS

Before examining the theories which he seeks to promulgate, the author first offers the following recollections as an observer of or a participant in roulette:

Scenario #1: *Trump Taj Mahal Hotel & Casino, Atlantic City, NJ*

At a roulette table the wheel was spun, the ball dropped and the first number was (00); second spin: the wheel spun, the ball dropped and the next occurrence was (00); third spin: the ball dropped to a black number; fourth spin: the ball dropped into (00). There was a collective, audible gasp among all of the players.

This scenario indicates the prevalence of the Universal principle detailed below under Elements Of The Occult In Roulette/Universal Principles. The Universal Principle which applies here is that the (0) and (00) are usually associated with black numbers. More often than not, these two will usually precede or follow black numbers. Further, the green numbers (0) and (00) and black numbers tend to precede and follow one another at precise intervals, more often than not. This can be seen in examining the Figures provided below and also each accompanying Narrative. A glaring example of this phenomenon can be observed in Figure 26.

1

Scenario #2: *Resorts Hotel & Casino, Atlantic City, NJ*

A player approached a roulette table, gave the dealer $35.00 and asked for seven red "nickels." The player placed all of the "nickels" on (9). The wheel was spun and the ball dropped into (9). The player departed with $1,260.00. The entire process took about three minutes.

In this scenario and also that following, note that the amount which the player collected included the amount won and also the bet. One should always remember that when one hits a number, the bet belongs to the winner. This is detailed in The Practice Of Roulette/Odds/Probability Of Winning, detailed below. This is also detailed under Types Of Bets within the same section. In this case the bet paid 35 x $35.00 or $1,225.00, plus the $35.00 bet, for a total of $1,260.00.

Scenario #3: *Wild, Wild West Casino, Atlantic City, NJ*

A player approached a roulette table, gave the dealer $200.00 and told the dealer to place the entire amount on (21). The wheel spun and the ball dropped into (21). The player collected $7,200.00 and departed after less than three minutes.

Here again the payoff on the "straight" bet was 35:1 or 35 x the $200.00 bet. The amount which the player collected also included the $200.00 bet, for a total of $7,200.00. Further, this scenario is offered because of the unusually large amount bet. Every gaming establishment has a maximum amount that players are allowed to bet. The amount in question was the maximum allowed in that establishment and in every casino in which the author has gamed in Atlantic City, NJ. These maximum bets are modified however at the discretion of each casino, depending upon the desires of selected clientele. See below.

Scenario #4: *The Sands Hotel & Casino, Atlantic City, NJ*

A player had placed a total of $1,000.00 on (17) and all of the eight surrounding numbers. The player had covered all of these numbers with "split" and "corner" bets while also covering the primary number with a "straight" bet. The wheel was spun and the ball dropped into (17). The player collected a total of $36,000.00 on all of the types of bets which he had made

It is indeed unusual for a bet of this magnitude to be allowed in any gaming establishment. As detailed below in The Practice Of Roulette/ Types Of Bets, each gaming establishment has a set minimum and maximum amount allowed for each type of bet. The usual practice in the gaming establishments of Atlantic City, NJ is to allow no more than $200.00 to be placed on a "straight" bet. All of the other types of the bets which the individual had made are likewise normally limited to a set amount, depending on the probability of winning. One must always remember however that the probability of winning a bet, irrespective of the type of bet made, is precisely the same, *relatively* speaking. This is detailed below under the same section. The point here is that the player must have secured special permission from the casino management in order to have placed such a large bet.

Scenario #5: *The Claridge Hotel & Casino, Atlantic City, NJ*

A player approached a roulette table, gave the dealer $1,500.00 and drew fifteen black chips. He then placed one chip on each of fifteen numbers. The wheel was spun and the ball dropped. What did the player win? Squat. The player immediately departed with an expression of tearful anguish.

In this scenario, the player obviously failed to avail himself of the game's attributes such as the symmetric nature of the game. If he had diluted his bet to allow for more spins, concentrating on fewer numbers, then he may have hit one of them. Further, he failed to consider the different types of bets allowed and apparently desired to make a "killing" by betting only "straight" bets. The player suffered handsomely. If he had formulated a strategy by "clocking" the wheel, he may have observed patterns in the numbers which may have allowed him to appreciate his starting bet handsomely.

Scenario # 6: *Trump Plaza Hotel & Casino, Atlantic City, NJ*

A player had placed $15.00 on the black ("outside" bet). The wheel spun and the ball dropped into one of the zeros: (0) or (00). Believing that all of the bet was lost, the player departed the table.

Here the bettor was guilty of a cardinal sin in any game of chance. He failed to familiarize himself with the rules of the game. Further, he declined to avail himself of the advice which each casino is required to provide players. He only needed to read the placard which is located on each roulette table which specifies that bettors who place an "outside" bet of this type, would be returned half of his bet in the event that one of the zeros occurs when one places a bet on either the red or the black.

Scenario #7: *Caesar's Palace Hotel & Casino, Atlantic City, NJ*

The author was observing a game of roulette when the (31) occurred. The (31) then repeated. The author concluded that it would behoove him to bet the (31). He then placed money on this number. The wheel spun and the ball dropped into (31).

Numbers do sometimes occur thrice in a row. Figure 40 gives the listing of the following numbers which the author has personally observed to occur thrice in a row: (4), (5), (6), (7), (10), (13), (15), (19), (23), (24), (27), (30), (31), (34) and (00).

Scenario #8: *The Wild, Wild West Casino, Atlantic City, NJ*

The author was engaged in the game when he observed the (10) occur and then the (3) immediately after. Not more than ten spins later, he observed the (10) again occur. Assuming that this was a "Recurring Pair," and that the (3) would recur immediately after the (10), he bet the (3). The next number was (3). As indicated in the Glossary, a Recurring Pair is two numbers which occur back-to-back or within a precise interval of one another at least twice within a certain interval, though not necessarily in the same order. An examination of the Figures provided later will confirm that this phenomenon occurs quite frequently. A player only needs to detect such a pattern and then take advantage of it.

Scenario #9: *Harrah's Hotel & Casino of Maryland Heights, MO*

The author was engaged in the game when he observed on the wheel opposite what he believed was the classic making of a "sandwich." The sequence of the numbers which occurred was: (30/26/16/16/26). He expected that the next number would be (30). The next number was

(30). As indicated in the Glossary, a "sandwich" is a number surrounded by two identical numbers, which are in turn surrounded by two other identical numbers. In this case, the "meat" of the sandwich was two identical numbers: (16). The "bread" was a group of four other numbers, two of which were identical. This last group of four numbers occurred in perfect reversed symmetry: (30/26/26/30). This author has further once observed a "green sandwich": (0/00/00/0).

II. The Purpose Of This Book

A. To Advocate Overcoming Adverse Odds

The general aim of this book is to inform the public that "You *can* beat the 'House'." The game of roulette has been structured so that each number which occurs should be completely random. Further, the odds against a player winning any money in this game are quite adverse: 38:1. This book will instruct the player on how to stack the aforementioned odds more in one's favor. Upon completion of this book, the reader should be informed how to interpret patterns which always occur in the numbers on any roulette wheel, anywhere. When these patterns are detected, one should then be able to determine, sometimes with pinpoint accuracy, when a number or a group of numbers will occur. The 5.26% advantage which the House has over the player in American-style roulette should therefore be eliminated. As detailed in The Practice Of Roulette below, the payoff on a "straight" bet, placed on one number of the thirty-eight possible, is 35:1. However, the odds of winning on such a bet is only 38:1. Accordingly, the odds favor any establishment in which one is gaming.

B. To Promulgate The Relationship Between Roulette And Numerology

With the publication of this book, the public will acquire a greater understanding of numbers and how they occur either naturally or supernaturally. The term *naturally* pertains merely to the numbers which the author observed occurring on various wheels in gaming establishments. He merely charted in a pre-arranged format the numbers as they occurred. No attempt was made to distort them or to manipulate these numbers. Here the apt phrase is "Whatcha see is what occurred."

The term *supernaturally* pertains to the patterns which can be seen in the numbers. Anyone with only a basic understanding of mathematics knows that each occurrence of a number on a roulette wheel is completely independent. In theory, no occurrence of a number has an effect upon any other occurrence. However, when one examines the multiple occurrences of the numbers occurring on a wheel, one can always see pronounced patterns. Many of these patterns can be quite astounding, as one can see by examining the Narratives and the chart associated with each Narrative. These are provided later in this book. Accordingly, this is indicative of the author's theory that such multiple occurrences which demonstrate such patterns may indeed be outside of the scope of the natural world. That is, the apparent forces which cause the numbers to form such distinct patterns can therefore be labeled *supernatural*, in that these forces cannot be seen or explained. The author will demonstrate that these forces are always present because the resultant persistent patterns cannot be ignored.

To reiterate, this game is theoretically one of numbers which are supposed to always be completely random. This author hereby contends that the numbers which occur in roulette are not always so. He further contends that there are supernatural forces continuously at work which cause the numbers in this game to show pronounced patterns. The author is convinced that these patterns cannot happen by chance.

With respect to the aforementioned supernatural forces, one of the most profound manifestations of these forces are labeled by the author

Equation Search Puzzles. (See Glossary). In examining the numbers provided herein, one can often see in a range of numbers pronounced mathematical equations. These the author has highlighted in the charts provided later in this book as Figures 1 through 37. These are also discussed in the narrative which accompanies each chart. Inasmuch as the numbers in each chart can be construed as counterparts to the word search puzzles which one can find in many books and newspapers, they deserve special merit.

In light of the above assertions, one purpose of this book is to advocate that roulette is a subset of numerology, or the occult study of the meaning of numbers. It does indeed mean something when a certain number on a wheel occurs often within a relatively short time frame. At other times, on the same wheel, one can observe that the number(s) in question are conspicuously absent. This can be observed in the charts of number occurrences which are found later in this book. It can therefore safely be stated that roulette is an example of occult or supernatural forces in action. For a more in depth discussion of the relationship between roulette and the supernatural, see Occultism As An Element Of Roulette, below.

III. Occultism As An Element Of Roulette

A. Occultism And Numerology Defined

The Encyclopedia Americana - International Edition (2001) defines occultism as:

> "The philosophy of hidden matters. It usually connotes unorthodox mystical beliefs and obscure magical practices, all implying the presence of some principle outside the scope of the natural world, and therefore inaccessible to scientific study."

Numerology is a subset of the occult, or occultism. This subject deserves to be part of this discussion because the "bottom line" is that roulette is a game about numbers. The same Encyclopedia Americana defines numerology as:

> "The occult study of the meaning of numbers. It is often used to uncover secret events or to forecast the future.

> When so used, numerology is a form of divination, or fortune-telling. As a form of divination, numerology is a type of magic. The Greek mathematician Pythagoras developed a number system which claims that all things are number. Accordingly, number influences the essence of things. Thus, number is the mediator between the divine and the earthly."

The author is not an advocate of occultism, *per se*. Further, he is an adherent to a religious faith which precludes a belief in sorcery, witchcraft and similar activities. He does however assert that there is a link between occultism and the game of roulette. Accordingly, because of his observances of number patterns in this game, the author is compelled to believe in numerology.

The author is convinced, as should the reader be upon completion of this book, that the number patterns which can frequently be observed in roulette cannot possibly have occurred by chance. This book will prove that there is an element of occultism in roulette, and that this game should therefore be afforded a place in the study of numerology. One aim of the author is therefore to promote access to the scientific study of phenomena which have heretofore been obscure, but which are quite obvious and which appear to influence numbers.

Lastly, in a distinct departure from the study of numerology as defined, this book will dwell on the *relationships* between or among numbers, not the *meaning* of numbers. The reader might concur however that when the numbers occurring on a roulette wheel show distinctive patterns, or that the wheel appears to be biased for or against certain numbers, then this must *mean* something within the "supernatural" realm. (For our purposes, the terms "numerology," "occult," "occultism," "powers that be," " the gods" and "supernatural" will be used interchangeably).

B. Elements Of The Occult In Roulette

1. The Validity Of Numerology

Pythagoras may have been onto something, if not also on something. Numbers don't lie. Often one can observe in roulette that the numbers appear to have a symmetry, or pattern, which the author does not believe had occurred by chance. He will provide herein strong evidence to support this contention. This book will demonstrate that there are obvious supernatural forces at work which cause the numbers in this game to behave the way that they do.

Refer for example to Recollections/Scenario # 1, above. The (00) occurred three times in four spins of the wheel. Also, the bias towards the (00) was interrupted only by one black number. The author has personally observed that the green numbers, both (0) and (00), and the eighteen black numbers frequently occur together. Refer to Figure 40 in which the (26), a black number, and (00) are listed as one of the Standard Pairs which can frequently be seen in this game. Refer also to Figure 26 which demonstrates how these two numbers are often paired. Accordingly, the occurrence of a black number between the occurrences of (00) was not a surprise when the author observed the sequence of numbers in Recollections/Scenario #1.

As indicated in the above definition of occultism, certain matters have heretofore been hidden. With the publication of this book, the public will acquire a greater understanding of numbers and how they occur naturally, or *supernaturally*. The occurrence of some of the numbers which will be examined herein may indeed be outside the scope of the natural world. The forces which cause these numbers to form distinct patterns can therefore be labeled *supernatural*, in that these forces cannot be seen or explained. However, the author will demonstrate that these forces are always present because the resultant persistent numerical patterns cannot be ignored. The reader is accordingly invited to examine the numbers which have been prepared in chart form in Figures 1 through 37. A description of the patterns therein is also provided in the narratives which accompany each figure.

2. The Relative Frequency Of Numbers

Refer to Scenario #4 above. The individual in question seemed to know that the (17) is a number which occurs frequently. The reader should be interested to know that the author observed the same individual in another casino some weeks prior, hitting the same number with the maximum bet allowed in that casino. He seemed to understand, as does the author and many frequent players, that the (17) occurs more often than the (1), for example. One should visit a casino and then observe that players will usually bet the (17) more often than the (1), as has the author observed. The author proves this contention concerning the relative frequency of the (1) as opposed to the (17) in Figure 38. According to the list of numbers in the roster in Figure 38 and their rankings, the (17) has been verified to occur 2.65% of the time. This is considerably more frequent than the occurrence of the (1) which occurs a mere 2.4% of the time. The aforementioned gentleman appears to be of the same mind as the individual detailed in the section below entitled *Roulette In The Popular Culture* concerning the (17). Accordingly, this phenomenon that certain numbers will occur more often than others is one of the most obvious manifestations of the influence of the supernatural in roulette.

3. Universal Principles

In addition to the charted observations in the Figures 1 through 37 which follow, there are other phenomena which the author has observed which are peculiar to this game. The phenomena which follow are general observations of the author and are indicative of principles which he believes can be universally applied. However, before examining the first five bullets below, one should keep in mind that in accordance with the general rules of probability, there should always be an equal occurrence of the various attributes of this game. That is, a black number should always be followed by one that is red, an even number should always precede one that is odd, etc. However, examination of the charted numbers in the Figures provided later should dispel this myth. Repetitive occurrences of numbers of a like attribute such as large numbers in the Figures are often quite astounding. For these reasons, the author hereby asserts that:

o   Like color usually follows like color. More often than not, a red number will follow one that is red. The same can be said for black numbers;

o   Even numbers will follow those which are even, more often than not. The same can be said of odd numbers.

o   Numbers of the same column tend to repeat themselves, more often than not. One only need examine the charts provided later in this book and observe that numbers occurring and then recurring within a short time frame in the same column is quite a common phenomenon;

o   Numbers in the same dozen tend to repeat themselves, more often than not. Likewise with the numbers within a column, one only need examine the charts provided later in this book and observe that numbers occurring and then recurring within a short time frame in the same dozen is quite a common phenomenon;

o   Bias in the numbers occurring on a particular wheel can always be seen. Such bias can be based on color (red/black), the column bias referenced above, consecutive bias, bias based on one of the ten digits 0 - 9, bias based on numbers with a common denominator or of a common multiple, the dozen bias referenced above, bias based on numbers divisible by two which is an even bias, or numbers not so divisible which is an odd bias, bias based on numbers straddling one of the six "lines" on the playing board, or bias based on one of the thirty-eight numbers on the wheel. Refer to Figures 1 through 37 and the accompanying narratives to see how these types of biases are always prevalent;

o   Numbers will often occur simultaneously on adjacent wheels. Refer to the three sets of Figures 16 & 17, 18 & 19 and 34 & 35 for a demonstration of this phenomenon;

o   Certain numbers will often occur in combination with one another. These common pairings are labeled Standard

Pairs. Refer to the list of Standard Pairs in Figure 40. Refer also to the charts in Figures 1 through 37;

o   The (0) and (00) are usually associated with black numbers. More often than not, these two will usually precede or follow black numbers. Further, the green numbers (0) and (00) and black numbers tend to precede and follow one another at precise intervals, more often than not.

o   Numbers will often repeat themselves, either immediately or at precisely defined intervals. The author therefore contends that the phenomenon which he has labeled "Kismet" is always apparent. This is in accordance with *The Rule Of Twenty*, below;

o   Numbers do occur thrice in a row. While this phenomenon is not exactly common, neither is it rare. (Refer again to Figure 40 for a listing of numbers which this author has personally observed to occur in such a manner);

o   Certain numbers tend to occur more often than others. The author has proven this in the *Vital Statistics* which are provided in Figure 38. (For a cinematic portrayal of a player's passion for a particular number, refer to *Roulette In The Popular Culture*, below).

o   In games of chance other than roulette where the numbers are supposedly random, one can also observe patterns. The author accordingly asserts that the supernatural influence in games of this type is therefore universal. (Refer to the numbers in Figure 40 under "*Dice Rolls*" which the author observed in a game of casino dice (craps));

o   Patterns are transitory. One should find that any patterns or observations of numbers occurring frequently at any point in time, only last for a limited interval. One may therefore become engaged in this game and appear to be having significant "luck" hitting certain numbers. Players are therefore cautioned that their "luck" will eventually subside, sooner or later. For further discussion of this subject, refer to the section entitled *Clocking*, below.

Knowledge of these Universal Principles might have been invaluable to the couple described in (6) below under Roulette In The Popular Culture/Popular Conceptions Concerning Roulette. Had the couple been familiar with these Principles, that couple would have understood the above principle that (0) and (00) are usually associated with black numbers. The couple would therefore have known that if they had waited for one of the green numbers, either (0) or (00), to occur before placing their bet, then this would likely have signified that the next number would be black. This couple would thereby likely have stood a better than even chance of doubling their "even money" bet. Further, if the couple was familiar with the casino rules which predominate in some casinos, then they would have stood some chance of recouping half of their bet. In every casino in which the author has gamed in Atlantic City, NJ, he has found the casino practice of reimbursing players half of their bet when the "even money" bet is placed on a color, and the number which occurs is one of the green, (0) or (00). Conversely, the author has gamed in five of the six casinos in metropolitan St. Louis, MO, and he has yet to encounter this practice. For an explanation of this rule, see Glossary under *En Prison*, *Reimbursement Rule* and *Surrender*.

C. The Numerology Of Gaming

1. Similarities between roulette and other games of random numbers

This book will address numerology as it pertains to gaming in general, not just as it pertains to roulette. The number patterns which can frequently be seen in this game can also be observed in other games of chance such as dice (craps), for instance. This book will not dwell at length on the numbers of that game, however. The author will leave the writing of a book about that game to "dice aficionados." However, one thing which these games, roulette and dice, have in common is that both center around the occurrence of numbers which are supposed to be always random. (See *The Practice Of Roulette*, below). To reiterate, one aim of this book is to dispel this myth of random numbers. Numbers are not always random because of supernatural forces which are continuously at work. To reiterate, upon completion of this book the player should be able to detect such patterns and thereby better stack the odds in one's favor.

a. Craps (Dice)

Refer to Figure 40. This figure shows that patterns can sometimes be observed in the rolling of dice, in addition to those which can be seen in roulette. Under the section entitled *Dice Rolls*, one can see that two sets of numbers were observed on two different days. The author cannot confirm that these numbers were observed at the same table. However, the author did observe pronounced patterns in each set of observations, which will be discussed below. Note that in Figure 40 the author recorded these numbers in the same manner as those which he observed on the roulette wheel. That is, he began at the top of each column and then he progressed down to the end of each column of twenty. The next column was then begun.

With respect to the observations on 28 September, it appears that "The Gods" decreed that the (8) would be the number which would show a pattern. Beginning at row twelve, one can see in all four columns that the shooter favored this number, though probably not by choice.

That is, "Kismet" (See Glossary) occurred four times, in that the (8) occurred four times at precise twenty roll intervals. What is doubly remarkable however is the fact that this pattern continued to the first two columns of the next row. What is triply remarkable is the (8) appearing at precise twenty roll intervals at row eight in columns three and four. For these reasons the (8) is highlighted in **bold** therein.

With respect to the observations two days later on 30 September, the "Powers That Be" seem to have declared that the (9) and the (11) were the numbers chosen by them to reflect their power to influence numbers. Note that in five instances which are concentrated in the first nine rows of the four columns, the (9) and the (11) are paired. This can be seen (a) at the first row in columns three and four, (b) at the fourth row in columns two, three and four, (c) at the fifth row again in columns two through four, (d) at the eighth row in columns one and two, and lastly at the ninth row in columns three and four. Also note that this pair can once again be seen at the bottom of the third column and at the top of the fourth column. Lastly, observe that these numbers were not charted on either 11 September or on 9 November. This is evidence, as the author states later in this book, that the date on which one plays this game does not necessarily influence the occurrence of particular numbers. As in the preceding example, each instance where the (9) and the (11) are paired is highlighted in **bold** therein.

D. The Numerology Of Roulette

1. The Prevalence Of Patterns

As it pertains to the game of roulette, numerology has special meaning. To reiterate, the numbers which one will observe in this game are not always random. A review of the numbers in the Occurrences, Figures 1 through 37 below should confirm this contention. Further, the patterns which one can see in this game frequently allow a player to determine approximately when a number or a group of numbers will appear. It could go without saying that doing so would give the player a substantial advantage over The House. Refer to Scenario #8 under *Recollections*, above. This is an excellent example which demonstrates that one can discern when a certain number will likely occur, and then "Beat The House." The author has labeled this phenomenon of two numbers occurring back-to-back or within a precisely defined interval of one another, and then recurring together in some form, a Recurring Pair. (See Glossary).

2. Mathematical Considerations

The author is not a mathematician. He is therefore not qualified to assess the mathematical odds for or against certain phenomena discussed herein occurring. For example, refer to Figure 21 and note that the (15) occurred and then recurred twice at precise twenty and forty spin intervals. This phenomenon is one of the most striking instances of *Kismet* which the author has observed. The odds against a number behaving in this manner must be quite astronomical. However, the author will leave the task of computing such odds to those who are competent in the fields of mathematics and in gaming. Further, the author solicits information from those who can compute such mathematical odds.

3. Clocking

a. Definition/Purpose

A Cardinal Rule in utilizing the theories herein is to "clock" any wheel which one intends to play. The general idea is to determine the "character" of the wheel at any particular point in time. This entails merely (1) observing the numbers which occur in order to determine which ones are then prevalent, or "hot," or (2) determining if any numbers appear to have any relationship with one another. In this regard the author has found that often certain numbers will appear together. That is, they frequently occur in close proximity with one another, or that they seem to appear at given intervals in relation to one another. These the author has labeled *Recurring Pairs* and *Standard Pairs*. A Standard Pair is two numbers which recur commonly, either together or within precise intervals of one another. A Recurring Pair is two numbers occurring back-to-back or within a precise interval at least twice, though not necessarily in the same order, for a limited interval. These two numbers do not normally occur together in this game, as do

Standard Pairs. This phenomenon can also occur for a trio of numbers. (See Glossary). The charted Occurrences in Figures 1 through 37 and also the listing of Standard Pairs in the chart of Special Numbers in Figure 40 which are provided later, should confirm these contentions.

b. Other Opinions

Frank Scoblete in his book *Guerilla Gambling: How To Beat The Casinos At Their Own Games*, substantially concurs with the author's position on this subject. He states therein that "There is only one sure way to beat a wheel and that is to clock it." Scoblete also concurs with the author's finding that "clocking" is quite a time-consuming, tedious task.

c. Devices

The author has made a regular practice of recording the numbers which he observes in this game. For this he uses a standard chart with twenty rows and any number of columns. The reason why this format is used is explained below under Occurrences/Methodology/Tools. Further, many casinos provide similar charts for the convenience of the players. Before commencing play, one should always ask.

Another device which can be helpful in "clocking" is the electronic monitor which one will find in all of the "world class" casinos of Atlantic City, NJ, for example. The author has found this device in use in all of the casinos in which he has gamed in that city. He has gamed in all of the casinos there, except one. Players are however advised that even an electronic device will malfunction periodically. The author has personally observed that these devices will frequently display numbers which did not occur, or else they will display multiple times the number(s) which did occur. In addition, the author is of the opinion that some of these electronic monitors have been programmed to display numbers other than those which have occurred. The author has noticed this phenomenon particularly in one mid-western casino. The apparent aim of the casino, or the manufacturer, is to confuse and thereby baffle players from detecting number patterns. Accordingly, if one habitually depends on the monitor, then one should also habitually monitor the monitor.

Players are further advised that the devices which portray numbers which have occurred on a wheel are quite limited in scope. The author has not found any of such devices which display more than eighteen of the previous numbers. This amount varies among casinos depending on the manufacturer of such devices. Accordingly, in order to acquire a functional idea of the numbers occurring on a wheel so as to adequately discern any useful patterns, players might be well advised to record their own numbers.

d. Caveats

A word of caution is in order here. The supernatural influence in the numbers is such that any patterns or numbers which frequently occur, can and do change. One may indeed detect a distinct pattern or relationship between or among certain numbers at one point in time. However, the "Powers That Be" are indeed whimsical, and they change the numbers at their will. In other words, one can expect to "clock" a wheel one day and observe pronounced patterns or frequently occurring numbers on that wheel. However, if one returns to the same wheel the next day, the patterns and frequent numbers which one observed previously, will likely have gone. The author uncovered this fact by concentrating his "clocking" primarily on one wheel in a particular casino. Accordingly, one cannot and should not expect to observe the same pattern of numbers on a particular wheel, all the time. In other words, "Clocking" is an ongoing activity.

e. Casino Decorum

One last word concerning "clocking" is in order. It has been the author's experience that casinos discourage activities which they construe as" loitering." That is, casinos do not like to observe persons in their establishments observing but not gaming over an extended period. Accordingly, one should not, or could not observe a wheel for the number of spins which Scoblete suggests would be necessary to adequately "clock" a wheel in order to discover any biases which the wheel might have. The establishment where one would attempt this activity would likely tell one in no uncertain terms to either commence play, or leave. Therefore, if one makes a habit of "clocking," as has the author, then one might be well advised to habitually limit the amount of time allocated to this activity, as has the author. In this respect, one might also be well advised to inform the floor person what one is doing if one has been there for some time without betting, and then ask how long one would be allowed to "clock" a wheel. Lastly, one might find that some casinos actually encourage this activity, though only on a limited basis.

Further on this subject of casino decorum, a favorite ploy of the author is to simply place one bet of five "lines" (see Glossary) upon first approaching the wheel which he intends to "clock." The author merely places a $1.00 chip on each line. He is therefore betting twenty-nine numbers. The author thereby has a 29/38 chance of hitting one of these numbers. He always bets the "top line" when betting in this manner. (See Glossary). If one of these numbers hits, then the author wins $1.00. If none of them do, then he has only lost $5.00 if he is "clocking" a $5.00 table. However, he has earned the right to "clock" the wheel. The casino's management cannot therefore accuse the author of loitering.

4. Special Numbers

Another example of the potential with which one can predict approximately when numbers will occur can be seen in the Special Numbers/Standard Pairs which are listed in Figure 40. To reiterate, the charted numbers therein frequently occur together, either back-to-back, in close proximity to one another or within precise intervals of one another. Accordingly, frequently one can observe that when one occurs, then the other will also occur soon after. Those who frequent gaming casinos are therefore invited to observe the roulette numbers which occur, in order to confirm this contention. For convenience here, wherever these numbers have occurred in combination in the Figures 1 through 37, they have been noted and have been designated a *Standard Pair*.

5. The Black Pentacle

This group of numbers is so named because: (1) they share a common color, (2) they are a group of five, and (3) they have special significance. The numbers (6/10/17/26/31) have been observed to have a special relationship with one another. From many years of playing this game, the author has uncovered this special relationship which he is compelled to individually address, and which he contends is the result of supernatural influences.

a. The special relationship among the numbers of The Black Pentacle

The special relationship among the numbers of The Black Pentacle is that: (1) these numbers seem to occur in clusters, and (2) they frequently occur within precise intervals of one another. Accordingly, one can frequently discern approximately when they will occur, or that these numbers should occur within a certain range. Refer to Figure 39 and the section therein labeled The Contiguous Black Pentacle. Observe that the five numbers in question occurred contiguously in column two at rows three through seven.

To make practical use of this special relationship among these five numbers, one of the author's favorite gaming techniques is to chart numbers in the usual manner in columns of twenty. When two of the numbers of The Black Pentacle are observed adjacent to one another in separate columns, then this is his signal to begin betting all five numbers using the system in Figure 42. The author has found that this technique seldom fails.

1. Other Theories

One other noted author on this game substantially agrees with the author in some respects. J. Edward Allen in his book *The Basics Of Winning Roulette* asserts his belief that two of the numbers in the author's Black Pentacle are special. He has stated that the (10) and the (26) are those to which the player should pay the most attention.

b. Sample wager of the numbers of The Black Pentacle

Further, the author has proven that one can bet only the numbers of The Black Pentacle and then increase one's beginning wager handsomely. This can be seen in Figure 43. Note that this Figure is a culmination of both Figures 29 and 42. The author merely took the actual occurrences in the former Figure and then adapted these to the generic system found in Figure 42. Figure 43 is the result. Here one can see that if one had bet only the five numbers in question over a certain interval, then one would have more than tripled one's beginning wager.

In Figure 42 the titles of the various columns and their purposes are thus:

Round is the basic interval which the author suggests should be used in gaming (see Glossary);

Spin is the attempt within the given round. Note in Figure 42 that one is allotted sixteen spins;

Number Hit is the number on which one has a winning bet. Note that the *round* ends when the desired number is *hit*. The end of the *round* is thereby signified by a "+" beside the *number* which one *hit*;

Bet is the amount allocated for the spin in question. Note that this number progresses throughout the *round*;

Cum. Bet is an abbreviation of the phrase *cumulative bet*. This is the amount of money which one has expended during the *round*. Note that this number progresses throughout the round;

Poss. Win is an abbreviation of *possible win*. This is the maximum amount which one can win, given the *spin* which one is on and the size of one's *bet*;

Net Win is simply the difference between the *cum. bet* and the *poss. win*;

Total Net Win is the total of all of the money which one has won since the first *round*. Note that this figure is the previous *total net win* plus the money which one has won in the current *round*.

Lastly, observe that this type of bet is the same as that detailed below under Systems/Symmetric Systems and in Figure 44. In this instance as in that, one merely selects five numbers and then bets them continuously.

Refer to Figures 1 through 37. Unless where otherwise indicated, the numbers of The Black Pentacle have been highlighted in order to demonstrate the frequency with which they occur, and their relationship with one another.

6. The Extreme Supernatural

Refer to Figure 39 under the heading The Extreme Supernatural. The author was compelled to provide these numbers in order to demonstrate the power that "The Supernatural" can exert over numbers. Note that two sets of numbers were observed on two different dates. The author cannot confirm that these two sets of numbers were observed on the same wheel. They were observed in the same casino. However, note the fact that the same numbers (shown in **bold**) occurred at the same intervals on both dates. This phenomenon was observed by the author quite by chance. He noticed this unusual phenomenon because he just happened to record the two sets of numbers side-by-side on the same chart.

7. A Potential "Red Pentacle"?

The author has considered the fact that there might be a "Red Pentacle," that is, a group of five red numbers which have a relationship similar to that which the author has observed among the aforementioned five black numbers. Although he has not yet uncovered this phenomenon, though he has earnestly tried to do so, he continues to search. He also solicits any information from readers who have discovered this or any similar phenomenon.

E. Natural vs. Supernatural

To reiterate, a primary purpose of this book is to advocate recognition of the presence of forces which cause the numbers in this game to behave abnormally, that is, not always in a completely random manner. Previously the author has mentioned the contention of others that these forces are "supernatural," in that they cannot be seen or explained. The author hereby modifies that contention. The forces in question may indeed be explained scientifically, and therefore be quite "natural."

It is a scientific fact that possibly the primary force which controls the Universe is *gravity*. Even the most cynical among us would have to concede that there must be a force which keeps our planet and the eight others which comprise our Solar System in perfect orbit around a huge ball of fire, without being consumed by such. In addition, it has been proven scientifically that the gravitational force which the moon exerts upon the earth causes the natural phenomenon called *tides*. These forces cannot be seen, but the effects that tides have on the earth are always observed and they have been explained in precise detail in almanacs, for example.

To expand upon these facts of natural phenomena, there may also be a *natural* force at work in the Universe which influences numbers in this and in other games where the numbers are supposed to be random. In other words, it is indeed possible that the gravitational force which holds our Universe together and also causes tidal action, is also that which causes numbers in games of chance to behave in the manner that they do. Further, it is possible that the position of our planet in the

Universe at any point in time will have some influence on the numbers here. The author welcomes any theories in this regard. He further offers this contention as food for thought.

Lastly on the subject of *natural* vs. *supernatural* forces, the author will leave it up to the reader to guess which force predominated when the following scenario occurred. He was playing the game at the Wild, Wild West Casino of Atlantic City, NJ and betting several numbers simultaneously. One of the numbers was (18). After several attempts to hit this number, he declined to bet it but continued to bet the others which he believed might occur. Incidentally, several other players at the crowded table were also betting heavily on the number in question. On the spin in which the author declined to bet that number, while several other players continued to bet heavily on it, also while continuing to chant "eighteen, eighteen!" loudly, the (18) occurred. It therefore may indeed have been possible that the chants of the several players who bet heavily on the number reached the ears of "The Gods" and caused it to occur. This scenario may also have been an effort on the part of the "The Powers-That-Be" to convey to the author that he should always adhere to his own guidelines.

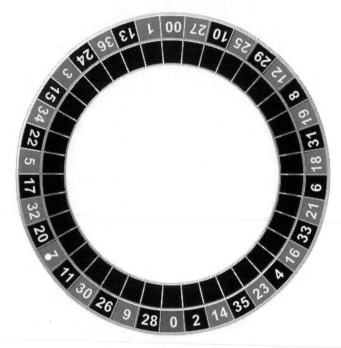

Effigy of a standard U.S. Roulette wheel

IV. Roulette In The Popular Culture

A. Popular Conceptions Concerning Roulette

This game has historically been an integral part of American culture, if not also world culture. This subject deserves discussion because the public is entitled to have misconceptions about this game dispelled, or to have general conceptions confirmed. Roulette has been showcased in motion pictures, for example. The following are titles of motion pictures in which roulette has been prominently portrayed:

(1) The Barbary Coast (1935)

(2) Casablanca (1942)

(3) The Big Sleep (1946)

(4) Dona Flor And Her Two Husbands (1978)

(5) Lost In America (1985)

(6) Indecent Proposal (1993)

In all of the above titled films a game of roulette was demonstrated. The game figured prominently in the plots and it was played by the characters therein according to the following scenarios:

In (1) above, a player bet heavily on "outside" bets of a certain color. He was apparently not aware that the wheel where he made these bets had been "fixed," that is, the wheel was altered to cause numbers or colors other than the ones which the player had made, to occur. The player thereby lost substantially.

In (2) above, a player was engaged in this game and was losing heavily. A casino executive approached and, aware of the individual's plight, subtly advised the player to bet the (22). The dealer who was conducting the game was also alerted. The (22) then occurred. The player was advised to let the bet ride. The number repeated. Another player, remarking at the "unusual" occurrence of a number repeating, questioned if the game was honest. He was assured that the game was as "honest as the day is long!"

In (3) above, a major character won over $14,000 at roulette and desired one more spin in order to make an "outside" bet on red. The casino owner reluctantly agreed to cover the proposed bet in even thousands. The wheel was spun and the ball dropped to a red number. The bet was doubled to $28,000. The wheel in this private club was obviously not "fixed."

In (4) above, a gentleman had a passion for playing roulette. His passion was for one number: (17). He won (and possibly lost) substantial sums betting this number.

In (5) above, an inexperienced player became heavily engaged in a casino game of roulette. She bet substantial amounts on (22) and likewise won substantially because this number was, at that point in time, a "hot" number. Then the number became "cold." Not only were the player's substantial wins eroded, but the player also lost most of her (and her husband's) life savings. The (22) was however a good choice to bet because this number occurs more often than most, having occurred 3.03% of the time in the 2,379 observations which the author took to prepare this book. The (22) is also the third most frequently occurring number which the author observed. See Figure 38 which lists the relative frequencies of all of the thirty-eight possibilities on the wheel which the author has uncovered.

Further concerning the (22), refer to Figure 22 and the accompanying Narrative. Observe that during the interval in which the author "clocked" the wheel, the (22) was indeed "hot," occurring seven times out of sixty spins, or better than 11% of the time. Observe further that the (22) was the mode. Lastly, observe that the (22) was only one of two numbers which experienced Kismet and therefore supported the author's Rule Of Twenty. (See Glossary).

In (6) above a couple in desperate need of money approached a roulette wheel in an effort to double their bet of $1,000. After some thought, but no attempt to "clock" the wheel, the couple decided to place an "outside" bet by which one could either double his money or lose it all (see Glossary). The couple then placed the entire bet on a color. The wheel was spun and the color opposite what was bet occurred. The bet was lost.

B. Correction Of Popular Conceptions Concerning Roulette

One should never encounter a "fixed" or a "biased" wheel in the United States and environs. Gaming in the U. S. is heavily regulated by each state government where it is practiced. Indeed, every responsible state government has very strict laws over gaming which both protect the public and ensure that taxes are properly levied against the casinos. This fact should dispel the myth of an intentionally biased wheel. Further, casinos do not have to "fix" wheels (or any other gaming devices) in order to "fleece" the public. As previously stated, gaming odds are stacked in favor of the "House" in roulette. In this and other games of chance such as dice, the number of players guarantees that gaming houses will always profit handsomely.

With respect to wheels which may be unintentionally biased, that is, those which may have a mechanical malfunction which might cause certain numbers to prevail, the public should likewise have no cause for alarm. One should also never be able to "clock" a wheel in order to determine if a wheel is biased for mechanical reasons in favor or against certain numbers (thereby enabling players to have a competitive edge over the House). Some authors have suggested that these scenarios can occur. State governments require regular testing of all of the devices in question in order to ensure that they are mechanically sound. This is the responsibility of each casino. The gaming authorities with whom the author has conversed have assured him that casinos have been made aware of their responsibility in this area and that they do adhere to applicable state regulations.

Lastly on the subject of unintentionally biased wheels, the author contends that the observations discussed herein prove unequivocally that such a wheel does not exist. The reason for this, to reiterate, is that most of the 2,379 observations which he took in order to prepare this book were observed substantially on one wheel. The author observed no consistent pattern each time he observed numbers. Further, when the author did notice a pronounced pattern on one day, he often noticed that the next day the previously observed and documented pattern was gone. The author played the wheel in question substantially for at least five days per week, over an extended interval.

V. The Practice Of Roulette

A. Fundamentals

1. "American-style" Roulette

To reiterate, this book will only address the game of roulette as it is practiced in the United States and environs, including the Caribbean. Though the author has not played the game in Europe, he has been informed upon good authority that roulette is played differently there than it is in the U. S. The primary difference is the inclusion of a (00) on roulette wheels in the Western Hemisphere. Most European wheels have only a (0). However, some of the "world-class" casinos in the U. S., particularly Bally's Hotel & Casino of Atlantic City, NJ have some wheels set aside for players who prefer the European style. Since the odds on these wheels are stacked more favorably towards the player, the houses which have these wheels usually require a minimum bet higher than that required for the other type of wheel.

2. "House" Advantage

With the inclusion of the (00) on the wheel, the percentage by which the "House" has advantage over the player is 5.26%. The reason for this advantage is that, though the wheel has thirty-eight numbers which can occur, and the chances of hitting a number is therefore 1:38, the pay out for hitting one number is only 35:1. The 5.26% advantage accounts for the difference. Accordingly, if one wants to play the game where the odds are better stacked in favor of the player, then one should seek out and frequent those establishments which have Single Zero (0) wheels.

3. Wheel Configuration

For the uninitiated, roulette is played with a wheel which has thirty-eight slots numbered from 1 – 36 and also the aforementioned (0) and (00). The numbers are often divided by slats which can vary in height (depending on the manufacturer) and which cause the ball to center on a number. The numbers are evenly divided between red and black numbers. Those numbers which are designated red and black are consistent among gaming establishments. The (0) and (00) are always green and are located opposite one another on the wheel. Further, the thirty-six numbers are always situated in designated spaces on every wheel. One will not find any deviation from this standard configuration among locales. Observe the diagrams of a modern roulette board and wheel which have been provided. Note that in most cases on the wheel consecutive numbers are located directly opposite (not adjacent) one another, (1) being opposite (2), (35) being opposite (36), etc.

Here a special word is in order concerning the slats which separate each of the numbers on the wheel. These of course vary with the manufacturer. Some authors on this subject have suggested that the width or the height of the slats may influence the numbers which occur on the wheel. Some have even suggested that certain wheels where the slats are of a certain height are preferable to others. In one Atlantic City casino the author has played on a wheel where the place where the ball rests was merely an indenture in the wheel. The wheel had no slats. This author disagrees with the aforementioned suggestion that numbers are influenced by the type of slats, or the existence thereof, for the simple reason that he has observed patterns on all wheels where he has played. These patterns he has observed on wheels where the slats are quite pronounced, and also on those where the slats are non-existent. In other words, one can always observe patterns on any wheel, irrespective of the type of slats on the wheel, or the existence thereof.

4. Board Configuration

The companion to the aforementioned wheel is the board upon which one places a bet. All of the numbers 1 – 36 are represented thereon, including the (0) and (00). Note in the effigy of a playing board which is provided that the board has a certain symmetry, with three vertical columns and also twelve horizontal rows. There is an equal amount of numbers (12) in each column and in each row (3). Each of the three groups of twelve rows is referred to as a "dozen." (See Glossary). One peculiarity concerning the board which differentiates it from the wheel is that the rows and columns are not perfectly symmetrical with respect to the amount of red and black numbers contained in each. Note that while each dozen has an equal amount of red and black numbers, the three columns differ in that they have an unequal amount of each. For instance, in the middle (second) column, one finds eight black numbers but only four red. Another peculiarity is that there are only two numbers which are adjacent to one another on both the wheel and on the board: (0) and (2).

5. Roulette Is Purportedly A Game Of Random Numbers

The obvious reason for the numbers being so situated on the wheel is that the numbers which occur when the game is being played should always be completely random. That is, both the red and the black, or the even and the odd, or the high and the low numbers should have an equal chance of occurring. The obvious rationale for configuring the numbers as such was to preclude a player from being able to predict the occurrence of a number, or of a group of numbers. To put it another way, theoretically one should never observe a "bias" in the occurrences. However, to reiterate, the author herein proves this contention wrong. The author contends that one can frequently observe a bias among the numbers. A primary purpose of this book is to demonstrate how to detect such bias in the numbers which will occur on any wheel at any point in time, and therefore improve one's game. The reason why the author so contends is because of the influence of the occult, or the "supernatural" referenced above. Evidence of this influence follows.

B. General Principles Concerning Types Of Bets

Besides dice (craps), the author is of the opinion that roulette is the most fascinating casino game because of the number and types of bets which one can make. A "Cardinal Rule" in roulette and any game of chance is that one should never place a bet without first thoroughly becoming familiar with the game rules including: (1) the types of bets allowable, (2) the odds of winning a bet and therefore (3) the payoff on a winning bet. The author's experience is that some people will do precisely that, i. e., bet without understanding the rules. However, one should further understand that the House provides assistance in this regard. Each table has a placard near the edge of the table which explains the basic rules of any game. On it one should learn (1) the minimum bet, and (2) the maximum bet allowable on each number. With respect to roulette, one should also learn the rule concerning "outside" bets, that is, bets in which the odds of winning on such a bet is less than 5:1. (See Glossary). Further in this regard, it is the dealer's job to advise players who do not fully understand the rules. Accordingly, if one is confused then one should ask. However, if one examines this book prior to gaming, then one should have been thoroughly familiarized with the rules and also indeed have a substantial advantage and thereby be in a position to "Beat The House" without having to contemplate how one should bet.

1. Outside Bets

a. The Practice Of "Surrender"

The last rule above concerning "outside" bets appears to be the most confusing, or the one which some players simply choose to ignore. Refer to Scenario #6 under Recollections, above. The standard rule in "world class" casinos is that when one places an "outside" bet on either the red or the black, and a green number (0/00) occurs, then the player will be reimbursed for half of the bet. This practice is known in some circles as *en prison*. In European gaming establishments this practice is known as *"surrender."* That is, if the scenario just described does occur, then one *surrenders* one half of one's bet. The author has actually observed on several occasions in Atlantic City, a center of "world class" casinos, where players actually were reimbursed for half of their losing bet, but they failed to realize this. They therefore departed with their money still on the table. These individuals were obviously not "world class" bettors. The author has observed this practice of reimbursing half of such a bet in every casino in which he has gamed in Atlantic City, NJ. However, this practice which is also known as the *reimbursement rule* is not standard among all U. S. casinos and it can vary widely by region. The author has not seen this practice in any Midwestern casino.

Also with respect to outside bets, the rules are not consistent among all casinos. For example, the general rule among the "world class" casinos is that the minimum bet must be on each outside bet, irrespective of any other bets which one has on the table. That is, if the minimum bet at the table is $15.00 (which is the usual minimum in such casinos during peak periods), one cannot place $13.00 on the "inside," and also $2.00 on an "outside" bet. Each bet on the inside *and* on the outside must be a least $15.00. Therefore, if one desires to bet inside and also on the red and also on the even numbers for example, then one must have a minimum of $15.00 on each bet. That is, the player must have at least $45.00 on the table.

However, there is some variation on the above rule concerning outside bets. At least one Midwestern casino allows a bettor to spread the minimum bet around the board in any manner which the bettor desires. That is, if the minimum table bet is $5.00, then one can bet $2.00 inside, $1.00 on the black, $1.00 on the even and $1.00 on a column. Again, if one is confused about the bets allowed, then one should ask.

b. Outside Bet Progression

These types of bets are quite popular and they can indeed pay off handsomely. This can be seen in several of the Figures which are provided later where a wheel seems to be biased in favor of numbers of like attributes. An excellent example can be seen in Figure 2 in column two from rows seven through sixteen. The wheel experienced a marked *even bias*. (See Glossary). For the convenience of the reader, the author also has provided in Figure 39 under the section Outside Bet Progression what one would have won if he had concentrated on an outside bet. Assuming that the occurrence of the (12) at row seven would have been the signal to commence concentration on betting even numbers, then starting with the next spin and letting the bet "ride" for the next nine spins, one would have turned a $5.00 bet into $2,560. The action would have and should have stopped there however because the next number after the (22) would have been odd. One would then have lost all of one's winnings and also the initial bet. Also, in a "world-class" casino such as those located in Atlantic City for example, the limit on outside bets is almost always $2,000. One would not have been allowed to let the bet "ride" any longer.

2. Odds/Mathematical Probability Of Winning

Also with respect to confusion about the types of bets, this author was admittedly initially confused about the payoffs on some kinds of bets. Based on his observations, he believes that others are also so confused. For this reason, one should realize that the odds of winning on each type of bet is governed precisely by simple arithmetic, or by mathematical formula. That is, it is safe to state that the probability of winning a bet at roulette, irrespective of the type of bet made, is precisely the same, *relatively* speaking. To give an example, a "straight bet with $1.00 on two adjacent numbers is precisely the same as a "split" bet of $2.00 on both numbers. This is because the payoff is exactly the same. The payoff on $1.00 bet straight on either of two adjacent numbers is $36.00 ($35.00 plus the bet). The payoff on a $2.00 bet split on the same two adjacent numbers is also $36.00 ($34.00 plus the $2.00 bet). Likewise, the payoff on $4.00 bet on a "corner" with four adjacent numbers is $36.00 ($32.00 plus the $4.00 bet). A general rule of thumb which one should always remember is that the greater the degree of risk, the larger the potential payoff. Or put another way, the greater the probability of winning, the lesser the potential win. These always go up or down in direct proportion to one another, in precise mathematical odds, irrespective of the type of bet.

3. Relative Desirability Of Different Types Of Bets

There appears to be some debate concerning what types of bets are desirable, or which are preferable over others. Walter I. Nolan, in his book *The Facts Of Roulette*, advises against the "Top Line" Bet (betting the "Top Line" consisting of (0/00/1/2/3). (This is the only way in which one can bet five adjacent numbers with one chip, incidentally). Nolan advises against this type of bet because, he contends, the odds are more greatly stacked against the bettor than in other types of bets. This author disagrees for two reasons: (1) the odds of winning this bet are no different than for any other type of bet because each number on the wheel has exactly a 1:38 chance of occurring, and (2) there is always the *supernatural* influence. Therefore, if the pattern of numbers which occur at any point in time indicates that any of the aforementioned five numbers are "hot," then it might be in one's best interests to bet any of them, or the entire Top Line. (See Glossary for the definition of a *hot* number).

C. Types Of Bets

Following are all of the types of roulette bets in descending order of risk:

1. **straight** - one number, paying 35:1; chance of hitting, 1:38;

2. **split** - two numbers, paying 17:1; chance of hitting, 1:19;

3. **three numbers**, paying 11:1; chance of hitting, 3:38. A special note is in order here. Should one choose to bet three adjacent numbers other than (0/00/2), this is commonly referred to in casino jargon as a "**street**" bet. A bet placed on (34/35/36) would be referred to as "34 street." It is always referred to by the number closest to the bettor. The (0/00/2) configuration is commonly called "the Basket." Note that a street bet or the Basket is the only means to place one chip on three numbers;

4. **corner** - four numbers, paying 8:1; chance of hitting 2:19. Note how the chance of hitting is precisely double that of the split bet;

5. **top line** - five numbers, paying 6:1; chance of hitting, 5:38. Note that the probability of hitting any five numbers would be precisely the same as those on the Top Line (0/00/1/2/3);

6. **line** - six numbers, paying 5:1; chance of hitting, 6:38. This bet is so named because it straddles one of the eleven lines dividing the streets, other than the Top Line. It is always referred to by

the two numbers on either side of the line closest to the bettor. Note also that the probability of hitting with this type of bet would be precisely the same as for any six numbers;

7. **column** - twelve numbers adjacent and horizontally, paying 2:1; chance of hitting, 6:19. Note that the probability of hitting is precisely quadruple that of the street bet. This and all those which follow are "outside" bets (see Glossary) which are considered by the House to be separate from others;

8. **dozen** - twelve contiguous numbers, paying 2:1; chance of hitting, 6:19. This is the exact counterpart to the column bet. The probability of hitting is also quadruple that of the street bet.

9. **even/odd** - (either the even or the odd) paying even money (1:1); chance of hitting 18:38 or 9:19;

10. **red/black** - (either the red or the black) paying even money; chance of hitting: 18:38. A special note is in order here. If one loses this type of bet and one of the green numbers (0 or 00) hits, then one is returned half the bet in many casinos; and

11. **high** (19-36)/**low** (1-18) - (either the high or the low) paying even money; chance of hitting, 18:38 or 9:19.

Types (1) through (6) are "inside" bets. Those remaining are "outside" bets. (See Glossary).

To reiterate, this game can vary widely by region within the U. S. One Midwestern casino offers at one of its tables what the casino labels an "action bet." For some reason the casino views the seven numbers (10 – 15) and also (33) as having special significance. This "action bet" allows players to bet all of the seven numbers simultaneously by placing the bet on a certain portion of the table. The payoff is 4:1. In consultation with a dealer at this table, the dealer labeled this bet "the worst bet on the table." This author tends to concur, in that he has never availed himself of this "action bet."

Lastly with respect to the types of bets which one can make, refer to Scenario #5 under Recollections, above. Recall that the bettor placed fifteen "straight" bets on the table in anticipation of hitting one. If the player had "split" his bet among thirty different numbers, then he stood an excellent chance (15:19) of receiving a 20% rate of return on investment. His $1,500 bet would have thus been spread to thirty numbers. If one of them had hit, then the player would have received $1,800.00 because the bet would have paid 17:1, plus his original bet.

D. Standard Table Practices

There is a certain decorum which is unique to this game. That is, roulette has certain practices which are standard. They are as follows:

Roulette Decorum - Roulette is the only game where each player may be assigned a unique color of chip. The reason for this should be obvious. With numerous players who can stack bets on one number, the dealer must have the means to determine who has won what. Accordingly, players may and frequently do request a certain color of chip. This is why one can hear at any roulette table that a player will call out: "Color!" This often means that the bettor is requesting a unique color of chip. Or a player is merely requesting to buy into the game. When the bettor finishes, he should again call out "Color!" and then redeem table chips for regular casino chips which can be used at any table. A player can play with regular (casino) chips but be advised that no more than one player is allowed to use casino chips at one time for inside bets. In most casinos any number of players may use casino chips for outside bets. However, at least one Midwestern casino only allows one player to bet with casino chips for both inside and outside bets.

In conjunction with the above, a table chip can be any value of one's choice. The usual practice at the table is to *place* one's money as close to the dealer as practicable. One should then watch the dealer count. The dealer should then announce the amount and ask the player what type of chips are desired. The player then informs the dealer whether table chips or casino chips are preferred. For example, if one wants to play with $5.00 chips and make "inside" bets, and one also wants a unique color, then one should tell the dealer: "Nickels inside." The term "nickel" is commonly used as a slang term for a $5.00 chip. The table chips which one selects will have a specifically defined value as long as one player uses them. When the player finishes and the chips are redeemed, the chips have no value. One is cautioned to always redeem table chips at the table where the chips were purchased. They have no value anywhere else in the casino or at any other roulette table. Also, refer to Scenario #2 under Recollections, above. The word "gave" was emphasized because one never hands anything to a dealer. They are instructed not to accept things handed to them. The author has been informed that this practice is for security purposes. The dealers are being watched by the floor persons who are being watched by the pit bosses or shift managers, who are constantly being monitored by the "eye in the sky" (security cameras). Every dollar which changes hands at each table must be observed and therefore recorded. Accordingly, one always *places* money on the table.

To elaborate on the above information concerning chips, if one does not want to appear ignorant, one should never approach a table and ask: "What are the _____ colored chips worth?" The author can confirm upon first-hand experience that this is a question which is frequently asked in casinos by persons who are either uninformed on the rules of this game, or who may be developmentally disabled. To reiterate, the colored chips can be of any value which one wants, depending upon the amount which one wants to bet and also the House rules for the table in question.

Betting - To reiterate, there is a limitation on the amount on the types of bets which one can place. All tables will have a placard situated near the edge of the table which normally describes the minimum and maximum amounts allowable on inside and outside bets. World-class casinos usually also spell out in detail the rule for outside bets on colors mentioned above. This jargon is not always readily understood, so if in doubt, then one should ask.

Refer to Scenario #4 under Recollections, above. All of the "world class" casinos of Atlantic City, NJ where the author has gamed limit the amount of an "inside" bet at $200.00 on any number. The reason for this is obvious: that they do not like to pay out more than $7,000.00 at a time. Accordingly, the irregularity in Scenario #4 under *Recollections* above is that the player was allowed to place such a large amount of money on an "inside" bet. It is obvious that the individual must have arranged with the casino beforehand in order to place such a large bet. A general rule of thumb is that casinos will modify their rules of gaming for special customers who are known to wager large amounts of money.

With respect to Scenarios #2, 3 and 4 under *Recollections*, above, note that the amount of winnings include the initial bet. When a player wins any bet, the bet belongs to the winner. Accordingly, in calculating winnings one should always figure on having the bet returned. This should be kept in mind when reviewing the generic systems which are provided later.

When the next spin is about to begin, the dealer will tell the players to "Place your bets." The dealer will then spin the wheel in one direction and then roll the ball in the opposite direction. A few seconds before it is apparent that the ball will drop into a number, the dealer will announce "No more bets," or simply wave their hand over the board to signify the same thing. If a player tries to place a bet after this announcement, dealers are required to remove the illegally placed bet. Some will actually throw the chips back at the player. When the ball lands, the dealer will announce the winning number, place a marker on top of the winning bets and then sweep all of the losing bets from the board. Winning bets are paid accordingly. Caution is in order here. Winning bets must not be touched on the board until the dealer takes the marker from the winning number. That is opposed to winnings which are often placed off the board in front of the winners.

Players are allowed to touch these types of winnings upon initial receipt.

Casino Chips - In conjunction with the above, one would be well advised to always select a unique color chip. In addition to the obvious reason mentioned above, having one's unique color would preclude another player from taking one's chips when one is distracted. However, if one desires to play with casino chips inside or outside, this is allowable. Chips of different denominations have different colors and these colors are substantially consistent among casinos. One may use chips in denominations of $1.00 (white), $5.00 (red), $25.00 (green) or $100.00 (black). Some world-class casinos such as Caesar's and Trump Plaza in Atlantic City have twenty dollar chips (yellow). It is also a common practice among such casinos to also have $2.50 chips (pink). These establishments will not usually allow one to play pink chips inside, however. For the truly "high rollers," such establishments also have $500.00 chips (purple), $1,000.00 chips (orange) and $5,000 chips (grey). At the Harrah's Hotel & Casino in Atlantic City, NJ this author observed something which he has not seen before or since: a $10.00 chip.

The author is not aware of the origin of the system of uniform color gaming chips. However, he has been informed that the reason for the $20.00 yellow chips which are used in the two above named casinos is that much of their clientele is East Asian. The $20.00 chip appeals to this ethnic group, especially in certain games such as baccarat. Perhaps the preference of East Asians for this denomination is in keeping with their reputation for intelligence and perception. Perhaps they are also aware of the significance of the Rule Of Twenty, discussed below, and this may be why they favor such chips.

Dealers - With respect to dealers, remember that they are only human and can therefore make mistakes. Sometimes their mistakes can be in one's favor. The author can recall an occasion where he finished his play and then "cashed out" (exchanged table chips for casino chips). He had exactly thirty-nine chips. The dealer counted them and called out to the floor person, "Forty!" On some occasions the dealer will also miscount the money which is placed before them before play commences. One should always therefore (1) *place* one's money as close to the dealer as is practicable, (2) do not take one's eyes off one's money, (3) watch the dealer count the money, and then (4) ensure that one's count agrees with the dealer's.

Further on the subject of dealers' fallibility, a player should not always rely on a dealer to place bets where they are told. It is common practice to put bets in front of dealers and ask that the dealer place the bet on a desired number. Some casinos encourage this practice. However, to reiterate, dealers are only human/fallible. The author can recall on one occasion where he put a bet before a dealer and asked that the bet be placed for him. He could not reach the desired number. After putting the bet in front of the dealer, he called out, loudly, "7!" The dealer apparently didn't hear. The author called out his desired number again, twice, while the ball was in motion. The dealer either did not hear or was not paying attention. Just before the dealer called off all bets when the ball was about to drop, the author then rose from his chair and hurriedly placed his bet on (7). The winning number was

(7). Players may therefore want to make a habit of positioning himself so that he may reach any desired number, if possible.

Further with respect to dealers, they do also sometimes give two players the same color table chips. If this would happen, then two players with money on the winning number would be distressed indeed. This actually happened to the author in an Atlantic City casino, twice. One should also beware of a "dirty stack" of table chips, that is, one which has more than one color.

Lastly with respect to dealers, the author has personally observed that some dealers, and not just roulette dealers, are not completely honest. He was on one occasion compelled to report the activities of a dishonest dealer to the casino's management. From what the author had observed, the dealer in question was not pocketing monies which he had "ripped off" from a player. This is virtually impossible. The author was of the impression that the individual merely got a "kick" out of shortchanging players. This was not the only instance of such behavior which the author has observed.

Accordingly, in order to mitigate against being "ripped off" by a dishonest dealer, one should always (1) count one's chips immediately after buying into a game but before commencing play, (2) count one's chips before "cashing out" at a table, (3) watch the dealer count the chips, and (4) make sure that both counts agree. If there is the smallest discrepancy, then it should promptly be brought to the attention of the dealer and/or the floorperson.

Roulette table

VI. The System Approach

A. General Theory Of Systems

It could go without saying that ideally, the roulette player wants to place one bet on one number, and then hit on the first attempt. This can and does happen occasionally. (Refer to Scenarios #2 and #3 under *Recollections*, above). With only a 1:38 chance of doing so however, the probability of doing this is slim indeed. Accordingly, those who are knowledgeable concerning these matters have advocated a "system" approach. The author concurs, primarily because roulette is amenable to systems. This is because of its mathematical/arithmetical/symmetrical nature. Moreover, the author has studied the numbers which occur in roulette over an extended period. He has uncovered the fact that often pronounced patterns materialize in these numbers. Accordingly, if one can observe such a pattern then this will likely enhance one's ability to predict approximately when a number or a group of numbers will occur. One then has an edge over the House. In order to demonstrate his contentions, the author has included the section "Occurrences" which is provided later in this book.

On the subject of systems, Allen has further stated:

> "The slow pace and variety of bets
> available has made the game a favorite

of system players for over 200 years. A system is merely a form of money management. Most systems are based on progression: increasing the size of the bet after a loss. The system player hopes to build up a series of small gains while avoiding a large loss."

This author substantially agrees with Allen's assessment. If one plays with real money, then one should have some means with which to manage one's hard-earned cash. This contrasts with what the author always observes in casinos: that most players do not appear to have any system to their play. One player which the author has met has admitted that his intention is to "have fun, not to win money." What the author sees mostly are players who indiscriminately place chips on a large amount of numbers in hopes of hitting one of them. Also what often occurs is that many players place large amounts of money on a few numbers in apparent hopes of making a "killing." These betting practices do often work. Quite often however they fail and players either lose large amounts of money or else make a "killing" and then continue playing and eventually give their winnings back to the House. Accordingly, the author has observed that these practices usually fail in the long run. For this reason the author advocates a more structured approach to the game. With a system, one can indeed do what Allen has suggested: build up a series of small gains while avoiding a large loss. Scoblete also substantially concurs with Allen and the author. He suggests that one be a "guerilla gambler," that is, one who "hits, wins and runs with the money."

Allen is also probably correct in his assertion that "most systems are based on progression." This author cannot dispute this statement because he is not aware of any systems which were created or which are advocated by others, with four exceptions. These follow:

1.Historic Systems
These systems are widely known to serious practitioners of roulette, or those who are widely read about gaming in general. If one were to research books which have been written about this game, then one should find them described therein.

a. The Martingale

This was supposedly used by an individual of the same name who "broke the bank" at Monte Carlo (possibly the premier gaming establishment on this planet). The system is based solely upon outside bets (odd/even). It requires that when one places such a bet and loses, then one should immediately double one's bet. However, to demonstrate that this "system" could be disastrous, refer to Figure 16. In the third column in particular, where the sequence beginning at row five is (30/2 9/00/9/7/29/22/17/28/1/16/29/26), one can see a pronounced altering of even and odd numbers. If for instance a player favored even numbers and began betting them at the fifth row, then he would indeed have doubled his even money/outside bet when the (30) hit. However, if he had continued betting the even and let the bet "ride" on the next spin, then he would have lost all of the initial bet and also his winnings. This is because the next number would have been the odd (29). The next number would have been one of the green, (00). Accordingly, if the casino in question had adopted the Reimbursement Rule, then the player would have been reimbursed half of that losing bet. The player would still be down from where he started. However, observe that the next three numbers would likewise have been odd. A player continuing to bet the even would have lost substantial amounts of money, even with a small beginning wager. The player in question would indeed have doubled his bet on the seventh attempt when the (22) hit. However, observe that for the next six spins after that win, the numbers alternated between the odd and the even. The player would likely have gotten nowhere and would likely have regressed into destitution.

b. The Grand Martingale

This is an extension of the above. When making any type of bet, and then losing, one should likewise double one's bet and then also increase it slightly.

c. The Inverse Martingale

This was supposedly developed for "optimists." (Whoever applied this term to gaming enthusiasts should know that we are all optimists, or we would not be gaming). This system requires that when one wins, one should let the bet "ride" for several spins. This increases the power of each winning bet.

d. The Labouchere

This system is supposedly scientifically based. The system requires that one write a series of at least three sequential numbers, then total the two outside numbers and thereby formulate the amount of the first bet. Accordingly, if one's sequence is (2/3/4/5), then the amount of the starting bet would be $7.00 (2+5). With each win the two outside numbers are eliminated. With each loss the amount of the bet is put at the end of the sequence. Therefore, if the first bet of $7.00 was a winning bet, then the next bet would be $7.00 (3+4). If the initial bet was a loss, then one would add (7) to the sequence. The sequence would therefore be (2/3/4/5/7). The next bet would therefore be $9.00 (7+2).

The author does not recommend the above "systems." He further can only assume that the individuals who devised them were eventually committed to an asylum for lunacy (after having gone broke, of course).

Allen has further stated that "systems have a history all their own." He is correct on this count. With the publication of this book, history will be made and the analysis of systematic play will have advanced to a new level. The author herein promulgates new systems which are more rational than those detailed above. The author will also provide the framework for implementing them.

B.Primary Considerations For Workable Systems

The general theory of the workable systems which are provided herein is based simply on betting as many numbers as possible over as many spins as are practicable. The laws of probability dictate that every one of the thirty-eight numbers on a wheel will materialize, eventually. Accordingly, the longer one can bet a number or series of numbers, then the greater the probability that the player will eventually hit these numbers.

The overall objective in gaming at roulette is of course to prolong the play as long as possible. Also, to concur with Allen's assessment of this game, this author suggests a progression of the size of one's bet at regular intervals throughout the play. See Figure 42 for suggested bet size progressions for gaming at a table where the minimum bet is $5.00. There are certain considerations which one should always keep in mind, however. These are:

minimum bet required - To reiterate, each table has a minimum bet. This amount varies from casino to casino, from table to table within each casino, and also with the time of day. Each gaming house expects a certain rate of return on investment. Each also caters to a clientele which will vary by region. (In this regard, the lowest minimum bet which the author has observed is $1.00 in one Midwestern casino). The various gaming establishments set their minimum bets accordingly. The author therefore knows from experience that on weekdays before noon at Bally's Hotel & Casino in Atlantic City for example, the minimums will be low (usually $5.00). He further knows from experience that in none of the "world class" casinos of that city at 11:00 p. m. on 31 December in any given year will one find a minimum bet required less than $15.00. The reader should also be interested to know that Caesar's Palace Hotel & Casino of Atlantic City, NJ has a table where players are required to bet with chips of at least $5 denomination. The usual table minimum was $10.00 as of this writing.

money - The primary factor which will dictate the system which one can use is of course the amount of funds available. One cannot for example use a four-number based system, betting the minimum with $1.00 chips on four different numbers if the minimum bet is $5.00. In this case, to use a four-number system one would have to bet at least $8.00 per spin in order to bet four numbers with an equal amount on each ($2.00 per number, per spin). This should always be kept in mind when using any generic system such as those provided in Figures 42 through 44.

patience - The player should always resolve at the beginning of play to be patient. This is of course more easily said than done. If one embarks on a certain system betting certain numbers and then observes that every number other than the ones which are being wagered are hitting, this can indeed be frustrating. One is therefore tempted to bet the numbers which are hitting. A player should therefore be patient and expect that the system will bear fruit, that is, that one's number will hit prior to one's funds being exhausted.

persistence - In conjunction with that immediately preceding, one should always resolve to be persistent. To reiterate, if one plays numbers long enough, they will materialize eventually. Once the intended numbers are in play, one should not deviate. The author knows from experience that when a gaming plan is deviated from, then disaster will usually strike and one will probably lose. This is possibly a message from "The Gods" that one should be persistent. Further, one will feel a complete ass when one bets certain numbers which fail to materialize over extended play, then stops betting one or more of those numbers, or decides to wait out one or more spins, then watches as the desired number hits before one has completed a round. For this reason, the following Cardinal Rule should always be observed: Do not skip spins.

Lastly on the subject of persistence, the author has learned from personal experience not to skip spins during a round. On several occasions he embarked on a round in order to hit certain numbers. When these numbers failed to materialize after many spins of the wheel, the author became frustrated. He then decided to not bet the number(s) in question for one spin, or else he decided that he would delete one number from his bet for one spin. The reader is invited to guess which number hit when the author failed to bet.

power of perception - One should acquire the ability to perceive patterns. Patterns are always apparent. Sometimes one can discern when a pattern *begins* to develop. Often one can observe a pattern which *has* materialized. One can then plan one's bets accordingly. The general idea is to select a system which is most appropriate to the pattern which one observes. In this regard, one should be aware that the House often provides substantial help. To reiterate, many casinos including all of the "world-class" casinos in Atlantic City, NJ for example, have attached to each wheel an electronic monitor which shows the numbers which have recently occurred.

To further reiterate, a word of caution is in order here. Any machine will malfunction periodically. Often the aforementioned monitors will portray numbers multiple times when the numbers occurred only once. Sometimes these machines will portray numbers which have not occurred. Further, this author is of the opinion that these machines have been engineered to display numbers other than those which have occurred. The apparent purpose of the machines having been so engineered is to confuse the players. This would preclude players from detecting patterns in order to get an edge over The House. Accordingly, one should make a habit of recording one's own numbers. In this regard, most casinos provide printed charts for the convenience of players. It was by use of such charts that the author recorded all of the numbers provided in the Charts provided later.

Collateral considerations to keep in mind when choosing a system are (1) the proximity of numbers on the wheel, (2) the configuration of numbers on the board, and (3) supernatural forces. Each of these factors will be discussed in turn below where actual systems are detailed or where specific occurrences of numbers are described.

C. Advantages Of Using Systems

There are several advantages to using systems: (1) facility in monitoring one's money and one's play; (2) facility in understanding the game and the various number patterns which often materialize; and (3) the fact that roulette is the casino game which is the most amenable to the system approach because of arithmetic/mathematical/symmetrical attributes. Or more simply put, the game of roulette *is* a system.

With respect to (1) above, the primary object of the game is of course to win money (unless one merely wants to be entertained). One should accordingly have some means to determine at any point in time how much one is ahead. If for instance one wants only to win a certain amount or receive a certain rate of return from one's initial bet, then one should of course create a system in order to accomplish this. The author therefore suggests that the player think in terms of gaming in *rounds*, and then placing one's winnings aside after each *round*. This is another area where Scoblete and the author are in agreement. He is also an advocate of gaming in *rounds*.

Here is an area where one should make an analogy between this game and the game of craps (dice). Craps is a game which is always measured in *rounds*, though this is not a term which the author has ever heard used in that game. At the beginning of each *round*, the shooter rolls a number. Depending on which number initially occurs, this determines the course of the *round*. If the shooter rolls a (7) before he makes his point after the initial "come out" roll, or if he makes his point, or if he rolls a (2), a (3), a (7) or an (11) on the initial roll, then this signifies the end of the *round*. In roulette also, the author advocates that a *round* should end when one hits one's number. Two examples of "*round* gaming" are provided in Figures 43 and 44. When one has learned to approach this game in terms of systematic *rounds*, then this should facilitate one's understanding of the game. The player will thereby likely have become conditioned to thinking systematically. It should logically follow that one will learn to look for number patterns, better to stack the odds in one's favor.

For the purpose of playing this game, a *round* is simply the number of spins that one is allowed according to the system one is using. When gaming at roulette in *rounds*, when a number is hit, then this signifies the end of the *round*. The process then repeats. If one sets aside one's winnings after each hit, then one can tell at any point in time how much one is ahead. Further, if a player configures his chips according to the system which he is using, with a specified amount of chips in each stack for every spin, then he can always at a glance see where he is within the *round*. If he has written his system down and has it within reach, then he can see precisely how much he has won, depending on the spin on which he has hit within the *round*. This incidentally is a favorite technique of the author.

D.Systems

This book will explore two basic types of systems: generic and number-based. Figure 42 is a generic system with which a player can bet any five numbers of his choosing. Every other system herein is number-based. However, with one exception all of these have common attributes. The one exception is the Rule Of Twenty, discussed below. Remember that there is always a myriad of patterns which one can observe in the numbers which occur on a particular wheel. A player is therefore limited only by his imagination concerning the systems which he can devise in order to "Beat The House."

1. Common Attributes

The system detailed in Figure 42 is designed around one basic unit - the *round* (see above). Each *round* is divided into *spins*. All of these systems were designed to allow the player to prolong the play for as long as possible. To reiterate, the general theory behind this system and the systems which are described later, is that the greater the number of *spins* one has in a *round*, the greater the probability that one will hit a desired number. Accordingly, these systems should be allocated a definite number of *spins*. The player must decide which system is appropriate according to the amount of numbers one wants to bet and how much cash he has on hand.

Note that each system referred to herein requires that one raise one's bet at definite intervals. The reason for this is to adhere to a Cardinal Rule: always bet so that one can recoup what one has already committed. Or conversely, one should never bet if one cannot recover the money that one has invested in the *round*.

Figures 42 is only a model for any generic system which one can devise. However, any system should have these attributes:

(1) the amount of spins (**spins**);

(2) the total amount bet each spin (**bet**);

(3) the cumulative amount bet up to and including the current spin (**cumulative bet**);

(4) the total amount that the player could possibly win on the current spin (**poss. win**);

(5) the total amount that the player could win on the current spin, minus the amount that has been sunk into the round (**net win = possible win - cumulative bet**);

(6) the total amount of numbers that have been bet up to and including the current spin (**cum. numbers bet**);

(7) the type of bet used in the current spin (**bet type**);

(8) the spin on which the player raises his bet (**raise**); and

(9) the total amount bet (**total bet**).

2. Generic Systems

These systems are so named because they were not designed around specific numbers on the board or on the wheel. With the exception of The Dynamic Duo, they all can be used with any numbers of one's choosing.

a. The Street System

An excellent example of a generic system is the Street System. The system is so named because it concentrates on the three numbers in any "street." (See *Types Of Bets,* above). This type of bet is popular with players and it has a good payoff with the probability of winning at 11:1. One possible reason for its popularity is that with one exception this is the only means to bet three numbers simultaneously with one chip.

b. The Digit/Last Digit System

This is a three, four or five number system which uses numbers that have the same last digit. The Digit System is a good example of how one can use the symmetry of the game. This system is also the best example of a hybrid which is both generic and also number-based. With this system the player bets only those numbers ending in a certain digit. Note that most of the numbers in this game can be sorted in groups of four each. That is, each of the numbers 1, 2, 3, 4, 5 and 6 can be sorted into one of six groups with four numbers in each group. There are four numbers which end in each of the aforementioned numbers. The numbers ending in (0) are five: (0/00/10/20/30). The numbers ending in (7), (8) and (9) are three each: (7/17/27), (8/18/28), and (9/19/29) respectively. With this system one can also observe the influence of the occult. The Occurrences provided later will show that often numbers occurring on a wheel will show a "bias" (see Glossary) in favor or against numbers ending in a certain digit. The author can state from experience that this system of concentrating only on numbers ending in a certain digit works more often than not.

c. The Board Section System

1. Non-contiguous numbers

With this system the player limits his bet to one of the twelve "sections" on the board. That is, the bet is centered on a third of one of the dozens, for instance, (27/30/33/36). Note that these numbers are contiguous on the board but not so in the usual sequence. The player can of course overlap the dozens at his option. However, one is reminded that it is easier to bet adjacent numbers if one wants to "split" a bet. This is therefore easier than betting four numbers which are dispersed around the board. This type of bet therefore requires a four-number system. This is in contrast with the Wheel Section System described below.

2. Contiguous numbers

On the subject of board sections, this is an area where the player is limited only by his imagination. There are several sections of the board on which the player can concentrate, depending on the amount of cash on hand and the minimum bet required. For instance, one can concentrate on "corners," or four numbers which are contiguous on the board. The payoff on this type of bet is 8:1. See *Types Of Bets*, above. Note that the greatest difference between this "contiguous number bet" and that described above is that with this type of bet one can bet four numbers with one chip.

d. The Wheel Section System

This is the counterpart to the Board Section System above. The difference is that this system centers around any given amount of contiguous numbers on the wheel. This is a popular system which is suggested by a prominent Midwestern casino in a brochure which it distributes to players. The player centers his bet around one number and also the four numbers on either side according to the numbers configured in Figure 41. The author accordingly labels this type of bet a "Radar Bet" because one number is that around which one *radiates* his bet. This system can be used with the five number, sixteen spin system described in Figure 42. It will be demonstrated later that sometimes the wheel will show a "bias" in favor of certain sections of the wheel. In instances such as these, the player might therefore be well advised to bet that section.

Further, in his travels to various parts of the country and also to numerous casinos, the author has found that there are substantial variations from one locale to another, and from casino-to-casino within each locale. For instance, one Midwestern casino has a table layout which was specifically designed for the Radar Bet mentioned above. Adjacent to the standard playing board, this casino offers players the opportunity to place a bet on any one of the numbers on the wheel. The numbers thereon are configured in the same manner as are the numbers on the wheel. The player simply gives the dealer the minimum bet (usually five dollars) which is then placed on one number. This central number and each of the two on either side of that number are all covered. If any of these five numbers occurs, then this signifies a "win." The dealer then places one winning chip on the regular board and then pays the player. Figure 41 is a configuration of all of the possibilities for placing a "Radar Bet."

e. The Rule Of Twenty

This system might also be labeled the Rule Of Multiples Of Twenty. This is not a system, *per se*. Rather, this is a means of detecting patterns. This Rule pertains to a general principle which the author has uncovered and which one might use to govern one's system of play. The Rule is that quite often numbers repeat themselves at precise intervals of twenty, or of forty, etc. The author does not claim that numbers will always act in such a manner. However, the Occurrences which are provided later demonstrate that this phenomenon does occur quite frequently. He will also examine the degree to which this phenomenon does occur. The author has labeled this phenomenon "Kismet." (See Glossary).

To give an example of the degree to which numbers will repeat themselves at precise intervals, refer to Figure 21. Observe that at row four in all three columns, the (15) repeated itself. This extreme example of *Kismet* is not the only extreme example of this phenomenon which the author observed.

To make use of this Rule, after observing and recording at least twenty numbers on a wheel, one simply bets the number which occurred twenty spins previously, or forty spins, etc. This is reiterated below under *The Floating Bet*. Or if one prefers, the number which occurred twenty spins, or forty spins, etc. previously is used to center one's "Radar Bet." Here is another area where the player is limited only by his imagination.

3.Number-based Systems

In these types of systems the player is again limited only by her/his imagination. There is literally a myriad of systems which one can use. Some of these with which the author has experimented to varying degrees of success, are detailed below.

a. The Dynamic Duo

With this system the player takes advantage of the Standard Pairs which are provided in Figure 40. When one of the numbers of a pair occurs, then one simply bets the other number or both numbers until one of them hits. The point here is that the occurrence of one of the numbers in the pair is often a signal to bet the other.

b. The Dynamic Bouncing Duo

This is a variation of the Dynamic Duo, above. In this system a player takes advantage of any Recurring Pairs which are observed. Recall that a Recurring Pair is two numbers occurring back-to-back or within a precise interval at least twice, though not necessarily in the same order, for a limited interval. When a player observes a number which has previously occurred, then this is a signal to bet the number which immediately followed when that number occurred previously, or both. Players might want to make a habit of charting numbers and observing the degree to which this phenomenon occurs, which is quite often.

c. The Floating Bet

With this system one merely bets a certain number or group of numbers which have just occurred. The idea is to alter the bet each spin according to a criteria of one's choosing. A favorite technique of the author is to bet the last five numbers which have occurred. The bet thereby "floats" depending on which five numbers have just occurred. Or, a player can just bet the last number which occurred. If numbers are frequently repeating themselves on the days that the player chooses to bet, then this system can indeed pay off handsomely. A variation of this system might be labeled "Floating Kismet" which takes advantage of the Rule Of Twenty. A player simply waits and observes at least twenty numbers while charting them in the same manner in which the author recorded the numbers in Figures 1 through 37. The player then bets the number which occurred twenty spins previously. Again, if *Kismet* is often prevalent on this gaming day, then this bet can indeed pay off handsomely.

To expand upon the "Floating Kismet" system referenced above, one of the most successful techniques which the author has used is to bet the number which occurred twenty spins previously, and also the number immediately following. He then added to his bet the two numbers on either side of those two numbers. Refer to Figure 16 and also the effigy of a wheel provided. The first two numbers in column one are (10) and (34). After having observed twenty numbers, play would have commenced at the top of column two. Accordingly, his bet would have consisted of the numbers (10), (25), (27) in one group, and also (22), (34) and (15). This is a six number system. As one can see by observing Figure 16, one would have hit the (25) on the fourth spin. The bet would then "float" to the number which occurred twenty spins previously, (9), and also the number immediately following, (15). Accordingly, the bet would "float" to the numbers (9), (28) and (26) and also (34), (15) and (3). Continuing play the player would have hit the (28) on the second spin. Choosing to stay on these same numbers, one would have hit the (28) three spins later. Upon first using this "Floating Kismet" system, the author was astounded by how well it worked. Astute observers would have seen that there was only one example of Kismet in the numbers charted in Figure 16. This can be seen at row fifteen in columns two and three where the (16) occurred. Observe further that Kismet did not occur within the interval in question. However, the "Floating Kismet" system did work without the Rule Of Twenty occurring. Use of this system *anticipates* that the Rule would occur. Just think how well this system would work if Kismet had indeed occurred within the interval in question. This system of "floating" a bet has been found by the author to be successful more often than not. Numbers frequently repeat themselves either immediately or shortly thereafter, or within a precisely defined interval. Accordingly, if one looks to capitalize on repeating numbers, then one might want to "float" his bet according to some criteria. By the way, a staple of casino jargon is: "There is nothing sweeter than a "repeater.""

d. Symmetric Systems

With these types of systems one takes advantage of the symmetry of the game. One merely finds a group of numbers to one's liking which have a common attribute such as the last digit (all numbers ending in (6) for example) and then chooses a generic system such as that provided in Figure 42. Figure 44 is an example of the implementation of such a system.

If one were to query players of this game, one should likely find those who prefer numbers which are multiples of (7). The possible reason for this is the belief promulgated by followers of the occult that the number (7) is lucky. The roulette numbers with this attribute are: (7/14/21/28/35). Accordingly, the generic system provided in Figure 42 is tailored to betting these types of numbers. Refer to Figure 11. The numbers which occurred on the wheel in question prove that one can concentrate only on numbers of a certain like attribute, i. e., those divisible by (7), and wager profitably.

Refer to Figures 43 and 44. Observe in these charts that the successful implementation of this system is contingent upon any one of the five numbers in question occurring at least once every sixteen spins. In Figures 11, 43 and 44 note that this has indeed occurred. Note also that when any one of the desired numbers is hit, then this signifies the end of the round. Note further that in actual implementation of the system in question and betting those numbers, in only one instance did the player have to proceed past the seventh spin. Perhaps this is another manifestation of supernatural forces at work. The "bottom line" is that one would have more than doubled one's money from the $190.00 initial outlay.

4. Negative Systems

The author has observed that many players will admit to betting numbers which they have *not* seen occur. The apparent rationale for this type of "system" is that if a number or a group of numbers has not occurred for an extended period of time, then such a number or numbers is/are due to occur. If one chooses to bet with this "system," then a word of caution is in order. Observe in Figures 1 through 37 that some numbers failed to materialize over an extended period. It could therefore be said that "The Gods" decreed that the day in question was not the day for the number(s) in question to occur. Accordingly, if one chooses to wager in this negative manner, then one might be well advised to first observe a number occurring, then wait for an extended period of time before betting that number. This is in keeping with the Theory Of Probability that over an extended period of time, a number has to occur on any wheel. Recall that "The Gods" in some cases have already sanctioned that the number(s) which one has seen that day, will occur.

However, "negative betting" does have its merits. *Not* betting a number or a series of numbers over an extended interval simply gives the bettor more chances to win. If one is certain that a number or group of numbers will occur at some point, then one can *not* bet these numbers for a given interval. Then, if these numbers have not occurred during this interval, and the player then starts to wager these, the number of spins over which the number(s) failed to occur and the player declined to bet, is the same as getting free spins.

VII. The Non-system Approach

The author has met many players who will readily admit to always betting their favorite numbers. Many will further admit to betting their birthdays or those of family members. Here again a word of caution is in order. However, first the author will provide his observation of how well this practice can work. On 17 September 2004 the author met a fellow player who was betting heavily on many numbers. On one spin he informed the author that he had a premonition that the number which coincided with the day of his birth, (25), would occur. He then placed $25.00 on (25). This incidentally was the maximum allowable bet at the casino in question. Also incidentally this was the biggest bet which the gentleman in question had on the table. The wheel spun and the ball landed in (25).

It would be an understatement that the above player's making a "killing" by betting his favorite number was remarkable. However, what is doubly remarkable is the fact that this is an excellent example of the aforementioned Rule Of Twenty working perfectly, and also an excellent example of the prevalence of *Kismet*. The gentleman in question was not "clocking" the wheel in question. However, the author was. He noticed that the occurrence of the (25) when the gentleman in question made his "killing" was precisely twenty spins after it had occurred previously.

Further, the above incident may be an additional manifestation of the power of the "Supernatural." It is remarkable that the gentleman in question appeared to have had a "brainstorm" at that point in time. This author is loathe to suggest that the individual was merely "lucky." A more apt designation would be that the person was divinely inspired. That is, "The Gods" or God may simply have been compelled to bless him so.

Now for the word of caution: one should never assume that one's favorite numbers or the numbers which one might expect to occur, will actually do so. For instance, one should not assume that the number which coincides with the day of the month would be a "Hot Number." (See Glossary). Refer to Figure 5 which charted numbers that occurred on the 1st day of the month. If one had assumed that the number (1) would frequently occur, then one would have been wrong and might possibly have lost a great deal of money by betting that number. Note that the (1) only occurred once. Likewise, if one had assumed that the numbers (13), (17), (26), (29) or (31) would occur, then one would likewise have been wrong. None of these numbers occurred in sixty spins. (A keen observer would note that this day was a virtual "Odd Black Drought." (See Glossary). This is remarkable because these numbers usually occur frequently according to the Vital Statistics which the author has provided in Figure 38. Refer also to Figures 13 and 20. The observances therein were recorded on 16 and 23 August, respectively. Note that in sixty occurrences neither of these two numbers occurred.

VIII. Occurrences

A. Methodology

In order to make his case that there is a supernatural element in roulette, *i. e.*, that the game is influenced by the occult, the author opted for a structured approach. Figures 1 through 37 are charted observances of the numbers which occurred mostly in one Midwestern casino. Except where noted in the Narrative accompanying each Figure/chart, each chart shows the occurrences on one wheel. Further, each group of numbers occurred over a short time span. This time span was not more than 1.5 to 2 hours. The numbers in each chart are therefore substantially contiguous. That is, the possibility that an extended time element influenced any patterns is virtually eliminated. Further, there was no pronounced lull between occurrences. However, in one set of occurrences the author specified that there *was* a pronounced lull between the occurrence of two numbers. Refer to Figure 27 and to the accompanying Narrative. The author's rationale for providing this set of occurrences was to demonstrate that a long interval between two occurrences does not necessarily mean that the sequence of numbers which were meant to occur, or actually did occur, was disrupted or influenced by an extended interval. To reiterate, an *occurrence* is a number occurring on a wheel. A *hit* signifies winning a bet on a number.

1. Tools

The sets of occurrences in Figures 1 through 37 were recorded by means of a printed chart provided by the casino where the numbers were observed. These charts contain nine columns of twenty rows each. The author merely recorded each number as it occurred. Accordingly, no electronic monitor was involved. There are none in the casino where the author recorded the numbers. To reiterate, most of the occurrences in question were observed substantially on one wheel which was always in operation in the casino in question. In only a few instances were numbers observed on other wheels. These are noted in each Narrative.

2. Documentation

The numbers in the sets of occurrences in Figures 1 through 37 are displayed as they occurred. The author began recording the numbers at the top of each column and then completed the column. The next column was then begun. Note that most of the sets of occurrences contain sixty numbers. The author had no predetermined rationale for recording the numbers in such groups of sixty, other than that he reasoned that this amount would allow any prevalent patterns to be detected.

In recording the numbers the author did have the reader in mind. He logically concluded that anyone who purchases this book might be distressed to have to observe more than sixty numbers at a time. In the Figures where other than sixty numbers are charted, the purpose was to highlight an unusual phenomenon or to make a point concerning the patterns. Further, the author saw fit to provide only thirty-seven sets of numbers because he believed that this amount would suffice to make his case for the theories which he seeks to promulgate.

3. Figure/Narrative Format

a. Figure Format

Each of the Figures from 1 through 37 have been standardized. On the left side of the chart are the numbers which were observed. To the immediate right of these numbers are those which failed to occur. These have been labeled *Non-occurs*. To the right of these "non-occurs" is the frequency distribution of all the possibilities on the wheel and also the frequency of each number which was charted. Each possibility has been highlighted in **bold**. At the bottom of each frequency distribution the Mode is provided. Note that by definition there can only be one mode. Accordingly, if two or more numbers shared the highest frequency, then there was no mode.

The author routinely recorded the date on which each set of observances was taken. Only rarely did he fail to record the date in question. The purpose was to determine if the date, including the day or the month would coincide with the numbers which occurred. That is, the author sought to determine if, for instance, the 14th of July would produce a bias towards the numbers (7) or (14). Accordingly, the purpose was to make the case for or against the presence of the "supernatural" on the wheel in question on the day of the observance.

Below each chart the Recurring Pairs or Recurring Trios are provided. Below these recurring numbers the Formulae which the author observed are provided. These formulae are the mathematical equations which the author observed in the charted numbers. These the author labels "Equation Search Puzzles." These are counterparts to the word search puzzles which one can find in many periodicals. Note that any numbers which comprise the Formulae do not have to be consecutive on the chart, that is, straight up or down a column or across in a row. Formulae can be seen in these numbers often at a right angle.

Lastly with respect to the format of the numbers, each occurrence where one can observe a "supernatural" influence has been marked with either a "*," a "**" (single or double asterisk) or a "+." (plus sign). A "*" only pertains to numbers in the formulae or in Recurring Pairs or Recurring Trios, or to any other unusual phenomenon. Only those occurrences which comprise Kismet are marked with a double asterisk, "**." Accordingly, if a number has both a "*" and a "**," then the number in question is an example of *Kismet*, or a Formula, or a Recurring Pair/Trio, or all of these. Only numbers which occurred simultaneously on two wheels are marked with a "+."

b. Narrative Format

The Narratives are provided in order to explain what the author perceived as unusual phenomena. These are generally a running narrative or explanation of what the author observed that was unusual, and what, generally, would dispel the myth of random numbers. The author did not see fit to organize the Narratives in any particular order. However, the general sequence which one will find are (1) biases, (2) hot numbers, (3) extraordinary phenomena, (4) Recurring Pairs or Recurring Trios, (5) Standard Pairs, (6) Formulae or (7) Kismet. Generally the last sentence of each Narrative describes what the author believes would have been the assessment of the ancient Greek mathematician Pythagoras, or those of his many disciples, of the formulae.

4. Simultaneous occurrences

Figures 16 and 17, 18 and 19 and also Figures 34 and 35 should be examined together as three distinct pairs. These three groups of numbers are the instances in which the author recorded the occurrences on two adjacent wheels simultaneously and then documented these numbers in separate figures. In Figure 37 the numbers were documented on two wheels and then presented as one Figure. The purpose in doing so was to demonstrate that often numbers will occur simultaneously on more than one wheel, or that patterns can sometimes be observed on two wheels simultaneously. This will further buttress the author's argument that the supernatural element, or the occult is always present in this game. Again, the rationale for including only three sets of such simultaneous occurrences was that this would suffice to solidify the author's argument.

Further, in this instance as the wheels were configured the author could not have recorded the occurrences on more than two wheels simultaneously if he had so wanted. The casino where the numbers were observed has only four wheels, with two each adjacent in two separate rooms. However, it is indeed possible that numbers will materialize on more than two wheels simultaneously. The author has personally observed a number occurring on three separate wheels simultaneously in a casino in Atlantic City, NJ.

B. Number Interpretation

The reader is of course welcome to interpret the occurrences in the charts provided in any manner in which she/he sees fit. Being a mere mortal the author has limited powers of perception. Accordingly, he cannot comment on what he has failed to perceive. The notations at the lower left of each set of occurrences are what the author deems noteworthy. The author invites the public to correspond with him concerning phenomena which it observes in the charts provided.

The reader will note that in many instances numbers repeat themselves. This may appear unusual to the uninitiated. In this regard the author is compelled to mention that he has seen a player accuse an Atlantic City casino of "fixing" a wheel. This individual could not contain her distress when she observed that the (0) repeated, and she had failed to bet that number. However, regular players of this game know that this phenomenon of numbers repeating occurs quite often. Indeed, this is indicative of a "system" which many, including this author, have used: betting only the last number which occurred. The author has found that this "system" often works well. The point here however is that numbers repeating themselves is not an unusual phenomenon. Accordingly, in the Narratives which follow no special mention will be made of repeating numbers.

However, a number occurring thrice in a row is quite an unusual phenomenon. For this reason the author was compelled to discuss in the following Narratives those numbers which he observed occurring thrice in a row. In addition, he has provided a listing of those numbers which he has personally seen occur thrice in a row in his experiences in casinos. These are provided in Figure 40 under *The Terrible Trios*.

In only one instance has the author observed a number occurring more than three times in a row. In one gaming session the author used a "system" which he believed would work: observing twenty numbers occur on one wheel and then choosing the one which he believed would recur within the next thirty-five spins. He had allocated enough funds to make the minimum bet for that interval. If the number recurred prior to the 35th spin, then the author would profit. If the number recurred on the 35th spin and the author raised his bet on that spin, then the author would likewise profit. After observing twenty numbers, one number, (24) looked promising. Refer to Figure 38 which charts the frequencies of all of the 2,379 numbers which the author recorded to prepare this book. Observe that the (24) is the twelfth most often occurring number of all of the thirty-eight possibilities, having occurred 2.61% of the time. The author then commenced betting that number and his presumption proved correct. The (24) indeed recurred on the twentieth attempt. The author then ceased play. Five spins after the author ceased, the (24) recurred. The number then repeated. The number then immediately repeated. Then the (24) repeated again. That is, the (24) occurred four times in a row. The author took this as a sign from "The Gods" that he should have stayed on that number. Incidentally, the play took place on the 25th day of the 10th month. (The author has never seen a number occur more than four times in a row. He has however been informed by a floorperson in an Atlantic City, NJ casino that he observed a number occurring five times in a row).

C. Nomenclature

Many of the words and phrases which one will encounter in the following Narratives concerning the Figures, are unique to this book. The reader is accordingly invited to refer to the Glossary included herein. The term *Kismet* which is included therein is a term of Middle Eastern origin which means *fate* or *destiny*. For our purposes this term refers to two or more occurrences of a number at precise intervals of twenty, or of forty or of sixty, etc. This is the realization of the Rule Of Twenty discussed earlier. The term "Kismet" is used to denote that the occurrence of the same number at such precise intervals is a phenomenon which was meant to occur. In other words, it appears that the number was predestined by the "Powers-That-Be" to occur in such a manner. The author uses the term *Kismet* for lack of one which is more apt.

D. Vital Statistics

The author's research culminated in a summation of all of the 2,379 observations which he observed. This summation is detailed in the Vital Statistics provided in Figures 38 and 38A. Note that only the numbers which are provided in Figures 1 through 37 are included in these Vital Statistics. The observations provided in Figure 40, for example, are not included.

Again the reader is welcome to interpret the Vital Statistics in any manner which she/he deems appropriate. However, one should note in Figure 38 that there is a wide disparity in these numbers. The mode, (11), was found to occur much more often than that which least occurs, (3). This is of course significant from a mathematical perspective. In examining these numbers one should always keep in mind that all of the thirty-eight possibilities on an American-style wheel *theoretically* have an equal chance of occurring. Accordingly, these Vital Statistics should forever destroy the theoretical myth that roulette numbers are random.

IX. Narratives/Charts

Figure 1

Biases

The occurrences began with a marked color bias. Eight of the first ten numbers, or 80%, were red: (30/19/7/7/12/32/25/23). The entire first column experienced this type of bias, in that fifteen, or 75% of all of the numbers in this column were the same color. This color bias continues to the first three rows of the second column.

There was a marked low bias in the third column at rows one through five. All of the first five numbers were below (18): (3/0/9/2/4).

There were two hot numbers. In the second column at rows two through six, the (27) occurred thrice. Also in the second column beginning at row eleven and continuing to the third column at row eleven, the (00) occurred four times, or 19% of the time within this range.

Recurring Pairs

The pairs which recurred here are first the (23/25) which two numbers first occurred back-to-back in column one at rows nine and ten. This pair then recurred in the same precise manner at row twenty of the same column and at row one of column two.

The (00/00) also occurred back-to-back in column two at rows eleven and twelve. This pair then recurred upon the appearance of another

(00) precisely twenty spins after the first part of the aforementioned pair, in column three at row eleven.

The (20/36) then remarkably occurred at a precise twenty spin interval of one another in columns two and three at row ten. This pair then recurred in the same precise manner at row twenty of the same two columns, though reversed.

The (11/32) also exhibited remarkable behavior when these two numbers first occurred back-to-back in column one at rows seven and eight. Upon the reappearance of another (11) in column two precisely twenty spins after the aforementioned (32), this pair then recurred. However, quite remarkably this pair recurred again upon the appearance of another (32) precisely twenty spins after the last (11), in column three at row eight.

Then the (3/20) emulated its cousins above when these two numbers first occurred back-to-back at row twenty of column two and at row one of column three. This pair then recurred when they reappeared back-to-back in column three at rows nine and ten.

The (2/15) then occurred first back-to-back in column two at rows four and five. Upon the reappearance of another (2) in column three at row four, opposite the aforementioned (15), this pair then recurred.

The numbers immediately preceding formed a quartet of sorts, and in the process formed two recurring pairs. Both of the aforementioned (2) were part of the (2/4) recurring pair which first occurred at a precise twenty spin interval of one another at row five. Upon the reappearance of another (2) in column three, at row four and immediately preceding the aforementioned (4), this pair then recurred.

The (00/32) emulated the (2/4) above when these two numbers first occurred at a precise twenty spin interval of one another at row twelve in columns two and three. Upon the appearance of another (00) in column three at row eleven and immediately preceding the aforementioned (32), this pair then recurred.

Likewise did the (11/14) behave as did the above two pairs when these two numbers first occurred at a precise twenty spin interval of one another in columns one and two at row seven. Upon the appearance of another (11) immediately following the aforementioned (14), this pair then recurred.

Formulae

A number of *formulae* were prepared by the "Powers-That-Be." First they clearly state that *(3 = 9 – 2 – 4)*. Then they tell us that *(31 – 6 = 25)*. They cleverly inform us that *((2 = 27 – (14 + 11))*. In a somewhat obtuse manner they state that *(30 + 19 = 7 x 7)*. Then they become mischievous when they tell us that *((3 + 0) x 9) – 2 = 4 + 0 + 21))*. Pythagoras himself might concede these universal truths.

Sandwiches

One rather thick sandwich can be seen here: (6/25/2/25/6).

Kismet

There were two occurrences of *Kismet*. In the first column at row eight, the (32) occurred. Precisely forty spins later in the third column at row eight, this number again occurred. Also, the (00) occurred in the second column at row eleven. It occurred again precisely twenty spins later in the third column at the same row.

FIGURE 1
NON-OCCURS

19-Jun

			NON-OCCURS				
30*	23*	3*	1	**1**		**19**	1
19*	27	0*	10	**2**	3	**20**	2
7*	27	9*	13	**3**	2	**21**	1
7*	15*	2*	16	**4**	1	**22**	
35	2*	4*	17	**5**	1	**23**	3
12	27*	OO*	22	**6**	2	**24**	
11*	14*	21*	24	**7**	2	**25**	4
**32*	11*	**32	26	**8**	1	**26**	
25*	33	3*		**9**	2	**27**	4
23*	36*	20*		**10**		**28**	1
8	**OO*	**OO*		**11**	3	**29**	1
18	OO*	32*		**12**	2	**30**	3
11	23	29		**13**		**31**	2
30	31*	34		**14**	2	**32**	3
28	6*	27		**15**	2	**33**	1
18	25*	5		**16**		**34**	1
30	2*	31		**17**		**35**	1
12	25*	9		**18**	2	**36**	2
14	6*	15		**0**	1	**OO**	4
25*	20*	36*				**MODE:**	

**Kismet
*Superna tural
Occurren ce

RECURRING PAIRS: (23/25) (00/00) (20/36) (11/32) (3/20)

(2/15) (2/4) (00/32) (11/14)

SANDWICH: (6/25/2/25/6)

FORMULAE: $(3 + 0 = 9 - 2 - 4) (31 - 6 = 25)$

$((2 = 27 - (14 + 11))$

$(30 + 19 = 7 \times 7)$

$((3 + 0) \times 9) - 2 = 4 + 0 + 21))$

Figure 2

Biases

A pronounced *color bias* is evident in the first column from row seven to row eleven. Five consecutive numbers were red: (12/32/7/23/25).

There was a noticeable *column bias* in the second column beginning at row six and continuing through row fourteen. Seven of the nine occurrences, or 77.7% of this range were in the *third column* (of the board): (9/12/6/6/18/24/12). This further means that this range of numbers experienced a pronounced *divisible bias*. All of these numbers were divisible by (3).

There was also a pronounced *even bias* in the second column, beginning at row seven and continuing to row sixteen. All of the ten numbers in this range were even: (12/14/6/6/18/24/26/12/20/22).

The bias became an *odd bias* beginning in the third column at row ten and continuing to row nineteen. With one exception, all of the ten numbers, or 90%, were odd: (3/19/7/9/17/7/7/31/33).

The same column experienced a *low bias* beginning at row twelve and ending at row seventeen. All of the six numbers were low (below (19)): (7/9/17/7/7/2).

Kismet

There were three occurrences of *Kismet*. In the first column at row seven the (12) occurred. The same number occurred again precisely twenty spins later in the second column at row seven. Also in the first column, the (2) occurred at row seventeen, occurring again precisely forty spins later in the third column at the same row. Further, in the first column the (5) occurred at the third row. Precisely forty spins later it again occurred in the third column at row three.

Recurring Pairs & Trios

The *recurring pairs* were quite evident as usual. First there was the (26/34) which occurred back-to-back at row twenty in column one and row one of column two. This pair recurred when they appeared again directly opposite one another at row four in columns two and three.

Then the (15/31) first occurred back-to-back in column one, at rows fourteen and fifteen. This pair then recurred in the same manner, back-to-back in column two at rows seventeen and eighteen, though reversed. This pair then remarkably recurred a third time upon the appearance of a (31) in column three at row eighteen, opposite the aforementioned (15).

Next the (2/31) first occurred at a precise twenty spin interval of one another in columns one and two at row seventeen. Upon the appearance of another (2) in column three at row seventeen, this pair again recurred at a precise twenty spin interval of one another. Then quite remarkably this pair recurred a third time upon the appearance of a (31) in column three at row eighteen, immediately following the aforementioned (2).

Then the (2/5) emulated its cousins above by also recurring as a pair thrice, first in columns one and two at row three at a precise twenty spin interval of one another. Upon the appearance of a (5) in column two at row two, immediately preceding the aforementioned (2), this pair then recurred again. Further, upon the appearance of another (5) in column three at row three, this pair then recurred a third time.

Next it was the turn of the (6/14) to recur as pair when these two numbers first occurred back-to-back in column two at rows eight and nine. Upon the appearance of a (6) in column three at row eight, opposite the aforementioned (14), this pair then recurred.

Then the (5/35) recurred as a pair by first occurring at a precise twenty spin interval of one another in columns two and three at row two. Upon the appearance of a (5) in column three at row three, immediately following the aforementioned (35), this pair then recurred.

The last pair to recur was the (5/26) which first occurred back-to-back in column two at rows one and two. This pair then recurred when these two numbers appeared again back-to-back in column three at rows three and four.

Quite remarkably one can see a recurring trio in column one at rows thirteen through fifteen where the (15/22/31) first occurred back-to-back. This trio then remarkably recurred, though in a different order, in column two at rows sixteen through eighteen.

Standard Pairs

One standard pair occurred at row twelve when the (22) and the (24) occurred directly opposite one another at row twelve in columns one and two, respectively.

Formulae

The *formulae* which appeared were also quite prolific, further indicating a strong presence of "The Powers-That-Be." First they inform us that *(18/6 = 3)*, and also that

(35 – 9 – 12 = 14). Then they tell us that *(6 + 18 = 24)*. Further they tell us that

(27 + 7 = 34), and also that *(6 x 1 = 6)*. They elaborate somewhat when they tell us that *((5 x 2) + 34 = 35 + 9))*. Then they matter-of-factly tell us that *(13 + 12 = 32 – 7)*. They become somewhat mischievous when they tell us that *(2 + 34 + 35 + 9 = 12 + 14 + 6 + 6 + 18 + 24)*. Lastly they become more subdued when they tell us that *(2 + 31 = 33)*. Pythagoras might accordingly be impressed with their logic.

FIGURE 2

	23-Jun		NON-OCCURS				
1	26*	35	8	1	2	19	1
28	5*	35*	10	2	3	20	2
**5*	2*	**5*	11	3	1	21	
15	34*	26*	16	4	1	22	3
36	35*	27	21	5	3	23	1
13	9*	6*	0	6	4	24	1
**12	**12*	1*	OO	7	5	25	1
32	14*	6*		8		26	3
7	6*	20		9	2	27	3
23	6*	3*		10		28	1
25	18*	19		11		29	1
22	24	7		12	3	30	1
22*	26	9		13	1	31	3
15*	12	17		14	1	32	1
31*	20	7		15	3	33	1
27	22*	7		16		34	2
**2*	31*	**2*		17	1	35	3
27*	15*	31*		18	1	36	1
7*	30	33*		0		OO	
34*	29	4			MODE:	7	

**Kismet
*Supernatural Occurrence

RECURRING PAIRS: (26/34) (15/31) (2/31) (2/5) (6/14) (5/35)

(5/26)

RECURRING TRIOS: (15/22/31)

FORMULAE: (18/6 = 3) (35 - 9 - 12 = 14) (6 + 18 = 24)

(27 + 7 = 34) (6 x 1 = 6)

((5 x 2) + 34 = 35 + 9))

(13 + 12 = 32 - 7)

(2 + 34 + 35 + 9
= 12 + 14 + 6 + 6 + 18 + 24)

(2 + 31 = 33)

Figure 3

Biases

The occurrences began with a marked digit bias in the first column, beginning at row ten and lasting for three spins. Three numbers ending in (6) occurred consecutively: (36/6/26). Note also that the occurrence of the (6) was part of a prolonged digit bias. Numbers ending in this digit occurred at precise twenty spin intervals in all three columns at rows eleven and twelve The sequences were (6/6/36) and (26/36/6) at both rows, respectively.

This was followed by a marked color bias starting at row eighteen of the first column and continuing to the fifth row of the second column. Seven of the eight numbers in this range, or 87.5%, were red: (32/34/18/30/19/7/21).

A digit bias of a different sort occurred in the second column. Beginning at the fifth row and continuing to row ten, all of the numbers began with a (2): (21/22/21/27/23/23).

The hot numbers in this round of occurrences were accordingly (6) and (36). The latter was the mode.

Recurring Pairs & Trios

The pairs which recurred were the (6/36) which first occurred back-to-back in column one at rows ten and eleven. This pair then remarkably recurred in the same manner in column two at rows eleven and twelve, though reversed. Then this pair recurred quite remarkably in the same manner a third time in column three at rows three and four, in the exact manner in which it had previously occurred. Then this pair again recurred a fourth time at a precise twenty spin interval of one another in columns two and three at row eleven. This pair then quite remarkably recurred a fifth and a sixth time, upon the appearance of a (6) in column three at row twelve. With the appearance of this number, this pair recurred both back-to-back with the (36) at row eleven, and also at a precise twenty spin interval of the (36) in column two at row twelve. This pair thereby holds the distinction of being the only pair which recurred six times in one round of observances. It could therefore be said that "The Gods" looked with great favor on this pair on this date.

Then the (00/36) first occurred back-to-back in column one at rows nine and ten. In the third column at rows seventeen and eighteen this pair recurred in the exact same manner.

Quite remarkably, the (00/18) occurred first back-to-back at row twenty in column one and at row one of column two. Upon the appearance of a (00) in column three at row one, this pair recurred. What is remarkable is the fact that the (00) would be paired with both the (18) and the (36), which comprise one of the Standard Pairs in Figure 40.

The (7/27) then occurred back-to-back in column one at rows seven and eight. Upon the appearance of a (27) in column two at row eight, this pair then recurred.

The (21/27) emulated its cousins above by occurring at a precise twenty spin interval of one another in columns one and two at row seven. Upon the appearance of a (27) in column two at row eight, this pair then recurred.

Standard Pairs

The standard pairs which can be seen here are, in addition to the aforementioned (6/36), the (8/11) which occurred in column one at rows four and five. In column three at rows sixteen and seventeen one can also observe a (0/00). Lastly, one can see one of the "Opposite Twins," a (23/32) in columns two and three at row nineteen.

Formulae

The formulae which the "Powers-That-Be" dictated should appear were first the mundane statement that *(11 + 11 = 22)*. Then we are treated to the statement that

(36/6 = 6). Next we are told unequivocally that *(20 + 1 = 22 − 1)*. These observances began with the clever statement that *((16 + 8 − 21) + 8 = 11))*. "The Gods" then become mischievous when they inform us that *((27 − 7) + 0 + (36 − 6) = 26 + 24))*. Could Pythagoras disagree?

Kismet

There were two instances of Kismet. In the first column at row eleven, the (6) occurred. It occurred precisely twenty spins later at the same row. Also, in the second column at row fifteen, the (12) occurred. This number again occurred precisely twenty spins later in the third column. Further note that only a (1) in column three at row ten kept the (36) from Kismet with the (36) in column one at row ten. Note also that the (36) in column three at row eleven kept the (6) from Triple Kismet at row eleven. Also note that the (6) in column three at row twelve kept the (36) from Kismet at row eleven.

FIGURE 3
NON-OCCURS

			NON-OCCURS				
16*	18*	OO*	9	1	2	19	1
8*	30	17	10	2	1	20	2
21*	19	6*	13	3	1	21	3
8*	7	36*	15	4	1	22	3
11*	21	0	29	5	2	23	3
25	22	4	31	6	4	24	1
27*	21*	20*		7	2	25	1
7*	27*	1*		8	2	26	1
OO*	23	22*		9		27	2
36*	23	1*		10		28	1
**6*	**6*	36*		11	3	29	
26*	36*	6*		12	2	30	1
24*	5	0		13		31	
11*	22*	35		14	1	32	2
11*	**12	**12		15		33	1
3	28	0		16	1	34	1
2	5	OO*		17	1	35	1
32	20	36*		18	1	36	5
34	23	32		0	3	OO	4
OO*	33	14				MODE:	36

**Kismet
*Superna tural Occurrence

RECURRING PAIRS: (6/36) (00/36) (00/18) (7/27) (21/27)

FORMULAE: (11 + 11 = 22) (36 / 6 = 6)

(20 + 1 = 22 - 1)

((16 + 8 - 21) + 8 = 11))

((27 - 7 + 0 + 36 - 6) = 26 + 24))

Figure 4

Biases

The occurrences began with a *hot number.* The (2) occurred three times in the first eleven spins, or 27.2% of all occurrences.

The occurrences in the first column are characterized by a marked color bias. The bias began at row nine and continued to row sixteen where seven of the eight numbers, or 87.5%, were red: (27/9/27/19/9/3/32).

A pronounced odd bias can also be seen in the first column starting at the seventh row and ending at row nineteen. With two exceptions, all of the numbers in this range, or 84.6%, are odd: (29/15/27/9/27/1 9/9/3/13/15/23).

The second column began with a marked digit bias. All of the first five numbers were biased in favor of the digit (3): (36/30/35/33/33). This range also indicates a high bias. All of these numbers were above (18).

The above was followed by an even bias. Beginning in the second column at row nine and continuing to row fourteen, all of the numbers were even: (6/36/12/30/4/26).

A color bias can also be seen beginning in the second column at row sixteen and continuing to the third column at row three. All of these eight numbers were red: (14/25/30/1/3/36/27/3). Note that this is further indicative of a column bias and also a divisible bias. Five of the last six numbers in this range were in the third column (of the board) and all are also divisible by (3): (30/3/36/27/3).

Another digit bias can be seen in the third column, beginning at row nine and continuing to row thirteen. All of these five numbers begin with (2): (25/20/24/25/2).

Recurring Pairs & Trios

Only three recurring pairs can be observed here, beginning with the (27/30) which first occurred at a precise twenty spin interval of one another in columns one and two at row twelve. These numbers reappeared in the exact same manner in columns two and three at a precise twenty spin interval of one another at row two, though reversed. Note also that these two numbers constitute a standard pair.

In addition, the (25/30) became a recurring pair when they first occurred back-to-back in column two at rows seventeen and eighteen.

When these two numbers subsequently reappeared at a precise twenty spin interval of one another in columns two and three at row twelve, this pair then recurred.

The (2/12) behaved quite extraordinarily when this pair first occurred at a precise twenty spin interval of one another in columns one and two at row six. This pair then duplicated this feat and reappeared in the same identical manner in the same two columns at row eleven, in the process becoming a recurring pair.

Standard Pairs

There were two standard pairs in addition to the aforementioned (27/30). The (18) and (36) occurred back-to-back at the bottom of the first column and at the top of the second column. The (3) and (36) occurred back-to-back at the bottom of the second column and at the top of the third column.

Formulae

The formulae to be found here show that "The Gods" continue to be on the case. First they state clearly that *(2 x 12 = 24)*. Then they matter-of-factly tell us that

(30 – 4 = 26). Need we also be reminded of the fact that *(34 = 2 + 30 + 2)*? Can anyone dispute their declaration that *(16 + 8 + 1 = 25)*? Then they cleverly inform us that

((22 + 28) – 16 – 8 – 1 = 25)). Finally, their propensity for being obtuse is again demonstrated when they tell us that *((27 + 3 + 22) – (28 + 16) = 8))*. With these universal truths, Pythagoras could not have any qualms.

Kismet

There were two instances of Kismet. At the top of the second column the (36) occurred. Precisely twenty spins later it again occurred at the top of the third column. Also, at row fourteen of the first column the (9) occurred. Precisely forty spins later it reappeared at the same row in the third column.

FIGURE 4

			NON-OCCURS				
23	**36	**36	5	**1**	2	**19**	1
16	30*	27*	10	**2**	4	**20**	2
34*	35	3*	11	**3**	3	**21**	
2*	33	22*	21	**4**	1	**22**	1
30*	33	28*	31	**5**		**23**	3
2*	12*	16*	0	**6**	1	**24**	1
29	28	8*	OO	**7**	1	**25**	3
15	**17**	1*		**8**	1	**26**	1
27	**6**	25*		**9**	3	**27**	3
9	36	20		**10**		**28**	2
2*	12*	24*		**11**		**29**	2
27*	30*	25*		**12**	2	**30**	4
19	4*	2		**13**	2	**31**	
**9	**26***	**9		**14**	1	**32**	1
3	**17**	33		**15**	2	**33**	3
32	14	7		**16**	2	**34**	1
13	25*	23		**17**	2	**35**	1
15	30*	13		**18**	1	**36**	3
23	1	29		**0**		**OO**	
18	3	20			**MODE:**		

**Kismet
*Superna tural Occurrence

RECURRING PAIRS: (27/30) (25/30) (2/12)

FORMULAE: (2 x 12 = 24) (30 - 4 = 26)

(34 = 2 + 30 + 2)

(16 + 8 + 1 = 25)

((22 + 28) - 16 - 8 - 1 = 25))

((27 + 3 + 22) - (28 + 16) = 8))

Figure 5

Biases

The occurrences began with a noticeable odd bias. Beginning in the first column at row four, all of the next six numbers were odd: (19/19/15/11/11/9).

Next one can observe a marked divisible bias. Beginning in the first column at row ten and continuing to row sixteen, five of the seven numbers were divisible by (10): (20/20/10/30/30).

Then there occurred a pronounced color bias. Beginning in the first column at row fourteen and continuing to row nineteen, all of the six numbers were red: (3/30/30/21/5/27). This color bias was again apparent in the second column beginning at row two and continuing to row nine. With the exception of the zeros, all of the six numbers in this range were red: (3/14/21/27/36/7).

There then began a low bias. Beginning in the second column at row eleven and ending at row sixteen, all of the numbers were low (below (19)): (9/15/1/14/5/6).

One can also observe a marked digit bias beginning in the first column at row ten and continuing to row eight in the second column. Eight of the nineteen numbers, or 42.1%, ended in the digit (0): (20/20/10/30/30/0/00/00).

A color bias can further be observed beginning in the second column at row twenty and continuing to row thirteen in the third column. Of the fourteen numbers in this range, eleven, or 84.6%, were red: (5/9/23/25/18/27/5/23/5/16/36).

Recurring Pairs & Trios

The pairs which recurred were first the (6/14) which occurred at a precise twenty spin interval of one another in columns one and two at row three. Remarkably this duo appeared again in the same manner, though reversed, in columns two and three at row fourteen.

Then the (4/5) first occurred at a precise twenty spin interval of one another in columns one and two at row twenty. This pair then recurred in column three at rows six and seven. Note also that only a (27) in column one at row nineteen precluded this pair from recurring a third time. Note further that only a (16) in column three at row eleven precluded this pair from recurring a fourth time. Further note that in each case the "louse" was a red number.

Then the (3/14) first occurred at a precise twenty spin interval of one another in columns one and two at row fourteen. This pair recurred, back-to-back, in column two at rows two and three.

Next the (7/9) behaved quite extraordinarily by first occurring at a precise twenty spin interval of one another in columns one and two, twice. The first instance was at row nine. The other instance where they were paired to recur at a precise twenty spin interval of one another was in the same two columns at row eleven. Remarkably this pair recurred a third time in column three at rows fifteen and sixteen.

Then the (4/36) occurred at a precise twenty spin interval of one another in columns two and three at row seven. This pair then recurred back-to-back in column three at rows twelve and thirteen.

The last of the pairs to recur was the (5/27) which first occurred back-to-back in column one at rows eighteen and nineteen. This pair then remarkably recurred in the same manner, back-to-back in column three at rows five and six.

Standard Pairs

The only standard pair which can be seen here is the (6/36) which occurred in column three at rows thirteen and fourteen.

Formulae

The formulae which can be seen here again attests to the presence of the "Powers-That-Be." They first tell us that $(24 - 9 = 15)$, and also that $(11 + 9 = 20)$. They then restate the axiom that $(15 - 1 = 14)$. Further, they insist that $(10 \times 3 = 30)$. Next they explain that $(4 + 0 + 3 + 14 = 21)$, and also that $(22 + 8 = 35 - 5)$. Then they remind us that $(9 - 7 = 2)$ and also that $(7 + 9 = 16)$. Must they further insist that $(23 - 2 = 5 + 16)$? Lastly, they state unequivocally that $(7 - 2 = 5)$. Pythagoras would have to submit to their dictates.

Kismet

There were two instances of Kismet. In the first column at row two, the (23) occurred. Precisely forty spins later, this number again occurred at the same row in the third column. Further, in the second column at row five, the (27) occurred. Precisely twenty spins later at the same row in the third column, this number again occurred.

Drought

There was a marked drought in two respects. First, one can see a virtual top black drought, in that four out of six of the top black numbers failed to occur: (26/28/29/31). Also, most of the numbers of The Black Pentacle were conspicuously absent: (17/26/31), revealing a virtual Black Pentacle drought.

FIGURE 5
NON-OCCURS

	1-Jul						
11	0*	9	13	1	1	19	3
**23	3*	**23	17	2	1	20	2
6*	14*	25	26	3	2	21	2
19	21*	18	28	4	3	22	1
19	**27	**27*	29	5	5	23	3
15	OO	5*	31	6	3	24	1
11	36*	4*	34	7	3	25	1
11*	OO	23*		8	1	26	
9*	7*	2*		9	4	27	3
20*	24*	5*		10	1	28	
7*	9*	16*		11	3	29	
20	15*	4*		12	1	30	2
10*	1*	36*		13		31	
3*	14*	6*		14	2	32	1
30*	5	7*		15	2	33	1
30	6	9*		16	1	34	
21	22*	19		17		35	1
5*	8*	33		18	1	36	2
27*	35*	32		0	1	OO	2
4*	5*	12			MODE:	5	

**Kismet
*Superna tural
Occurren ce

RECURRING PAIRS: (6/14) (4/5) (3/14) (7/9) (4/36) (5/27)

FORMULAE: (24 - 9 = 15) (11 + 9 = 20) (15 - 1 = 14)

(10 x 3 = 30) (4 + 0 + 3 + 14 = 21)

(22 + 8 = 35 - 5) (9 - 7 = 2) (7 + 9 = 16)

(23 - 2 = 5 + 16) (7 - 2 = 5)

Figure 6

Biases

The occurrences began with a noticeable color bias. Starting in the first column at the first row, the numbers were biased in favor of the red. Nine of the first twelve numbers, or 75%, were red: (18/9/21/23/36/32/14/12/34).

There was a marked digit bias in the second column. Beginning at row six and continuing to row twelve, six of the seven numbers, or 85.7%, began with (2): (27/22/26/26/20/24).

Within the second column one can also observe an even bias. Beginning at row seven and ending at row twenty, with three exceptions all of the numbers, or 78.5%, were even: (22/12/26/26/20/24/18/16 /34/14/8).

A most unusual phenomenon occurred in the third column at rows thirteen through nineteen. This range experienced a double digit bias. Four of the seven numbers, or 57.1%, were double digit: (22/11/22/33). Note also that the first (22) is opposite an (11) in column two at row thirteen.

Lastly, one can see in all three columns a consecutive bias at row four where the numbers fell in perfect descending order: (10/9/8).

Recurring Pairs

The recurring pairs to be seen here are the (8/17) which remarkably occurred back-to-back at row twenty in column two and at row one of column three. This pair remarkably recurred shortly thereafter in the same manner, back-to-back in column three at rows nine and ten.

Also remarkably, the (18/29) emulated its cousins above when this duo first occurred back-to-back in column one at rows one and two. This pair remarkably recurred in precisely the same manner in column three at rows eleven and twelve.

Next, two consecutive numbers, (9/10) first occurred back-to-back in column one at rows three and four. This pair recurred upon the appearance of a (9) in column two at row four, opposite the aforementioned (10).

Then two additional consecutive numbers, (17/18) also occurred back-to-back in column one at rows thirteen and fourteen. Remarkably this pair recurred in the exact same manner in column three at rows ten and eleven.

The last of the pairs to recur was the (9/17) which first occurred at a precise twenty spin interval of one another in columns one and two at row three. Upon the appearance of a (9) in column two at row four, immediately following the aforementioned (17), this pair then recurred.

Standard Pairs

Three standard pairs were observed. In the first column at rows twelve and thirteen the (34/17) occurred back-to-back. In the second column at rows seventeen and eighteen the (00/0) occurred in the same manner. Also, in the third column at rows five and six the (16/32) occurred back-to-back.

Formulae

The formulae which can be observed prove once again the enduring presence of the "Supernatural." First it tells us that *(18 = 35 − 17)*. Next it tells us that

(15 + 8 + 16 − 32 = 7). Elaborating upon that axiom, we are then informed that

(32 − 7 + 18 = 8 + 17 + 18). Further elaborating upon that statement, we are then informed that *(7 + 18 − 8 = 17)*. Then it cleverly tells us that *(15 + 30 + 7 = 16 + 0 + 0 + 35 + 1)*. Further we are reminded that *(17 − 9 = 8)* and also that *(16 − 7 − 0 = 9)*. Need we also be reminded that *(18 + 16 = 34)*? Pythagoras would have to concur.

Kismet

There was one instance of Kismet. In the first column at row fourteen, the (18) occurred. This number occurred again precisely twenty spins later in the second column.

FIGURE 6

14-Jul			NON-OCCURS					
18*	35*	**17***	2	**1**	1	**19**	1
29*	1*	33	5	**2**		**20**	1
9*	**17***	15*	6	**3**	1	**21**	1
10*	9*	8*	13	**4**	1	**22**	3
21	4	16*	25	**5**		**23**	1
10	27	32*	28	**6**		**24**	1
23	22	7*	31	**7**	2	**25**	
36	12	18*		**8**	3	**26**	3
32	**26**	8*		**9**	3	**27**	1
14	**26**	**17***		**10**	2	**28**	
12	20	18*		**11**	2	**29**	2
34	24	29*		**12**	2	**30**	1
17*	11	22		**13**		**31**	
**18*	****18***	3		**14**	2	**32**	2
15*	16*	11		**15**	2	**33**	2
30*	34*	22		**16**	3	**34**	2
7*	OO*	9*		**17**	4	**35**	1
16*	0	19		**18**	5	**36**	1
OO*	14	33		**0**	1	**OO**	3
OO*	8*	**26**			**MODE:**	18	

**Kismet
*Superna tural Occurrence

RECURRING PAIRS: (8/17) (18/29) (9/10) (17/18) (9/17)

FORMULAE: $(18 = 35 - 17)$ $(15 + 8 + 16 - 32 = 7)$

$(32 - 7 + 18 = 8 + 17 + 18)$

$(7 + 18 - 8 = 17)$

$(15 + 30 + 7 = 16 + 0 + 0 + 35 + 1)$

$(17 - 9 = 8)$ $(16 - 7 - 0 = 9)$ $(18 + 16 = 34)$

Figure 7

Biases

The occurrences began with a marked column bias. Precisely half of the occurrences in the first column were in the middle (second) column of the board: (35/2/23/2/8/35/17/20/2/8). Note that with one exception, all of these occurrences are black numbers, revealing a marked color bias: black.

The occurrences also ended with a noticeable column bias. In the third column, beginning with row twelve, five consecutive numbers occurred in the middle column of the board: (32/11/20/23/14). Note also that here one can observe a unique example of column bias. In the third column from row twelve to row twenty, all of the red numbers in the middle column of the board occurred: (5/14/23/32). That is, 44.4% of the nine numbers in this range were red numbers in the middle column.

There was one hot number. The (8) occurred five times, at rows nine and twenty of the first column, and at rows nine, thirteen and fourteen of the second column. It is all the more remarkable that this number should repeat itself in the second column and also be an example of Kismet. Note that the (8) occurred precisely twenty spins apart in columns one and two at row nine. Accordingly, the wheel in question experienced a marked number bias for a prolonged interval.

Kismet

In addition to the aforementioned example of Kismet, there were four others. In the first column at row six, the (16) occurred. Precisely twenty spins later it again occurred in the second column at row six. Also in the first column the (20) occurred at row fourteen. Precisely forty spins later it occurred in the third column. Again in the first column the (1) occurred at row nineteen. It recurred precisely twenty spins later in the second column at the same row. The last example of Kismet was the occurrence of the (24) in the second column at row three. Precisely twenty spins later it reappeared in column three at row three. This set of sixty occurrences might therefore be labeled "Kismet City."

Recurring Pairs & Trios

Recurring pairs were five. To reiterate, the (16/16) occurred at a precise twenty spin interval of one another in columns one and two at row six. Upon the appearance of another (16) in column two at row five, immediately preceding the aforementioned (16) in column two, this pair then recurred.

Next it was the turn of the (0/7) to recur as a pair, first occurring back-to-back in column one at rows eleven and twelve. Upon the appearance of another (7) in column two at row twelve, opposite the aforementioned (0), this pair then recurred.

The (20/36) quite extraordinarily first occurred back-to-back in column one at rows fourteen and fifteen. This pair then recurred in precisely the same manner exactly six spins later at rows one and two in column two.

Then the (8/8) remarkably occurred within a precise twenty spin interval of one another at row nine in columns one and two. This pair remarkably recurred back-to-back in column two at rows thirteen and fourteen.

Next the (8/20) also behaved extraordinarily when these two numbers first occurred at a precise twenty spin interval of one another in columns one and two at row fourteen. Then this duo recurred back-to-back at row twenty of column one and at row one of column two. Quite remarkably, this pair then recurred a third time upon the appearance of another (20) in column three at row fourteen, opposite the aforementioned (8) in column two.

Note further that each of the above three pairs are also part of a most unusual phenomenon of a recurring trio. Observe the occurrence of the (8/20/36) in column one at rows fourteen and fifteen, coupled with the (8) at row fourteen in column two, opposite the aforementioned (20). This trio recurred when these three numbers then occurred back-to-back from row twenty in column one, continuing to row two in column two.

Formulae

The formulae which can be seen reveal that "The Powers-That-Be" were quite prolific in this set of occurrences. First they remind us that *(1 – 1 = 0),* and also that

(8 + 8 = 16). Then they remind us that *(32 + 11 – 20 = 23).* They

then cleverly tell us that *((28/7) x 2) x 1 = 8))*. Sublimely they tell us that *((24/2) + 7 = 19))*. They then blandly state that *(5 + 2 = 7)*. Need they also remind us that *((2 + 24) = (24 + 2))*? They then make their point quite succinctly when they tell us that *((23 + 5) – 2 – 7 = 19))*. Pythagoras would have to submit to their dictates.

FIGURE 7

15-Jul			NON-OCCURS				
35	20*	29	3	1	2	19	1
4	36*	10	6	2	4	20	3
2*	**24*	**24*	9	3		21	
23*	5*	2*	13	4	2	22	
28	16*	7*	21	5	2	23	2
**16*	**16*	19*	22	6		24	3
2	25	OO	27	7	4	25	2
15	33	30	34	8	5	26	1
**8*	**8*	16*		9		27	
35	4	25		10	2	28	2
7*	24	12		11	1	29	1
0*	7*	32*		12	2	30	2
17	8	11*		13		31	1
**20*	8*	**20*		14	1	32	1
36*	30	23*		15	2	33	1
7*	26	14		16	4	34	
28*	18	15		17	1	35	2
2*	31	12		18	1	36	2
**1*	**1*	OO*		0	1	OO	2
8*	10	5			MODE:	8	

**Kismet
*Superna tural Occurrence

RECURRING PAIRS: (16/16) (0/7) (20/36) (8/20) (8/8)

RECURRING TRIO: (8/20/36)

FORMULAE: (1 - 1 = 0) (8 + 8 = 16) (32 + 11 - 20 = 23)

((28 / 7) x 2) x 1 = 8))

(24 / 2 + 7 = 19) (5 + 2 = 7)

(2 + 24 = 24 + 2) ((23 + 5) - 2 - 7 = 19))

Figure 8

Biases

Here one can see a most unusual example of a number occurring thrice in a row. In column three at rows eighteen through twenty the (10) occurred and then recurred twice. Note that this number is listed as one of The *Terrible Trios* in Figure 40.

One hot number was observed in addition to the aforementioned (10). In the second column at row seventeen, the (36) occurred. It recurred three more times after that occurrence, in the third column at rows one, six and nine, or 30.7% of the time within this interval.

Other biases to be observed are, first, a wheel bias in column two at rows five through seven. Three consecutive numbers, (34/3/22) are in a small section of the wheel. In column three one can also see a marked column bias. Half of the numbers in the third column are in the first column of the board: (4/4/28/1/34/19/4/10/10/10). Also, six of the final ten occurrences or 60%, are in the first column: (34/19/4/10/10/10).

Lastly, one can see a most extraordinary example of wheel bias. At row nineteen the sequence of numbers was (29), (25) and (10) in columns one through three, respectively. Observe on the effigy of a roulette wheel provided on p. 28 that these numbers are in perfect counterclockwise order. That is, at precise intervals numbers of a small section of the wheel occurred consecutively.

Recurring Pairs & Trios

The recurring pairs to be observed here are first the (6/14) which first occurred at a precise twenty spin interval of one another at row eight in columns one and two. Upon the appearance of another (14) at row nine in column two, immediately following the aforementioned (6), this pair then recurred.

Then the (00/36) recurred as a pair, first occurring back-to-back in column two at rows seventeen and eighteen. This pair then recurred when they reappeared at a precise twenty spin interval of one another at row one of columns two and three.

The (5/36) showed remarkable behavior when this duo first occurred back-to-back in column one at rows five and six. This pair remarkably recurred again back-to-back in column two at rows sixteen and seventeen.

Then the (4/36) first occurred at a precise twenty spin interval of one another in columns two and three at row seventeen. This pair recurred when this duo occurred back-to-back in column three at rows one and two. Note also that these two numbers occurred at a precise forty spin interval of one another in columns one and three at row nine.

The (14/20) emulated its cousins above when these two numbers first occurred back-to-back in column two at rows three and four. Shortly thereafter this pair recurred in the same manner and in the same column at rows nine and ten. Likewise did the (1/12) behave in the same manner when these two numbers first occurred back-to-back in column one at rows two and three. This pair then recurred when they repeated this feat and occurred back-to-back in column two at rows fourteen and fifteen.

The (20) and the (33) exhibited one of the most profound examples of a recurring pair which the author has yet observed. In the first column at row ten the (20) occurred, followed by the (33). These two numbers recurred in the precise same order in the next column in the same two rows.

The final pair to recur here is the (4/14) which first occurred back-to-back in column one at rows eight and nine. Upon the appearance of another (14) in column two at row nine, opposite the aforementioned (4), this pair then recurred.

Kismet

The most profound phenomenon to be seen here is a most extraordinary example of Kismet. In the first column at row ten the (20) occurred. Then the (33) occurred immediately following. Precisely twenty spins later these two numbers repeated in exactly the same order at the same two rows in column two. To reiterate, these two numbers therefore comprise one of the recurring pairs in this set of observations.

Formulae

The formulae which can be seen show that "The Gods" never relent in dictating universal truths. First they reaffirm that *(2 + 4 + 14 = 20)*.

Then they reassert the fact that *(32 + 2 + 0 = 34)*. Next they obtusely inform us that *((5 x 2) + 14 – 4 = 20))*. They continue to be clever when they reiterate that *((29 – 15) + 0 + 0 = 14))*. Then they reaffirm the fact that *(14 + 20 = 34)*. They further inform us in no uncertain terms that

(6 + 14 = 20). Lastly they cleverly tell us that *((22/2) x 1 = 11))*. Could Pythagoras contend with these universal truths?

Standard Pairs

The standard pairs to be seen are, first, at the top of the second column at rows one and two where the (0/00) occurred back-to-back. The only other standard pair to be seen is the (3/36) which occurred opposite one another in columns two and three at row six.

Drought

Lastly, these numbers reveal an unusual phenomenon of "street drought." In the list of Non-Occurs note that none of the numbers of the "7 Street," that is, (7), (8) or (9), occurred.

FIGURE 8

	4-Aug		NON-OCCURS				
22	OO*	36*	7	1	3	19	1
1*	0*	4*	8	2	2	20	3
12*	14*	35	9	3	1	21	
0	20*	4	16	4	4	22	2
36*	34*	28	17	5	2	23	
5*	3	36	21	6	1	24	1
2*	22*	1*	23	7		25	1
14*	6*	11*	30	8		26	1
4*	14*	36	31	9		27	2
**20*	**20*	29		10	3	28	2
**33*	**33*	32*		11	2	29	2
11	34	2*		12	2	30	
18	27	OO*		13	1	31	
28	1*	34*		14	3	32	1
13	12*	OO		15	1	33	3
27	5*	19		16		34	3
26	36*	4*		17		35	1
33	OO*	10*		18	1	36	5
29*	25	10*		0	2	OO	4
15*	24	10*				MODE:	36

**Kismet
*Super natural Occurrence

RECURRING PAIRS: (6/14) (00/36) (5/36) (4/36) (14/20) (1/12)

(4/14)

FORMULAE: (2 + 14 + 4 = 20) (32 + 2 + 0 = 34)

((5 x 2) + 14 - 4 = 20))

(29 - 15 + 0 + 0 = 14) (14 + 20 = 34)

(6 + 14 = 20) (22 / 2 x 1 = 11)

Figure 9

Biases

A most unusual phenomenon occurred (or failed to occur) in that of the Non-Occurs, there were two sets of consecutive numbers: (6/7/8) and (33/34/35). Astute observers will also see that both these sets of consecutive numbers began with a black number in the third column and ended with a black number in the middle column. Note also that the middle number in each trio is a red number from the first column. "The Gods" therefore demonstrated a consecutive bias.

Recurring Pairs & Trios

These occurrences also began with quite a rare phenomenon. Further, this set of occurrences is unique in that this is the only instance in which the author has observed more than one trio of numbers recur. These occurrences might therefore be labeled "recurring trio city." Here one can observe three recurring trios. One can first observe this phenomenon in column one in the first three rows where the sequence was (11/29/4). This trio of numbers repeated itself, though not in the same order, nine spins later at rows twelve through fourteen.

This highly unusual phenomenon of a recurring trio occurred again in column two when the (31/32/26) occurred at rows three through five. This trio recurred in the third column at rows ten through twelve when it materialized again (though not in the same order): (32/31/26).

The last of the recurring trios to be observed here is the (4/11/26) which first occurred in column one at rows thirteen through fifteen. Remarkably this trio recurred in columns two and three at row fourteen, including the (4) at row fifteen in column three.

There were five recurring pairs. The first of these was the (4/14) which first occurred back-to-back in column one at rows three and four. This pair then remarkably recurred in the same order at row twenty in column one and at row one in column two.

The (4/29) emulated its cousins above when these two numbers first occurred back-to-back in column one at rows two and three. Remarkably this pair then recurred in the same order, back-to-back in the same column at rows twelve and thirteen. This pair then recurred a second time when these two numbers occurred at a precise twenty spin interval of one another at row twenty in columns one and two.

Quite remarkably the (16/24) recurred as a pair, twice in column three at rows six through nine. This is a very rare instance of a consecutive recurring pair.

The (12/24) formed what might be labeled a "Siamese recurring pair." These two numbers first occurred at a precise twenty spin interval of one another at row ten in columns one and two. This pair then recurred at row nine in columns two and three. Note that each pair is separate. However, the fact that the (12) repeated itself to form another recurring pair is quite extraordinary.

The last of the pairs to recur was the (4/22) which first occurred at a precise twenty spin interval of one another in columns one and two at row seventeen. This pair recurred when they occurred back-to-back in column two at rows seven and eight. Note also that these numbers appeared at a precise forty spin interval of one another at row twenty in columns one and three.

Unusual Phenomena

Further, this last set of numbers also comprised a phenomenon which the author has never before observed: a quintet. The five numbers in question are highlighted in **bold** and also in *italics* at rows thirteen through fifteen: (4/11/26/11/4). Ordinarily this would be labeled a sandwich. However, in view of its most unusual and unique nature, the author was compelled to use a different term.

Kismet

One can also observe two examples of Kismet. In the first column at row two the (29) occurred. Precisely forty spins later it recurred in the same row in the third column. The second example can be seen also in the first column at row fourteen when the (11) occurred. It recurred precisely forty spins later at the same row in the third column. It is also worth noting that both of these numbers are odd, black and in the middle column.

Sandwich

One sandwich materialized. Beginning in column two at row nineteen and continuing to row three in column three, one can observe (9/29/12/29/9).

Formulae

The formulae which can be seen reaffirm the presence of the "Powers-That-Be." First they dictate that *(19 + 21 − 16 = 24)*. The message which they convey within that message is that *(19 + 21 = 16 + 24)*. Then they elaborate on that theme when they tell us that *(16 + 24 − 16 = 24)*. Further elaborations are also in order when they inform us that

(16 + 24 + 16 = 24 + 32). Lastly, they state unequivocally that *(18 = 36 − 4 − 14)*. Even Pythagoras would have to concur with these sentiments.

FIGURE 9

9-Aug			NON-OCCURS				
11*	14*	12*	2	**1**	1	**19**	2
**29*	27	**29	3	**2**		**20**	
4*	**31***	9*	6	**3**		**21**	2
14*	32*	19*	7	**4**	6	**22**	4
OO	**26***	21*	8	**5**	1	**23**	1
21	**17**	16*	20	**6**		**24**	3
11	22*	24*	28	**7**		**25**	1
17	4*	16*	30	**8**		**26**	4
23	12*	24*	33	**9**	2	**27**	1
24*	12*	32*	34	**10**	2	**28**	
OO	15	**31**	35	**11**	4	**29**	4
29*	18	**26**		**12**	3	**30**	
4*	13	0		**13**	2	**31**	2
11	**26***	***11***		**14**	2	**32**	2
26	25	4*		**15**	1	**33**	
5	**10**	19		**16**	2	**34**	
4*	22*	1		**17**	2	**35**	
18*	**10**	13		**18**	2	**36**	1
36*	9*	22		**0**	1	**OO**	2
4*	29*	22			**MODE:**	4	

**Kismet
*Superna tural Occurrence

RECURRING PAIRS: (4/14) (4/29) (16/24) (12/24) (4/22)

RECURRING TRIOS: (4/11/29) (26/31/32) (4/11/26)

QUINTET: (4/11/26/11/4)

SANDWICH: (9/29/12/29/9)

FORMULAE: (19 + 21 - 16 = 24) (19 + 21 = 16 + 24)

(16 + 24 + 16 = 24 + 32) (18 = 36 - 4 - 14)

Figure 10

Biases

The occurrences began with a marked digit bias. At rows one, two, thirteen, sixteen, seventeen and nineteen, one can see numbers which ended in (1). That is, six of the numbers in the first column, or 30%, were those which ended in this digit.

These occurrences also began with a marked bias in favor of The Black Pentacle, in that the first three numbers were of this group: (31/31/10).

Other biases which can be seen here are in column two at rows four through six where three numbers which are multiples of three occurred, though not in the usual order: (6/3/9). The same type of phenomenon can be seen in all three columns at row thirteen where the numbers show a descending pattern of numbers at intervals of two: (11/9/7). An odd/consecutive bias is therefore apparent at regular intervals.

Two additional instances of consecutive bias are also apparent. In column two at rows eleven through thirteen, the sequence is: (10/11/9). Also, this set of observances ends with another trio which demonstrates a consecutive bias in column three at rows eighteen through twenty: (18/20/19).

Lastly, an odd bias can be seen in the second column at rows twelve through twenty. With one exception, all of the nine numbers in this range, or 88.8%, were odd: (11/9/27/13/13/19/29/21). An odd bias can again be observed in the third column at rows twelve through seventeen. All six of these numbers were odd: (1/7/17/29/23/3).

Kismet

There was one example of Kismet. In the first column at row nine, the (32) occurred. It occurred again precisely twenty spins later in the second column at the same row.

Recurring Pairs & Trios

The recurring pairs were first the (6/30) which first occurred at a precise twenty spin interval of one another at row four in columns one and two. This duo then recurred as a separate pair when they appeared back-to-back in column one at rows five and six.

The (2/32) did substantially the same as the numbers above when they first occurred at a precise twenty spin interval of one another in columns two and three at row nine. Note that the (32) was a part of Kismet. Then this duo recurred as a pair when they occurred back-to-back in column two at rows nine and ten.

Likewise did the (2/34) emulate the numbers above when they first occurred at a precise twenty spin interval of one another in columns two and three at row ten. This pair then recurred when these two numbers occurred back-to-back in column three at rows nine and ten.

The (9/11) completed this quartet of numbers which behaved substantially the same when these two numbers first occurred at a precise twenty spin interval of one another in columns one and two at row thirteen. Upon the appearance of another (11) in column two at row twelve, immediately preceding the aforementioned (9), this pair then recurred.

Formulae

"The Gods" reaffirmed their eternal presence when they state first that *(25 = 32 − 7)*, and also that *(30 − 6 = 24)*. They further inform us that *(21 = 22 − 1)*. Then they matter-of-factly state that *(6 + 3 = 9)*. The power of "The Gods" to multiply is apparent when they state that *(17 x 2 = 34)*, and also that *(2 x 10 = 11 + 9)*. They also demonstrate a little mischief when they state unequivocally that *((29 − 23) x 3 = 18))*. Could Pythagoras dispute these universal truths?

Standard Pairs

With respect to standard pairs, these observances began with (31/10) in column one at rows one through three. One can also observe a (27/30) in column two at rows fourteen and fifteen. Then one can see a (4/18) in column three at rows two and three. Also, one can see one of the "Opposite Twins," (12/21) in columns one and two at row twenty.

FIGURE 10
NON-OCCURS

	Aug 18						
31	25	0	5	1	2	19	2
31	3	4	8	2	3	20	1
10	17	18	16	3	3	21	2
30*	6*	24*	26	4	1	22	1
30*	3*	25	28	5		23	3
6*	9*	34	35	6	2	24	1
15	14	36	OO	7	2	25	3
25*	13	17*		8		26	
**32*	**32*	2*		9	2	27	1
7*	2*	34*		10	2	28	
23	10*	2		11	3	29	2
33	11*	1		12	1	30	3
11*	9*	7		13	3	31	2
23	27	17		14	1	32	2
18	30	29*		15	1	33	1
11	13	23*		16		34	2
21*	13	3*		17	3	35	
22*	19	18*		18	3	36	1
1*	29	20		0	1	OO	
12	21	19				**MODE:**	

**Kismet
*Superna tural Occurrence

RECURRING PAIRS: (6/30) (2/32) (2/34) (9/11)

FORMULAE: (25 = 32 - 7) (30 - 6 = 24) (21 = 22 - 1)

(6 + 3 = 9) (17 x 2 = 34) (2 x 10 = 11 + 9)

((29 - 23) x 3 = 18))

Figure 11

The primary purpose of examining these occurrences is to demonstrate the predominance of numbers of a certain attribute. In this case the common attribute is perfect divisibility by (7). Observe that the author has departed from his usual practice of highlighting the numbers of The Black Pentacle. In the accompanying chart and also in Figure 44 which demonstrates the implementation of a system which concentrates only on five designated numbers, only the numbers divisible by (7), that is, (7/14/21/28/35) are highlighted in **bold.**

Biases

The occurrences began with a noticeable digit bias. In addition to the fact that three of the first four numbers, or 75%, end in (4), one can see that four of the twenty numbers in the first column, or 20%, end in this digit: (4/34/4/14).

There was one noticeable hot number. Beginning in the first column at row fifteen, the (14) occurred five times over the next thirty-eight spins, or 13.1% of the time within this range.

The frequent occurrence of the (14) was merely part of a general bias in favor of the digit (4). Twelve of the sixty occurrences were numbers ending in (4): (4/34/4/14/14/14/24/34/14/4/24/14). That is, 20% of all sixty occurrences were numbers ending in (4). Note that numbers ending in (4) represent only 10.5% of all of the numbers possible. Accordingly, the numbers ending in (4) occurred about twice as often as they should have.

The second column experienced a marked column bias. The bias began at row eight and continued to row seventeen where seven of the ten numbers in this range, or 70%, were in the third column of the board: (18/33/24/15/12/12/33).

The occurrences then experienced an even bias. Beginning in the second column at row eighteen, all of the occurrences were even: (34/10/14/28/30/22).

Lastly, close scrutiny reveals that these sixty numbers favor those divisible by (7). Fifteen, or 25% of these occurrences have this attribute: (35/28/14/14/35/7/14/14/28/21/7/35/14/28/7). One can therefore observe a marked divisible bias. For this reason the author was compelled to prepare Figure 44 in order to demonstrate how the utilization of a particular system will be to a player's benefit under circumstances such as this.

Recurring Pairs & Trios

The pairs which recurred here were the (14/15) which first occurred back-to-back in column two at rows five and six. This pair then recurred when they appeared again at a precise twenty spin interval of one another in columns two and three at row twelve.

Then the (6/14) first occurred back-to-back in column one at rows fifteen and sixteen. This pair then recurred at a precise twenty spin interval of one another in columns two and three at row twenty.

The (11/12) behaved in the same manner as those preceding when these two numbers first occurred back-to-back in column one at rows thirteen and fourteen. Upon the appearance of a (12) in column two at row fourteen, opposite the aforementioned (11), this pair then recurred.

Then it was the turn of the (4/7) to recur as a pair when these two numbers first appeared at a precise twenty spin interval of one another in columns one and two at row four. This duo then appeared back-to-back in column three at rows six and seven, becoming in the process a recurring pair.

The only standard pair to be seen here is the (13/33) in columns two and three at row ten.

There were three recurring trios, two of which were of an extraordinary nature. First the (9/11/12) occurred consecutively in column one at rows twelve through fourteen. This trio then recurred extraordinarily in all three columns at precise twenty and forty spin intervals beginning at row fourteen in column one. Further note that this trio recurred in precise reverse order than that in which it first occurred.

The second recurring trio materialized in column one at rows six through eight when the sequence was (8/9/28). Most extraordinarily this trio recurred in the exact same order in column three at rows thirteen through fifteen. Note also that each trio occurred exactly five spins after, and also five spin before the beginning and the end of this set of numbers.

The last recurring trio comprised two right angles. The (8/14/15) first occurred in columns one and two, with the (8) occurring in column one at row six, and the (14/15) occurring back-to-back in column two at rows five and six. This trio recurred in substantially the same format in columns two and three, with the (15) occurring in column two at row twelve and the (8/14) occurring back-to-back in column three at rows twelve and thirteen.

Kismet

There were two examples of Kismet. In the first column at row three, the (35) occurred. Precisely twenty spins later it recurred at the same row in column two. Also in the first column at row nineteen, the (10) occurred. Precisely twenty spins later it materialized at the same row in column two.

Formulae

With respect to the formulae which materialized here, the influence of the supernatural is quite apparent. This pervading force tells us first that *(8 = 15 –7)*. Then it tells us that *(33 – 14 = 19)*. We are then informed that *((7 = (14 + 15) – 22))*. Then we are subtly informed that *((34 = - (10 + 14) + (28 + 30))*. Lastly, the force tells us that *(7 + 4 = 11)*. Pythagoras might concede these mathematical truths.

Drought

With respect to the numbers which failed to occur, it is quite remarkable that three are consecutive. These occurrences experienced a "1 street drought," in that neither the (1), (2) nor (3) occurred. It is further quite remarkable that of all the numbers which failed to occur, four of these are in one small section of the wheel. Refer to the effigy of the roulette wheel which is provided on p. 28. Observe that the (5), (17), (20) and (32) are contiguous. None of these numbers materialized in sixty spins. The wheel therefore experienced a marked section drought.

These sixty occurrences further experienced a drought of a most unusual nature. Seven of the ten numbers which failed to occur were in the second column of the board: (2/5/17/20/23/29/32). We can therefore see a virtual middle column drought.

FIGURE 11

	Aug 11		NON-OCCURS				
4	14	28*	1	1		19	3
34	18	30*	2	2		20	
**35	**35	22	3	3		21	1
4*	7*	21	5	4	3	22	2
33*	14*	19*	17	5		23	
8*	15*	7*	20	6	2	24	2
9*	22*	4*	23	7	3	25	1
28*	18	11*	29	8	2	26	2
36	19	24	32	9	3	27	1
0	33	13	OO	10	3	28	3
26	24	35		11	3	29	
9*	15*	14*		12	3	30	1
12*	16	8*		13	1	31	1
11*	12*	9*		14	5	32	
14*	31	28*		15	2	33	3
6*	12	10		16	1	34	2
27	33	26		17		35	3
19	34*	7		18	2	36	1
**10	**10*	11		0	1	OO	
25	14*	6*			MODE:	14	

**Kismet
*Superna tural Occurrence

RECURRING PAIRS: (14/15) (6/14) (11/12) (4/7)

RECURRING TRIOS: (9/11/12) (8/9/28) (8/14/15)

FORMULAE: $(8 = 15 - 7)$ $(33 - 14 = 19)$

$((7 = (14 + 15) - 22))$

$((34 = -(10 + 14) + 28 + 30))$ $(7 + 4 = 11)$

Figure 12

Note that this Figure is unique in that it contains the observations on the same date in two different years. The author provides these two sets of observances in order to demonstrate that the numbers which occur on the same date and on the same wheel in two different years are not necessarily similar. Further note that the second set of observations on 13 August 2005 are not examined as were those from the preceding year. No Recurring Pairs or Formulae were highlighted, for instance. Accordingly, the narrative below only pertains to the observations from 2004. Also, the observations from 2005 are not included in the Vital Statistics in Figures 38 and 38A.

Biases

The occurrences began with a marked low bias. All of the first five numbers in the first column were low (below (19)): (14/1/14/9/1).

The first column also experienced a digit bias. At rows one, three, seventeen and nineteen a number ending in (4) occurred: (14/14/4/14). That is, 20% of the occurrences in the first column were biased in favor of (4).

In the second column at rows four through six one can observe a consecutive bias. The sequence therein was (10/9/11) which numbers are consecutive, though not in the usual order.

One hot number can also be observed in the second column. At rows two, eight and fifteen the (34) occurred thrice, or 15% of the time. For the range from rows two through fifteen, the (34) occurred 21.4% of the time.

Near the top of the third column one can see a marked high bias. From row two through row seven, six consecutive numbers were high (above (18)): (22/25/23/31/20/36).

From row seven in column two to row nineteen in column three, the (36) was a hot number, occurring four times within this range, or 12.1% of the time.

Though it is difficult to detect, this set of sixty observances was characterized by a line bias. Twelve of the sixty numbers were centered around the last line of the board which includes the numbers (31 – 36): (35/32/35/34/36/34/34/35/31/36/36/36). What is even more remarkable is the fact that ten, or 16.6% of all sixty observances were in the last "street" of the board (34/35/36). This is of course indicative of a 34 street bias.

Recurring Pairs & Trios

The pairs which recurred here were first the (1/14) which occurred in column one at rows two and three. This pair then recurred in the same column and in the same order at rows eighteen and nineteen.

Then the (0/36) occurred at a precise twenty spin interval of one another in column two and three at row nineteen. This pair then recurred back-to-back in column three at rows seven and eight.

The (3/22) behaved similarly when these two numbers first occurred back-to-back in column two at rows nine and ten. This pair recurred when they occurred at a precise twenty spin interval of one another in columns two and three at row eighteen.

The (1/9) also behaved similarly as those preceding when these two numbers first occurred back-to-back in column one at rows four and five. Upon the appearance of a (9) in column two at row five, opposite the aforementioned (1), this pair then recurred.

The (3/34) behaved extraordinarily when these two numbers occurred back-to-back in column two at rows eight and nine. This pair then quite extraordinarily recurred in the same column, also back-to-back at rows fourteen and fifteen, though not in the original order.

Also extraordinarily the (3/9) occurred at a precise twenty spin interval of one another in columns one and two at row nine. This duo then quite extraordinarily recurred as a pair in the same manner in column two and three at row fourteen.

The last of the pairs to recur here was the (9/10) which first occurred at a precise twenty spin interval of one another in columns one and two at row four. Upon the appearance of another (9) in column two at row five, immediately following the aforementioned (10), this pair then recurred. In addition, this is one of the rare instances in which a pair recurred a second time. These two numbers also appeared again back-to-back in column three at rows fourteen and fifteen. This pairing is even more extraordinary in view of the fact that these two numbers are consecutive.

The latter two pairings of the (9) and (10) must be considered separately in that they are part of a rare instance in which a trio recurred. Observe in column two that the sequence at rows three through five is:

(18/10/9). This trio quite extraordinarily recurred in column three at rows thirteen through fifteen where the sequence was (18/9/10).

The only standard pair to be observed here is the (3/36) which occurred back-to-back in column three at rows eighteen and nineteen.

Formulae

The "Powers-That-Be" were on the case as usual in telling us in formulae that

(10 + 16 = 26), and that *(16 = 34 – 18).* They were also compelled to inform us that

(14 x 1 = 14). Their mischief becomes apparent when they inform us that

((0 = (35 + 12) – (22 + 25)). Then they cleverly tell us that *(1 + 14 + 35 = 16 + 34).*

Disciples of Pythagoras would have to capitulate to these dictates.

Kismet

There were three examples of Kismet. In the first column at row twenty, the (35) occurred. It occurred again precisely twenty spins later in the same row of column two. In the second column at row seven the (36) occurred. It recurred precisely twenty spins later at the same row in column three. Also in the second column one can observe the (26) at row seventeen. This number recurred precisely twenty spins later at the same row in column three. Lastly, it is worth noting that all of these numbers are large numbers in the third dozen.

Drought

With respect to the numbers which failed to occur, three of these numbers were black numbers in the third column of the board: (6/24/33). That is, the entire set of observances experienced a virtual third black drought. Only the (15) occurred, being the last number in the range in column three at row twenty.

Lastly, it is worth noting also that of the numbers which failed to occur, three of these numbers were consecutive. Neither the (6), nor the (7), nor the (8) occurred.

FIGURE 12

Aug 13	2004	NON-	OCCURS
14*	16*	12*	6
1*	34*	22*	7
14*	18*	25*	8
9*	10*	23	21
1*	9*	31	24
27	11	20	33
28	**36	**36*	
5	34*	0*	
9*	3*	4	
2	22*	29	
27	17	36	
OO	30	23	
19	0	18*	
18	3*	9*	
35	34*	10*	
32	13	16*	
4	**26	**26*	
1*	22*	3*	
14*	0*	36*	
**35*	**35*	15	

#		#	
1	3	19	1
2	1	20	1
3	3	21	
4	2	22	3
5	1	23	2
6		24	
7		25	1
8		26	2
9	4	27	2
10	2	28	1
11	1	29	1
12	1	30	1
13	1	31	1
14	3	32	1
15	1	33	
16	2	34	3
17	1	35	3
18	3	36	4
0	3	OO	1
		MODE:	

**Kismet   *Supernatural Occurrence

RECURRING PAIRS: (1/14) (0/36) (3/22) (1/9) (3/34) (3/9) (9/10)
RECURRING TRIO: (9/10/18)
FORMULAE: (10 + 16 = 26) (16 = 34 - 18) (1 x 14 = 14)
((0 = 35 + 12) - (22 + 25))
(1 + 14 + 35 = 16 + 34)

Aug 13	2005			#		#	
28	27	12		1	2	19	4
7	2	30		2	2	20	
3	28	33		3	2	21	
23	17	27		4	1	22	
34	0	17		5	3	23	4
31	3	7		6		24	
13	11	23		7	4	25	1
13	25	19		8	1	26	2
7	23	19		9	1	27	2
32	5	12		10	3	28	3
23	17	33		11	3	29	
11	19	10		12	3	30	1
9	11	28		13	2	31	1
1	7	19		14		32	1
5	4	1		15		33	4
26	0	33		16		34	1
10	35	12		17	3	35	1
0	36	33		18	1	36	1
8	10	18		0	3	OO	
5	26	2				**MODE:**	

Figure 13

Biases

The occurrences began with a marked digit bias. Four of the numbers in the first column, or 20%, which are located at rows three, six, seven and fourteen ended in (6): (36/36/6/36). Another digit bias can be observed from rows ten through twenty in this column. Five of the numbers in this range of eleven, or 45.45%, ended in (7): (17/27/17/17/17).

One can further observe that there were two hot numbers in the first column. Three of the first fourteen numbers, or 21.4%, were (36). Also, the (17) occurred four times, or 20% of all occurrences in this column. For the range from rows ten through twenty, the (17) occurred 36.36% of the time.

In the second column one can also observe a digit bias. Five of the occurrences, or 25%, were numbers ending in (1): (21/11/1/11/21). Further, all of the last four numbers in the column ended in (1): (11/1/11/21). This column also experienced a column bias of the board. Nine of the twenty occurrences, or 45%, were in the middle column of the board: (5/14/23/17/5/23/14/11/11).

There was also a low bias from the fifteenth row of the second column to the first row of column three. All of the seven occurrences were low numbers (below (19)): (15/14/11/1/11/21/10).

The third column began with a marked even bias. With one exception, all of the first seven numbers from rows one through ten, or 85.7%, were even: (10/22/12/2/26/2).

The third column then continued with a color bias. With one exception, all of the first eight numbers from rows one through ten, or 87.5%, were black: (10/22/31/2/26/2/33).

With respect to the numbers which failed to occur, four of these numbers were small (below (19)) and in the first column of the board: (4/7/13/16).

Recurring Pairs & Trios

The recurring pairs to be seen here are (1/34) which duo occurred at a precise twenty spin interval of one another in columns one and two at row eleven. This pair then extraordinarily recurred in the same manner in columns two and three at row eighteen.

Then the (17/23) occurred at a precise twenty spin interval of one another in columns one and two at row ten. This pair then recurred when these two numbers occurred back-to-back in column two at rows five and six.

Next the (5/21) recurred as a pair when these two numbers first occurred back-to-back in column two at rows eight and nine. Upon the appearance of a (21) in column three at row nine, opposite the aforementioned (5), this pair then recurred.

Then the (12/15) recurred as a pair and also emulated its cousins above when this duo first occurred at a precise twenty spin interval of one another in columns two and three at row fifteen. Upon the appearance of a (15) in column three at row sixteen, immediately following the aforementioned (12), this pair then recurred. Note also that only a (36) in column one at row three kept this pair from recurring a second time.

The (21/28) recurred as a pair when these two numbers first occurred back-to-back in column two at rows seven and eight. Then this pair recurred at a precise twenty spin interval of one another in columns two and three at row twenty.

The last of the pairs to recur was the (12/31) which quite extraordinarily first occurred back-to-back in column three at rows three and four. This pair then recurred back-to-back in the same column shortly thereafter at rows fourteen and fifteen, though reversed.

The standard pairs to be seen here are first the (6/36) which occurred back-to-back in column one at rows six and seven. Also, the (10/31) occurred at a precise twenty spin interval of one another in columns two and three at row four.

Formulae

"The Gods" again made their presence known by first reminding us that

(1 x 34 = 34). They then state unequivocally that *(27 − 15 = 12)*. Then they flatly state that *(30 = 36 − 6)*. We are then reminded that *(11 = 21 − 10)* and further that

(10 = 22 −12). They become somewhat more eloquent when they tell us that

(22 + 27 − 34 = 15). Lastly, they become somewhat mischievous

when they tell us that *((11 – 1) + 11 = 21))*. Pythagoras would have to recognize these universal truths.

Kismet

There was one instance of Kismet. In the second column at row eleven, the (34) occurred. This number occurred again in the third column at the same row precisely twenty spins later.

FIGURE 13
NON-OCCURS

	Aug 16						
20	33	**10***	3	**1**	2	**19**	1
12	5	**22***	4	**2**	3	**20**	1
36	14	**12***	7	**3**		**21**	3
15	**10**	**31***	8	**4**		**22**	2
30*	23*	2	13	**5**	2	**23**	2
36*	**17***	**26**	16	**6**	2	**24**	
6*	28*	2	18	**7**		**25**	1
35	21*	33	24	**8**		**26**	1
32	5*	21*	29	**9**	1	**27**	2
17*	23*	25	OO	**10**	4	**28**	2
1*	**34*	**34*		**11**	2	**29**	
9	22*	**10***		**12**	3	**30**	1
31	27*	**6**		**13**		**31**	3
36	34*	**31***		**14**	2	**32**	1
27*	15*	**12***		**15**	3	**33**	2
17	14	15*		**16**		**34**	4
17	11*	2		**17**	5	**35**	1
19	1*	34*		**18**		**36**	3
10	11*	0		**0**	1	**OO**	
17	21*	28*				**MODE:**	17

**Kismet
*Superna tural Occurrence

**RECURRING
PAIRS:**　　　　(1/34) (17/23) (5/21) (12/15) (21/28)(12/31)

　　　　　　　　(10/22)

FORMULAE:　　(1 x 34 = 34) (27 - 15 = 12) (30 = 36 - 6)

　　　　　　　　(22 + 27 - 34 = 15) ((11 - 1) + 11 = 21))

　　　　　　　　(11 = 21 - 10) (10 = 22 - 12)

Figure 14

Biases

The (30) was obviously the hot number of the first column, occurring three times, or 42.8% of the occurrences within the range of the first seven numbers. Then it became completely cold, not occurring again until row nine of column three.

Also, here one can see a most extraordinary example of wheel bias. Refer to the effigy of a roulette wheel on p. 28. In the second column beginning at row twelve and continuing to row seventeen, all of the six numbers occurred in a small, contiguous section of the wheel: (22/15/34/5/15/17).

Recurring Pairs & Trios

The pairs which recurred were first the (11/30) which duo first appeared in column one at rows one and two, and then repeated this feat at rows three and four. This is quite a rare phenomenon.

The next pair to recur was the (5/15) which duo first occurred in columns one and two at a precise twenty spin interval of one another at row sixteen. This pair then recurred when this duo appeared again back-to-back in column two at rows fifteen and sixteen. Observe that this second pairing is separated only by a (34) in column two at row thirteen which would have made this pair recur a third time.

The next pair to recur was the (19/22) which first occurred at a precise twenty spin interval of one another in columns one and two at row twelve. Upon the appearance of a (19) in column two immediately preceding the aforementioned (22), this pair then recurred.

The last pair to recur was the (14/30) which first occurred at a precise twenty spin interval of one another at row one in columns one and two. This pair then recurred in approximately the same manner when this duo appeared again at row nine in columns two and three, again at a precise twenty spin interval of one another. Observe also that only the (26) in column three at row eighteen kept this duo from recurring a third time.

Kismet

Note that the (22) of the last recurring pair mentioned above is part of the only instance of Kismet here. The (22) occurred again in column three at row twelve.

Formulae

"The Gods" again reasserted their authority to influence numbers when they first inform us that *(1 + 12 = 13).* Then they tell us that *(9 + 11 = 20).* They then tell us that *(19 = 10 + 9).* Further they tell us that *(30 + 11 – 30 = 11).* Next they unequivocally state that *((30 + 11 + 9) – 20 = 30)).* Then they state that *(9 = 17 – 8).* They demonstrate their usual obtuseness when they cleverly inform us that *((25 + 22) – 6) – 23 = 18)).* Must they also remind us that *((33 – 8) + 5 = 30))*? Pythagoras' disciples would be confounded but compliant with these dictates.

Supernatural Phenomena

The unusual "supernatural" phenomenon to be seen here is that the first eight numbers alternated colors, beginning with red: (30/11/30/11/9/20/30/24). This is of course the way that roulette numbers are *theoretically* supposed to occur. However, as one can observe in the Narratives provided later, the numbers seldom occur in this theoretical manner. This is why this observed phenomenon is unusual.

Standard Pairs

Remarkably, there was only one standard pair. In columns two and three at row twenty the (3/36) occurred.

FIGURE 14

	18-Aug		NON-OCCURS				
30*	14*	24	2	1	2	19	2
11*	23	7	16	2		20	1
30*	OO	21	31	3	1	21	1
11*	24	9*	32	4	1	22	2
9*	27	17*		5	3	23	3
20*	10	8*		6	2	24	3
30*	1	33*		7	2	25	1
24	12	5*		8	1	26	1
35	14*	30*		9	3	27	1
1*	12*	13*		10	2	28	1
23	19*	25*		11	2	29	2
19*	**22*	**22*		12	3	30	5
10*	15	6*		13	1	31	
9*	34	23*		14	3	32	
29	5*	18*		15	2	33	1
5*	15*	28		16		34	1
7	17	14		17	2	35	1
29	4	26		18	1	36	1
6	12	30		0	1	OO	1
0	36	3			**MODE:**	30	

**Kismet
*Superna tural Occurrence

RECURRING PAIRS: (11/30) (5/15) (19/22) (14/30)

FORMULAE: (1 + 12 = 13) (11 + 9 = 20) (19 = 10 + 9)

(30 + 11 - 30 = 11)

((30 + 11 + 9) - 20 = 30))

(9 = 17 - 8) ((25 + 22 - 6) - 23 = 18))

((33 - 8) + 5 = 30))

Figure 15

Biases

The first unusual phenomenon to be seen here is the hot number, (19), which occurred four times in eighteen spins from row six in column one to row three in column two. The (19) thereby occurred 22.2% of the time within this range. Note also that the (19) is the mode.

There was also a hot number beginning in the second column at row nineteen and continuing to row eight of column three. Within this range of ten numbers, the (13) occurred three times, or 30% of the time.

A marked wheel bias can be seen in column two at rows eighteen through twenty and continuing to row one of column three. Each of these four occurrences are contiguous on the wheel: (36/13/13/1).

The second column demonstrated a pronounced color bias beginning at row seven and continuing through row sixteen. With two exceptions, all of the numbers in this range of eight numbers, or 80%, were red: (16/34/5/27/34/7/32/21).

Note also the color bias which began near the top of the third column. With one exception, all of the numbers in this range of eight numbers from row two through row nine, or 87.5%, were black: (26/17/31/29/10/13/29).

The third column also demonstrated a marked column bias beginning at row ten and continuing to row nineteen. With three exceptions, all of the numbers in this range of ten numbers, or 70%, were in the first column of the board: (25/16/4/22/1/7/19).

The third column demonstrated a remarkable presence of the Black Pentacle (6/10/17/26/31). Six of the numbers in this column were of the Pentacle, beginning at row two and continuing to row eighteen: (26/17/31/10/6/17). All of the numbers of The Black Pentacle were thereby represented. Note that the (00) is included in this range, which, to reiterate, is usually associated with black numbers.

Recurring Pairs & Trios

The pairs which recurred here were first the (13/36) which duo occurred back-to-back in column two at rows eighteen and nineteen. Remarkably this pair recurred separately with the (13) repeating itself and also occurring at a precise twenty spin interval of one another in columns two and three at row twenty.

Next the (2/27) occurred at a precise twenty spin interval of one another in columns one and two at row fourteen. Then this pair recurred separately in column two when they occurred back-to-back at rows ten and eleven.

Then the (10/11) occurred back-to-back in column two at rows five and six. Upon the appearance of a (10) in column three at row six, opposite the aforementioned (11), this pair then recurred.

The (2/7) emulated its cousins above when this duo first occurred back-to-back in column two at rows thirteen and fourteen. This pair then recurred separately in columns two and three at row seventeen.

Next the (17/19) recurred as a pair when this duo first occurred at a precise twenty spin interval of one another in columns two and three at row three. This duo then occurred back-to-back and thereby recurred as a pair in column three at rows eighteen and nineteen.

Then the (10/36) recurred as a pair when this duo first occurred back-to-back in column one at rows seventeen and eighteen. Upon the appearance of a (36) in column two at row eighteen, opposite the aforementioned (10), this pair then recurred.

The last of the pairs to recur was the (2/36) which duo first occurred within a twenty spin interval of one another at row seventeen in columns one and two. Upon the appearance of a (36) in column two at row eighteen, immediately following the aforementioned (2), this pair then recurred.

Sandwich

One sandwich materialized. In column one from rows twelve through fifteen, the sequence was: (19/27/27/19) by which "The Gods" prepared a rather thick sandwich with a rather thin bun.

Formulae

The formulae which materialized indicates that the "Powers-That-Be" again exerted their influence when they stated that *(1 + 6 = 7)*, and that *(17 + 19 = 36)*. They then reaffirm the fact that *(34 – 5 – 2 = 27)*. Next they tell us that *(24 – 5 = 19)* and that *(13/13 = 1)*. They elaborate on that theme when they state that

$((13 + 13) \times 1 = 26))$. Lastly, they reaffirm the fact that $(27 = 34 - 7)$. Pythagoras himself could not have better stated these universal truths.

Standard Pairs

There was one standard pair in column one. The (3) and (36) occurred back-to-back at rows sixteen and seventeen.

Drought

Lastly, this set of occurrences is quite remarkable in that it is characterized by an (8) *drought*. None of the numbers containing an (8) occurred.

FIGURE 15

19-Aug			NON-OCCURS				
35	5*	1*	8	1	2	19	5
9	24*	26*	12	2	3	20	1
9	19*	17*	14	3	1	21	1
25	24	31	18	4	1	22	1
20	10*	29	33	5	2	23	1
19	11*	10*	0	6	1	24	2
31	16	OO		7	2	25	2
OO	34*	13		8		26	1
30	5*	29		9	2	27	3
15	2*	25		10	4	28	
10	27*	16		11	1	29	2
19*	34*	4		12		30	2
27*	7*	22		13	3	31	2
27*	2*	30		14		32	1
19*	32	1*		15	1	33	
3	21	6*		16	2	34	2
36*	2*	7*		17	2	35	2
10*	36*	17*		18		36	3
23	13*	19*		0		OO	2
35	13*	36*			**MODE:**	19	

**Kismet
*Superna tural Occurrence

RECURRING PAIRS: (13/36) (2/27) (10/11) (2/7) (2/36) (10/36)

(17/19)

FORMULAE: (1 + 6 = 7) (17 + 19 = 36) (34 - 5 - 2 = 27)

(24 - 5 = 19) ((13 + 13) x 1 = 26))

(27 = 34 - 7) (13 / 13 = 1)

SANDWICH: (19/27/27/19)

Figure 16

The reader should first note that this is a special set of observations. The numbers on two adjacent wheels were simultaneously observed. As such, this set of sixty occurrences should be considered with those in Figure 17. Some numbers did occur simultaneously on both wheels. These were first, the (34) and also the (18) and are marked with a "+." They are detailed below.

Observe also that in a slight departure from his usual methodology the author was compelled to highlight numbers in bold in addition to the numbers of The Black Pentacle. This is because of a most extraordinary occurrence of a recurring trio: (7/22/29). This trio is marked on the chart in **bold** and also in *italics.*

Simultaneous Occurrences

At row two of column one the (34) occurred. Simultaneously it occurred on the adjacent wheel. Next in the same column at, coincidentally, row eighteen, the (18) appeared simultaneously with the appearance of the same number on the adjacent wheel.

Biases

The unusual phenomena also to be observed here are in the first column which ended with a marked color bias which extended into the second column. The bias began at row eighteen of column one and ended at row five of the next column. Six of the numbers within this range of eight, or 75%, were red: (18/27/21/19/25/7). Note that these six numbers were further evenly divided between the first and third columns of the board.

Note that there was a marked column bias in column two. The bias began at row nine and continued to the end of the column. With three exceptions, all of the numbers in this range of twelve numbers, or 75%, were in the first column of the board: (28/22/7/10/16/25/16/19/1). Put another way, 65% of all the numbers in column two were biased in favor of the first column.

One can also see a marked divisible/column bias beginning in column one at row eighteen and continuing to row one in column two: (18/33/27/21). All of these numbers are in the third column and are divisible by (3).

Recurring Pairs & Trios

Recurring pairs to be observed here are the (11/16) which first occurred at a precise twenty spin interval of one another in columns one and two at row seventeen. Then this pair recurred twice, remarkably in the same manner in columns two and three at row two. Also, with the appearance of another (11) in column three at row one, immediately preceding the aforementioned (16), this pair then recurred a second time.

Then the (22/29) occurred at a precise twenty spin interval of one another in columns two and three at row ten. This pair then recurred upon the appearance of a (22) in column three at row eleven, immediately following the aforementioned (29).

Further, the (7/28) first occurred back-to-back in column two at rows five and six. This pair then recurred when this duo occurred at a precise twenty spin interval of one another in columns two and three, at row nine. Note also that only the appearance of a (17) in column three at row twelve kept this pair from recurring a third time.

In addition, the (22/36) occurred back-to-back in column two at rows ten and eleven. This duo then recurred as a pair upon the appearance of a (22) in column three at row eleven, opposite the aforementioned (36).

Next the (11/21) emulated its cousins above when this duo first occurred back-to-back in column two at rows one and two. This pair then recurred upon the appearance of an (11) in column three at row one, opposite the aforementioned (21).

The last of the pairs to recur was that (7/29) which first occurred at a precise twenty spin interval of one another in columns one and two at row twelve. This pair then recurred back-to-back in column three at rows nine and ten. Inasmuch as the first occurrence of this pair was separate from the aforementioned recurring trio, the additional occurrence of this pair must also be addressed.

To reiterate, there was also a quite astounding appearance of a recurring trio. The last of the pairs to occur above was also part of this trio: (7/22/29). This trio can be seen at row ten in all of the three columns. It can again be observed in the third column at rows nine through eleven where the trio recurred, though not in the original order. The occurrence and recurrence of this trio in the tenth row and also in the third column is accordingly highlighted in *italics* and in **bold**.

Standard Pairs

The first standard pair to be observed here is the (26/29) which occurred back-to-back in column three at rows sixteen and seventeen. Next, one can see in the first and second columns at row eleven a (6/36). Then one can observe an (18/36) also in columns one and two at row eighteen.

Kismet

There was only one example of Kismet. In the second column at row fifteen, the (16) occurred. It recurred precisely twenty spins later in the third column.

Formulae

The "Powers-That-Be" were on the case as usual. They first tell us that

(0 = 16 − 16) and that *(10 = 21 − 11)*. They then state succinctly that *(7 + 22 = 29)* and that *(18 = 36/2)*. Next, they inform us that *(9 + 15 = 24)*. We are then reminded that

(16 = 36 − 19 − 1) and that *(11 + 16 = 27)*. Need they also remind us that *(27 + 3 = 30)*, or that *(7 = 29 − 22)*? Lastly, they obtusely convey their point when they state that

((17 + 28 = 1 x (16 + 29)). Pythagoras might concur with these universal truths.

Drought

Note that of all the numbers which failed to appear, all of the red numbers of the middle column of the board were among these: (5/14/23/32). There was accordingly a middle red drought.

With respect to the numbers which failed to appear, in addition to the aforementioned middle red drought, note that six of the numbers which failed to appear were in the middle column of the board: (5/8/14/23/32/35).

FIGURE 16
NON-OCCURS

20-Aug							
10*	21*	11*	4	**1**	2	**19**	2
34+	11*	16*	5	**2**	2	**20**	1
9	19	27*	8	**3**	2	**21**	2
9*	25	3*	13	**4**		**22**	2
15*	7*	30*	14	**5**		**23**	
24*	28*	29	23	**6**	1	**24**	2
29	2	OO	32	**7**	4	**25**	2
0	21	9	35	**8**		**26**	1
3	28*	**7***		**9**	3	**27**	2
7*	**22***	**29***		**10**	2	**28**	3
6	36*	**22***		**11**	3	**29**	5
29*	7*	**17***		**12**	1	**30**	1
12	0	28*		**13**		**31**	1
20	**10**	1*		**14**		**32**	
OO*	**16*	**16*		**15**	1	**33**	1
24	25	29*		**16**	4	**34**	1
11*	16*	**26**		**17**	2	**35**	
18*+	36*	2*		**18**	1	**36**	2
33	19*	**31**		**0**	2	**OO**	2
27	1*	**17**				**MODE:**	29

**Kismet

*Superna tural Occurrence

    + signifies simultaneous occurrence on the opposite wheel

RECURRING PAIRS: (11/16) (22/29) (7/28) (22/36) (11/21) (7/29)

RECURRING TRIO: (7/22/29)

FORMULAE: (0 = 16 - 16) (10 = 21 - 11) (7 + 22 = 29)

     (18 = 36 / 2) (9 + 15 = 24)

     (16 = 36 - 19 - 1)

     (11 + 16 = 27) (27 + 3 = 30) (7 = 29 - 22)

     ((17 + 28 = 1 x (16 + 29))

Figure 17

The reader should first note that this is a special set of observations. The numbers on two adjacent wheels were simultaneously observed. As such, this set of sixty occurrences should be considered with those in Figure 16. Some numbers did occur simultaneously on both wheels. These were first the (34) and also the (18) and are marked with a "+." They are detailed below.

Simultaneous Occurrences

At row eleven of column one the (34) occurred. Simultaneously it occurred on the adjacent wheel. Next, in the second column at row two the (18) appeared simultaneously with the appearance of the same number on the adjacent wheel.

Biases

The occurrences began with a pronounced column bias. Beginning at row six, all of the next five occurrences were in the middle column of the board: (23/35/11/8/29).

There was a hot number in column one. Beginning at row four, the (13) occurred four times in fourteen spins, or 28.4% of the time within this range. Observe also that the (13) occurred 20% of the time in the first column

In column one can also be seen a marked wheel bias. Refer to the effigy of a roulette wheel on p. 28. Beginning at row eleven and continuing to row nineteen, seven of the nine numbers in this range, or 77.7%, were substantially in one area of the wheel from (13) through (34): (34/3/13/36/13/13/3).

The observances then experienced a pronounced color bias beginning at row nineteen of the first column and continuing to the fourth row of column two. All of the six numbers in this range were red: (3/27/30/18/5/9). Note that with one exception, all of these numbers were in the third column of the board.

In the second column can also be seen an even bias. Starting at the ninth row and continuing through row fourteen, all of the numbers except one were even: (34/12/8/4/10). Note also that twelve of the numbers in column two, or 60%, are even: (30/18/28/32/34/12/8/4/10/24/30/10).

A color bias was also prevalent in column two from rows twelve through eighteen. All of the numbers in this range are black: (8/4/10/29/11/11/24).

Kismet

There were three instances of Kismet, two of which were contiguous numbers. First one can see at row eight the (11) occurring at a precise twenty spin interval of one another in columns one and two. The next instance of Kismet was the (10) which can be observed in columns one and two at row fourteen. Lastly, there was the (36) which occurred at a precise forty spin interval of one another in columns one and three at row fifteen.

Recurring Pairs & Trios

The pairs which recurred here were the (11/24) which first occurred at a precise twenty spin interval of one another in columns one and two at row eighteen. Upon the appearance of an (11) in column two at row seventeen, immediately preceding the aforementioned (24), this pair then recurred. Remarkably this pair recurred a second time when this duo appeared back-to-back in column three at rows four and five.

The (11/13) emulated its cousins above by also recurring twice, first occurring at a precise twenty spin interval of one another in columns one and two at row sixteen. Remarkably this pair recurred in the same relationship to one another at the next row, in the same two columns. Also quite remarkably this pair then recurred a second time upon the appearance of an (11) in column one at row eighteen, immediately following the aforementioned (13) at the previous row. Finally, note also the appearance of this duo at a precise forty spin interval of one another in columns one and three at row four. "The Gods" apparently looked upon this duo with favor on the date in question.

Then it was the turn of the (3/11) to recur as a pair when this duo first occurred back-to-back in column one at rows eighteen and nineteen. This pair then recurred at a precise twenty spin interval of one another at row eight in columns two and three.

The (11/11) then behaved as did its cousins above when this duo first occurred at a precise twenty spin interval of one another in columns one and two at row eight. This pair then recurred back-to-back in column two at rows sixteen and seventeen.

Next the (11/34) behaved as did its cousins above when this duo first occurred back-to-back in column two at rows eight and nine. This pair then recurred at a precise twenty spin interval of one another in columns two and three at row sixteen.

Then the (10/17) occurred back-to-back at row twenty in column two and at row one of column three. This pair then recurred at a precise twenty spin interval of one another in columns two and three at row fourteen.

Next the (24/30) occurred back-to-back in column two at rows eighteen and nineteen. This pair then recurred upon the appearance of a (24) in column three at row nineteen, opposite the aforementioned (30).

The (8/22) likewise occurred at a precise twenty spin interval of one another in columns two and three at row twelve. Upon the appearance of an (8) in column three at row thirteen, immediately following the aforementioned (22), this pair then recurred.

Lastly on the subject of recurring pairs, observe that five of these contain an (11), which was the mode. "The Gods" apparently decided that this number would be deserving of their favor on this date.

Standard Pairs

With respect to standard pairs, first one can see an (8/11) in column one at rows eight and nine. Then one can see a (27/30) in column one at row twenty, continuing to row one of column two.

Formulae

"The Gods" again reaffirmed several universal truths, first in telling us that

$(13 + 11 + 3 = 27)$, and also that $(12 = 0 + 8 + 4)$. Next they reaffirm that

$((10 + 17 + 6) - 22 = 11))$, and also that $(17 + 36 = 34 + 19)$. Further they remind us that $(34 = 3 + 31)$. Then they remind us that $(17 + 7 = 24)$. Need they also tell us that

$(13 + 11 = 24)$, and also that $(3 + 27 = 30)$? Their last utterance conveys the generally accepted truth that $(14 = 22 - 8)$. Pythagoras' disciples would be unamazed but accepting of these truths.

Unusual Phenomena

This set of occurrences also contained quite an unusual phenomenon of a number repeating itself in adjacent columns at the same interval. At rows sixteen and seventeen in column one the (13) repeated itself. At the same two rows in column two the (11) likewise repeated itself .

FIGURE 17

	20-Aug		NON-OCCURS				
14	30*	**17***	2	**1**	1	**19**	1
1	18+	**6***	15	**2**		**20**	1
35	5	**22***	16	**3**	3	**21**	
13	9	**11***	21	**4**	1	**22**	2
6	28	**24***	25	**5**	1	**23**	1
23	**17***	**7***	33	**6**	2	**24**	3
35	32	**26**		**7**	1	**25**	
**11*	**11*	**3***		**8**	4	**26**	2
8	34*	**31***		**9**	1	**27**	1
29	12	**26**		**10**	3	**28**	1
34+	0	**14***		**11**	6	**29**	2
3	8*	**22***		**12**	1	**30**	2
13	4	**8***		**13**	4	**31**	1
**10	**10*	**17***		**14**	2	**32**	1
**36	29	****36***		**15**		**33**	
13*	11*	**34***		**16**		**34**	3
13*	11*	**19***		**17**	3	**35**	2
11*	24*	**20**		**18**	1	**36**	2
3*	30*	**24***		**0**	1	**OO**	
27*	**10***	**8**			**MODE:**	11	

**Kismet
*Superna tural Occurrence
+ signifies simultaneous occurrence on the opposite wheel

RECURRING PAIRS: (11/24) (11/13) (3/11) (11/11) (11/34)

(10/17) (24/30) (8/22)

FORMULAE: ((10 + 17 + 6) - 22 = 11))

(17 + 36 = 34 + 19)

(34 = 3 + 31) (17 + 7 = 24) (13 + 11 = 24)

(3 + 27 = 30) (14 = 22 - 8)

Figure 18

This was a special set of observances, in that the numbers on two adjacent wheels were simultaneously observed. As such, this set of sixty occurrences should be considered with those in Figure 19. The numbers which occurred simultaneously on both wheels were: (22), (31), (0), (23) and (30). These are marked with a "**+**." They are detailed below.

Simultaneous Occurrences

The (22) occurred at row two of column one. Simultaneously it occurred on the adjacent wheel. Next, the (31) occurred at row ten in column two. Simultaneously it occurred on the adjacent wheel. Next, the (0) occurred at row nineteen in the same column. Simultaneously it occurred on the adjacent wheel. Next, the (23) occurred at row one in column three. Simultaneously it occurred on the adjacent wheel. Lastly, the (30) occurred at row five in column three. It occurred simultaneously on the adjacent wheel.

Biases

The first column was characterized by a marked even bias. Fourteen of the numbers in this column, or 70%, were even: (8/22/32/20/16/12/8/30/10/4/16/22/16/6). Note also that all of the first seven numbers in this column were even.

There was also a marked column bias in the first column. Beginning at row ten and continuing through row nineteen, with two exceptions all of the numbers in this range of ten numbers, or 80%, were in the first column of the board: (19/10/4/16/13/25/22/16).

There was one hot number in column one. The (16) occurred three times, or 15% of the time. For the range in which it occurred from row five through row nineteen, the (16) occurred 20% of the time.

The second column experienced a pronounced odd bias. Beginning at row two and continuing through row twelve, with three exceptions all of the numbers in this range, or 66.6%, were odd: (1/21/29/13/1/25/31/29).

Note also the double occurrence of the (00) in the second column during which this column experienced a prolonged color bias in favor of black numbers. Refer to the section above entitled "Elements Of Occultism In Roulette/The Validity Of Numerology/Universal

Principles" which states that the (0) and (00) are usually associated with black numbers. Beginning at row nine and continuing to the end of the column, the sequence including the (00/0) was: (8/31/00/29/24/2/00/22/20/33/0/29). The contention of the author that both the (0) and (00) are usually associated with black numbers is thereby affirmed.

Beginning at row ten of the third column, one can see a consecutive bias. Three consecutive numbers occurred over three spins, though not in the usual order: (34/35/33). This sequence was part of an occurrence of high bias which ended at row thirteen. All of the numbers in this range were high (above (18)): (29/34/35/33/20).

Lastly, note that four numbers failed to occur on this wheel as they also failed to occur on the wheel which was simultaneously "clocked" in Figure 19, below: (3/5/26/36). "The Gods" apparently looked upon this quartet with disfavor on the date in question.

Kismet

The first occurrence of Kismet can be seen in columns one and three in which the (9) occurred at row eight in the first column and then recurred precisely forty spins later. In the second and third columns one can also see an occurrence of the (1) at row six and then its recurrence in the third row precisely twenty spins later. It is also worth noting that these two examples of Kismet are both red, odd and in the first dozen.

Recurring Pairs & Trios

Four pairs of numbers recurred, the first being the (13/16) which occurred at a precise twenty spin interval of one another in columns one and two at row five. This duo then recurred as a pair in column one, back-to-back at rows fifteen and sixteen.

Next the (20/33) recurred as a pair when this duo first occurred back-to-back in column two at rows seventeen and eighteen. This pair then recurred back-to-back in column three at rows twelve and thirteen, though reversed.

Then the (8/29) recurred remarkably by first occurring at a precise twenty spin interval of one another in columns two and three at row nine. This duo recurred as a pair in the same manner in the same two columns at row twenty, though reversed.

The (19/30) emulated its cousins above when this duo first occurred back-to-back in column one at rows nine and ten. This pair then remarkably recurred when they appeared again back-to-back in column three at rows fifteen and sixteen.

The last pair to recur was the (00/29). At row eleven in column one the (29) occurred. Precisely twenty spins later the (00) occurred in the second column at row eleven. This pair recurred when the (29) recurred immediately after the (00) at row twelve in column two.

Standard Pairs

The standard pairs which can be seen here are first the (12/21) which occurred at a precise twenty spin interval of one another in columns two and three at row three. Then the (13/33) likewise materialized at a precise twenty spin interval of one another in the same two columns at row eighteen.

Formulae

"The Gods" were again quite active in conjuring formulae. First they tell us that

$(30 + 1 = 31)$ and also that $(16 = 6 + 10)$. Then they inform us that $(2 + 0 = 22 - 20)$. They then elaborate on the previous declaration to tell us that $(24 = 2 + 0 + 22)$. They become somewhat more clever when they tell us that $((4 = (16 + 13) - 25))$. Their obtuseness is quite apparent when they convey that $((13 + 25) - 22 = 16))$. They continue with their antics when they tell us that $((33 - 0 - 29) + 23 = 27))$. Need they also remind us that $(22 = 16 + 6)$ or that $(19 = 29 - 10)$? Finally they unequivocally reassert their authority when they tell us that $((32 = (20 + 16) - 12) + 8))$. Again "The Gods" have forced Pythagoras' disciples to submit to their will.

FIGURE 18

	21-Aug		NON-OCCURS				
8	**10***	23*+	3#	**1**	3	**19**	2
22+	1	27*	5#	**2**	1	**20**	4
32*	21	12	7	**3**		**21**	2
20*	29	11	14	**4**	1	**22**	3
16*	13*	30*+	17	**5**		**23**	1
12*	**1	**1*	18	**6**	1	**24**	1
8*	0	**31***	26#	**7**		**25**	2
**9	25	**9	28	**8**	4	**26**	
30*	8*	29*	36#	**9**	2	**27**	1
19*	**31+**	34		**10**	2	**28**	
29*	OO*	35		**11**	1	**29**	5
10*	29*	33*		**12**	2	**30**	3
21	24*	20*		**13**	3	**31**	2
4*	2*	15		**14**		**32**	1
16*	OO*	19		**15**	1	**33**	2
13*	22*	30		**16**	3	**34**	2
25*	20*	34		**17**		**35**	1
22*	33*	13		**18**		**36**	
16*	0*+	20		**0**	2	**OO**	2
6*	29*	8*			**MODE:**	29	

**Kismet
*Superna tural Occurrence
    + signifies simultaneous occurrence on the opposite wheel

RECURRING PAIRS: (13/16) (20/33) (8/29) (19/30) (00/29)

FORMULAE: ((32 = (20 + 16) - 12) + 8)) (22 = 16 + 6)

(19 = 29 - 10) (30 + 1 = 31) (16 = 6 + 10)

((4 = (16 + 13) - 25)) ((13 + 25) - 22 = 16))

(24 = 2 + 0 + 22) (2 + 0 = 22 - 20)

((33 - 0 - 29) + 23 = 27))

Figure 19

This was a special set of observances, in that the numbers on two adjacent wheels were simultaneously observed. As such, this set of sixty occurrences should be considered with those in Figure 18. The numbers which occurred simultaneously on both wheels were: (22), (31), (0), (23) and (30). They are marked with a "+."

Simultaneous Occurrences

The (22) occurred at row seventeen of column one. Simultaneously it occurred on the adjacent wheel. Next, the (31) occurred at row six in column two. Simultaneously it occurred on the adjacent wheel. Next, the (0) occurred at row twelve in the same column. Simultaneously it occurred on the adjacent wheel. Next, the (23) occurred at row sixteen in column two. Simultaneously it occurred on the adjacent wheel. Lastly, the (30) occurred at row three in column three. It occurred simultaneously on the adjacent wheel.

Biases

The first column began with a noticeable color and odd bias. All of the first five numbers (7/9/7/25/27) were red and odd.

Here one can also see in column one a marked divisible bias. All of the numbers in the range from rows eight through eleven are divisible by (7): (28/7/7/14).

Further, one can also observe that the first column began with a hot number. Of the first ten occurrences, the (7) occurred four times, or 40% of the time within this range. Refer also to the effigy of a roulette wheel on p. 28. Observe that the (0) and the (28) are next to one another. One can therefore see a remarkable wheel bias at row twelve in all three columns. The sequence therein is (0), (0) and (28). Accordingly, two adjacent numbers occurred at precise twenty spin intervals.

The first column also began with a column bias. Seven of the first ten numbers, or 70%, occurred within the first column of the board: (7/7/25/13/28/7/7). In addition, half of the numbers in the first column, or 50%, were in the first column of the board: (7/7/25/13/28/7/7/22/22/4).

Another hot number can be seen beginning in the first column at row seventeen and continuing to the second column at row three. The (22) occurred three times out of seven spins, or 42.8% of the time.

The second column was also characterized by a pronounced section bias. Refer to the effigy of a roulette wheel on p. 28. Beginning at row six and continuing to row fifteen, the occurrences centered substantially around the section of the wheel from (12) through (6). Seven of the ten occurrences in this range, or 70%, were within this section: (31/6/12/8/6/12/31).

The end of the second column saw the beginning of a hot number. From row twenty therein to row three of column three, the (30) occurred three times in four spins, or 75% of the time.

Column three also demonstrated a marked even bias beginning at row twelve and continuing through row sixteen. All of the five numbers in this range are even: (28/8/2/18/22).

Lastly, note that as in the preceding Figure 18, four numbers failed to occur on this wheel as they also failed to occur on the wheel which was simultaneously "clocked": (3/5/26/36). "The Powers-That Be" apparently looked upon this quartet with disfavor on the date in question.

It is further worth noting that row seventeen is biased in favor of three of the four double digit numbers: (22), (33) and (00).

Lastly it is also worth noting that all of the numbers at row nineteen are large, red, odd and in the third column.

Recurring Pairs & Trios

With respect to the pairs which recurred here, the (22/33), two of the four "Double Digits," first occurred at a precise twenty spin interval of one another in columns one and two at row seventeen. This duo then recurred as a pair back-to-back in column three at rows four and five.

Also, the (22/30) first occurred at a precise twenty spin interval of one another in columns two and three at row three. Then this duo recurred as a pair upon the appearance of a (22) immediately following the aforementioned (30) in column three at row four.

Then the (12/17) recurred as a pair when these two numbers occurred at a precise twenty spin interval of one another in columns two and three at row eight. Remarkably this duo then recurred as a pair when they appeared again in the same manner in columns one and two at row thirteen, though reversed.

Next it was the turn of two numbers of the third black, (6/33) to recur as a pair when this duo occurred at a precise twenty spin interval of one another in columns two and three, at row eleven. Upon the appearance of a (6) at row ten in column three, immediately preceding the aforementioned (33), this pair then recurred.

Then the (20/22) recurred as a pair when this duo occurred back-to-back in column two at rows three and four. Upon the appearance of a (22) in column three at row four, opposite the aforementioned (20), this pair then recurred.

Kismet

There were two examples of Kismet. In the first column the (27) occurred at row nineteen. Precisely twenty spins later this number recurred in the second column at row nineteen. Also, in column one the (0) occurred at row twelve. Precisely twenty spins later this number recurred in column two in the same row.

Standard Pairs

The only standard pair which can be seen here is the (27/30) which occurred back-to-back in column two at rows nineteen and twenty.

Formulae

The presence of formulae again reveal the influence of "The Powers-That-Be." They first remind us that *(7 + 7 = 14)*. Then we are reminded that *(1 x 17 = 17)*. In close proximity we are then reminded that *(33 + 1 = 17 + 17)*. They also state unequivocally that *((28 − 7) − 7 = 14))*. Need we also be reminded that *(28 − 8 − 2 = 18)*? We are further cleverly reminded that *((2 + 18 + 22) − 0 − 21 = 21))*. Lastly they remind us how strong their influence is when they dictate that *((20 + 9 + 31) − 6 − 12 − 8 = 34))*. Pythagoras' disciples might be confounded by but compliant with these dictates.

FIGURE 19

	21-Aug		NON-OCCURS				
7	0	30	3#	**1**	1	**19**	1
9	25	13	5#	**2**	1	**20**	2
7	22*	30*+	10	**3**		**21**	3
25	20*	22*	15	**4**	1	**22**	5
27	9*	33*	16	**5**		**23**	1
20	**31*+**	1*	26#	**6**	3	**24**	1
13	**6***	**17***	29	**7**	4	**25**	2
28*	12*	**17***	35	**8**	2	**26**	
7*	8*	19	36#	**9**	2	**27**	3
7*	34*	**6***		**10**		**28**	2
14*	**6***	33*		**11**	1	**29**	
**0	**0+	28*		**12**	2	**30**	3
17*	12*	8*		**13**	2	**31**	2
21	34	2*		**14**	2	**32**	1
14	**31**	18*		**15**		**33**	3
11	23+	22*		**16**		**34**	2
22*+	33*	OO*		**17**	3	**35**	
22	32	21*		**18**	1	**36**	
**27	**27	21*		**0**	3	**OO**	1
4	30	24				**MODE:**	22

**Kismet

*Superna tural Occurrence

+ signifies simultaneous occurrence on the opposite wheel

RECURRING PAIRS: (22/33) (22/30) (12/17) (6/33) (20/22)

FORMULAE: ((28 - 7) - 7 = 14)) (7 + 7 = 14)

(1 x 17 = 17) ((2 + 18 + 22) - 0 - 21 = 21))

((20 + 9 + 31) - 6 - 12 - 8 = 34))

(33 + 1 = 17 + 17) (28 - 8 - 2 = 18)

Figure 20

Unusual Phenomena

The occurrences in column one began with a phenomenon which might best be labeled alternating digits. The first five numbers alternated between numbers ending in (2) and (1): (2/11/12/11/22). With respect to the (2), this phenomenon is all the more extraordinary in light of the fact that the next column contained only one number ending in (2).

Biases

The first column also experienced a column bias in favor of the numbers in the middle column. Twelve of the numbers in the first column, or 60%, were in the middle column: (2/11/11/14/14/5/2/32/11/5/14/5). Accordingly, there were two hot numbers in the first column. These were the (11) which occurred three times at rows two, four and thirteen, and the (14) which also occurred three times at rows six, seven and sixteen. Both numbers occurred 15% of the time within the range in question.

The second column further experienced a divisible bias at rows six through fourteen. With two exceptions, all of the nine numbers in this range, or 77.7%, were divisible by (5): (20/15/15/25/35/35/30).

Another hot number can be seen beginning in the second column at row eleven and ending at the top of the third column. Within this range, the (35) occurred three times or 27.2% of the time within the range in question.

In column three one can also observe a remarkable color bias. Beginning at the ninth row and continuing to the nineteenth row, all of the numbers except the (0), or 90.9% were red: (25/30/16/25/18/34/3/9/30/18). Note that the last four numbers in this range were red numbers in the third column. All are divisible by (3).

Recurring Pairs & Trios

The recurring pairs which materialized here were the (5/15) which first occurred at a precise twenty spin interval of one another in columns one and two at row eight. Remarkably this duo recurred as a pair in precisely the same manner in the same two columns at row twenty.

Next, the cousins to the above, the (5/14) did substantially the same when these two numbers first occurred back-to-back in column one at rows seven and eight. Remarkably this duo recurred as a pair in the same column at rows fifteen and sixteen, though reversed.

Then the (18/30) first occurred at a precise twenty spin interval of one another in columns two and three at row fourteen. This pair then recurred back-to-back in column three, separately, at rows eighteen and nineteen.

The (15/20) emulated its cousins immediately preceding when this duo first occurred back-to-back in column two at rows six and seven. Then this pair recurred by occurring at a precise twenty spin interval of one another in columns two and three at row twenty.

Standard Pairs

With respect to standard pairs, those which can be seen here are first the (16/32) which occurred in column one at rows eleven and twelve. Then in the second column one can see the (8/11) occur at rows four and five.

Kismet

There were three occurrences of Kismet. In column one at the fourth row, the (11) occurred and then recurred precisely twenty spins later. Also in column one at the nineteenth row the (31) occurred and then subsequently recurred precisely twenty spins later. Lastly, in the second column at the ninth row the (25) occurred and then recurred precisely twenty spins later.

Formulae

The "Supernatural" gave another demonstration of its power when it stated clearly that *(5 = 10/2)* and that *(5 + 15 = 20)*. Then they state succinctly that *(2 = 32/16)*. They further tell us that *(31 − 5 = 26)* and that *(3 = 11 − 8)*. In addition, they dictate that

(21 + 4 = 25). However, this force clearly manifests its power when it states quite obtusely that *((8 x 20) − 15 − 15 − 25 = 1 x (35 x 4) − 35))*. This is the most complex formula which the author has yet observed in roulette numbers. Accordingly, both the author and Pythagoras must hereby bow to the power of The "Supernatural."

Drought

The third column also experienced a (2) drought. No number in the third column ended in (2). "The Gods" apparently looked upon the (2) with disfavor on that date.

Also, with respect to the numbers which failed to occur, note that five of these numbers were in the third column: (6/24/27/33/36). This indicates a virtual third black drought. The "Powers-That-Be" apparently disfavored the black numbers in the third column on this date.

FIGURE 20

	23-Aug		NON-OCCURS				
2	**26***	35	6	1	1	19	
11	13	**17**	19	2	2	20	2
12	3*	8	23	3	2	21	4
**11*	**11*	28	24	4	3	22	2
22*	8*	21	27	5	3	23	
14	20*	0	29	6		24	
14*	15*	21*	33	7	1	25	3
5*	15*	4*	36	8	2	26	1
10*	**25*	**25*	OO	9	1	27	
2*	1*	30		10	1	28	1
32*	35*	16		11	4	29	
16*	4*	0		12	1	30	3
11	35*	25		13	1	31	3
4	30*	18*		14	3	32	1
5*	21	34		15	3	33	
14*	**31**	3		16	2	34	2
34	21	9		17	1	35	3
7	22	30*		18	2	36	
**31	**31	18*		0	2	OO	
5*	15*	20*			**MODE:**		

**Kismet
*Superna tural Occurrence

RECURRING PAIRS: (5/15) (5/14) (18/30) (15/20)

FORMULAE: (5 = 10 / 2) (5 + 15 = 20) (2 = 32 / 16)

(31 - 5 = 26) (3 = 11 - 8) (21 + 4 = 25)

(11 + 11 = 22) (5 X 10 = 25 + 25)

((8 X 20) - 15 - 15 - 25 = 1 x (35 x 4) - 35))

Figure 21

Biases

This set of observances begin with a pronounced column bias which can be seen in column one at rows five through nine. All of the five numbers in this string are in the same first column: (25/34/7/4/28). This same type of bias can be seen in column two from rows five through eleven, interrupted only by a (00): (23/29/11/14/5/5).

In column three one can see a marked color bias/black from row three through row fourteen, interrupted only by a (00) and a (21) at rows eight and ten. All of the other numbers, or 83.3% of the twelve numbers in this string, are black: (8/15/2/29/10/28/28/26/28/33). Note also that the (28) was a hot number in this range, occurring three times, or 25% of the time within this range.

Note also that there is a marked example of digit bias which can be seen in rows one and twelve. Observe that consecutively in both of these rows at precise twenty and forty spin intervals after initially occurring, each number in these rows favor the (6): (26/16/26), and (6/6/26).

Recurring Pairs & Trios

This set of numbers is offered primarily as an excellent example of recurring pairs. The pair which recurred here most often is the (5/28) which recurred in a most extraordinary manner. It is detailed below. For another prime example of such a pair, see Figure 30, below.

The recurring pairs which one can see here are first the (5/28) which remarkably occurred four times in the same manner. These two numbers were paired opposite one another and at a precise twenty spin interval at rows nine, eleven and thirteen in all three columns. Because of the extraordinary nature of the pairing of these two numbers, each of the four instances of this pair is highlighted in **bold**, in addition to the usual highlighting of The Black Pentacle.

Then it was the turn of the (5/19) to recur as a pair, first at a precise twenty spin interval apart at row eleven in columns one and two, and then back-to-back in column two at rows thirteen and fourteen.

Also quite remarkably the (8/15) first occurred back-to-back in column one at rows three and four. This pair then recurred in the same exact manner precisely forty spins later in column three at the same two rows.

Further, the (8/9) also remarkably occurred first back-to-back in column one at rows two and three. In the same column at rows nineteen and twenty this pair then recurred back-to-back in the same precise manner. It is also noteworthy that these are two consecutive numbers.

Next it was the turn of the (5/6) to recur as a pair in the same manner as its cousins above when these two consecutive numbers first occurred back-to-back in column one at rows twelve and thirteen. Precisely twenty spins later this pair recurred back-to-back in column two at the same two rows. Again it is noteworthy that these two numbers are consecutive.

The last of the pairs to recur here is the (15/25) which first occurred back-to-back in column one at rows four and five. These two numbers then recurred as a pair when they occurred precisely twenty spins apart in columns one and two at row fifteen.

Formulae

The "Powers-That-Be" demonstrated their influence and informed us that

(25 = 23 + 2). They also told us in no uncertain terms that *(15 + 5 = 20)*. Then they matter-of-factly convey the fact that *(7 x 4 = 28)*, and that *(5 − 0 = 5)*. They become rather mischievous however when they cleverly state that *((11 + 14) = (5 x 5))*. Then they become quite mischievous when they tell us that *((27 + 1 + 8) − 12 = 24))*. Could Pythagoras find fault with these universal truths?

Kismet

Here one can observe several remarkable instances of Kismet. It is highly unusual for a number to occur and then recur twice at precise forty and sixty spin intervals, as did the (15) in all three columns at row four. One can also see the (8) occur in column one at row three and then recur precisely forty spins later in column three at the same row. Also, the (29) occurred in column two at row six and then recurred precisely twenty spins later in column three at the same row. Likewise did the (26) occur at row one of the second column and then recur precisely forty spins later at row one of the (truncated) fourth column.

Note that the (26/29) are listed in Figure 40 as a standard pair. Note also that all of the above numbers which demonstrated Kismet are black numbers. Three are in the middle column.

Then the (6) behaved similarly as did its black cousins above when it occurred first in column one at row twelve. This number then appeared again at the same row in column two. Its red opposite, the (5) behaved in the same manner when it first occurred in column one at row thirteen. Then it reappeared precisely twenty spins later in column two at the same row.

The final instance of Kismet to be observed here is the occurrence of the (12) in column two at row nineteen, and then its reappearance precisely twenty spins later at the same row in column three. Note also that both of these instances of red Kismet are small and in the first dozen.

FIGURE 21

	26-Aug			NON-OCCURS				
13	**26	16	**26	3	1	2	19	2
9*	17	32		18	2	1	20	1
**8*	36	**8*		30	3		21	1
**15*	**15	**15*		31	4	2	22	1
25*	23*	2*		35	5	5	23	1
34	**29	**29		0	6	2	24	2
7*	11*	10			7	1	25	3
4*	14*	OO			8	4	26	3
**28*	5*	**28			9	2	27	1
24	OO*	21			10	1	28	4
19*	5*	28*			11	2	29	2
**6*	**6*	26			12	2	30	
**5*	**5*	28*			13	1	31	
16	19*	33			14	1	32	2
15*	25*	1			15	4	33	1
5*	4	27*			16	2	34	1
20*	32	1*			17	1	35	
22	25	8*			18		36	1
9*	**12	**12*			0		OO	2
8*	11	24*				MODE:	5	

**Kismet
*Superna tural Occurrence

RECURRING PAIRS: (5/28) (5/19) (8/15) (8/9) (5/6) (15/25)

FORMULAE: (25 = 23 + 2) (15 + 5 = 20) ((11 + 14) = 5 x 5))

(7 x 4 = 28) ((27 + 1 + 8) - 12 = 24)) (5 - 0 = 5)

Figure 22

Biases

Possibly the most obvious attribute which one can see here is the fact that there were so many numbers which failed to occur. The wheel was therefore quite biased against these numbers. Ten numbers out of the thirty-eight possibilities failed to materialize. What is doubly odd however, is the fact that these ten numbers are equally divided between the red and black numbers.

Note also that of the ten numbers which failed to occur, three of these numbers were of The Black Pentacle: (17/26/31). Note further that the other two numbers of The Black Pentacle, (6) and (10), only occurred once each, in column two at row two, and also in column three at row six, respectively. This is accordingly another good example of the influence of The Supernatural in this game. It could therefore be said that the "Powers-That-Be" looked with disfavor on The Black Pentacle at that time.

Conversely, one can say that the "Powers-That-Be" did favor at least one number, the (22), which one could say was "red" hot, in that it occurred far more than all others. This number occurred seven times out of the sixty, or 11.5% of the time. One could also say that this number was "white" hot in the first column, occurring four times therein from row seven through row twenty, or 28.5% of the time. Note also that this number represented one of only two instances of Kismet, the other being the (7) in columns one and three at row eight.

Bias can also be seen most notably in three areas. First one can see a remarkable example of wheel bias at row eight. Note that all of the three numbers in this row, (7/11/7), are located adjacent to one another on the wheel. What is remarkable is the fact that the wheel seemed to be biased towards one small section therein at regular intervals.

Further, here is a rare instance in which one can see a marked consecutive bias. In the third column from row seventeen through row nineteen, all of the numbers in this string are consecutive: (20/21/22). What is remarkable is the fact that they are in perfect ascending order.

Lastly, if one closely observes this set of numbers, in the third column one can see a marked divisible bias. Note that 50% of the numbers in this column are divisible by (5): (30/5/20/10/30/5/15/15/20/5).

Recurring Pairs & Trios

There were however a generous number of recurring pairs. First there was the (22/32) which first occurred back-to-back in column one at rows fourteen and fifteen. Upon the reappearance of another (22) in column two at row fifteen opposite the aforementioned (32), this pair then recurred.

Then the (22/30) occurred precisely within twenty spins of one another in columns one and two at row seven. These numbers then duplicated this feat when they recurred as a pair in the same manner in columns two and three at row nineteen, though not in the same order. It is also noteworthy that the first coupling of these two numbers was part of a "mini-sandwich," in that the (30) was "sandwiched" between two occurrences of (22).

The (7/16) then had its turn to be influenced by "The Gods," when they first occurred at a precise twenty spin interval apart in columns one and two, at row three. These two numbers then recurred as a pair when they reappeared back-to-back in column three at rows eight and nine.

The (27/30) was the only recurring pair which was also a standard pair. These two numbers occurred back-to-back, twice, in column two at rows eighteen and nineteen, and then again in column three at rows ten and eleven, though reversed.

Then the (18/27) occurred back-to-back in column two at rows eleven and twelve. Upon the reappearance of another (27) in column three at row eleven, opposite the aforementioned (18), this pair then recurred.

The (5/15) then emulated its cousins immediately preceding when these two numbers first occurred at a precise twenty spin interval apart in columns two and three at row twenty. Then these two numbers recurred as a pair when they reappeared again separately, back-to-back, in column three at rows thirteen and fourteen.

The (15/20) also behaved similarly as those immediately preceding when these two numbers occurred at a precise twenty spin interval apart in columns two and three at row sixteen. Upon the reappearance of another (20) in column three at row seventeen, immediately following the aforementioned (15), this pair then recurred.

The last of the recurring pairs to be observed here is the (7/22) which first occurred back-to-back in column one at rows seven and eight. This pair then remarkably recurred in precisely the same fashion, exactly forty spins later in column three at the same two rows.

Formulae

The formulae which the "Powers-That-Be" devised for our amusement were, first their declaration that $(9 = 22 - 0 - 6 - 7)$. Then they inform us that $(14 = 27 - 13)$. They further inform us that $(14 + 8 = 22)$. Their last dictum was that $(15 - 0 = 15)$. Pythagoras himself would be amazed but compliant at these dictates.

FIGURE 22

	27-Aug		NON-OCCURS				
28	0*	7	2	1	2	19	
21	6*	30	3	2		20	4
16*	7*	5	12	3		21	3
16	20	34	17	4	1	22	7
5	35	20	19	5	4	23	1
23	OO	10	25	6	1	24	1
**22*	30*	**22*	26	7	4	25	
**7*	11	**7*	31	8	1	26	
32	9	16*	33	9	2	27	3
29	21	30*	36	10	1	28	1
1	18*	27*		11	1	29	2
14*	27*	13*		12		30	4
8*	29	5*		13	1	31	
22*	4	15*		14	1	32	2
32*	22*	OO*		15	3	33	
1	20*	15*		16	3	34	2
34	24	20*		17		35	1
22	27*	21		18	1	36	
9*	30*	22*		0	1	OO	2
22*	15*	5*			MODE:	22	

**Kismet
*Superna tural Occurrence

RECURRING PAIRS: (22/32) (22/30) (7/16) (27/30) (18/27)

(5/15) (7/22) (15/20)

FORMULAE: (9 = 22 - 0 - 6 - 7) (14 = 27 - 13)

(14 + 8 = 22) (15 - 0 = 15)

Figure 23

This set of observances is not unusual but for the fact that the number which has been shown to occur most often, (11), failed to occur. Refer to Figure 38 which gives a listing of all the possibilities on the wheel and the frequencies which the author uncovered. In addition, the most striking phenomenon here is the numbers and complexity of the formulae which materialized, relative to the total number of occurrences.

Recurring Pairs & Trios

The recurring pairs to be observed here are first the (5/7) which two numbers occurred at a twenty spin interval of one another in columns two and three at row six. Upon the reappearance of another (5) in column three at row seven, immediately following the aforementioned (7), this pair then recurred.

The next pair to recur, (8/32) can be seen at row twelve when the (32) occurred in column two. Its match, (8) occurred precisely twenty spins later in column three. At row fifteen this pair recurred when the (8) occurred in column two. Precisely twenty spins later the (32) recurred.

Then the (8/33) demonstrated their affinity for one another when they first occurred back-to-back in column two at rows fifteen and sixteen. This pair then duplicated this process and recurred when they reappeared again back-to-back in column three at rows eleven and twelve, though reversed.

The (5/10) showed a perfect mating by first occurring at a precise twenty spin interval apart in column one and two at row six. These two numbers then showed that they are perfect "soul mates" by duplicating this relationship in the same manner in columns two and three at row four, thereby recurring as a pair and also producing identical twins.

Likewise did the (4/33) demonstrate a perfect "love match" by emulating its cousins above and occurring at a precise twenty spin interval apart in columns one and two at row sixteen. This pair then duplicated its initial coupling and also produced an identical set of twins when they recurred in the same precise manner in columns two and three at row eleven.

The final pair which recurred was the (3/5) which first occurred back-to-back in column two at rows six and seven. This pair recurred when another (5) appeared in column three at row seven, opposite the aforementioned (3). Note also these are part of a "Red Septet" of seven consecutive red and odd numbers: (3/5/5/7/7/9/9).

The aforementioned "Red Septet" is part of a pronounced bias towards consecutive/red/odd numbers at row seven: (7/3/5).

Formulae

"The Gods" have shown that they can be quite clever at conveying a message. In this first instance, they pronounce most obtusely that $((14 + 14) - 3 = 25))$. Then in quite a lengthy statement they tell us that $(5 + 3 + 9 + 2 + 9 + 4 = 32)$. The antics of "The Gods" continue with their assertion that $((35 - (5 \times 3) - 9 = 2 + 9))$. Further, they cleverly proclaim that $((7 - 5) + 17 + 1 = 20))$. Also quite cleverly they inform us that $((26 - 17) + 5 = 2 \times 7))$. They do ease up a bit when they state that $(5 + 2 = 7)$. However, they again become mischievous when they obtusely reaffirm that $(9 + 9 = 17 + 1)$. Disciples of Pythagoras might concede to these universal truths.

Standard Pairs

Standard pairs to be seen here are the (13/33) in column two at rows eighteen and nineteen. Also one can see a (16/19) at row twenty in columns one and two.

Kismet

The only instance of Kismet to be observed here is the occurrence of the (9) at row eight in column one, and its recurrence precisely twenty spins later in column two.

FIGURE 23
NON-OCCURS

			NON-OCCURS				
30	23	**26**	6	**1**	3	**19**	2
1	21	**26***	11	**2**	2	**20**	1
0	13	**17***	12	**3**	3	**21**	2
34	**10***	5*	22	**4**	2	**22**	
27	35*	2*	28	**5**	3	**23**	1
10*	5*	7*	OO	**6**		**24**	1
7	3*	5*		**7**	2	**25**	1
9*	**9***	**17***		**8**	2	**26**	3
31	2*	1*		**9**	3	**27**	2
1	9*	20*		**10**	2	**28**	
19	4*	33*		**11**		**29**	1
14*	32*	8*		**12**		**30**	2
14*	15	35		**13**	2	**31**	1
3*	29	0		**14**	3	**32**	2
25*	8*	32		**15**	1	**33**	3
4*	33*	21		**16**	1	**34**	1
3	**26**	27		**17**	2	**35**	2
30	13	14		**18**	1	**36**	1
36	33	24		**0**	2	**OO**	
19	16	18			MODE:		

**Kismet
*Superna tural Occurrence

RECURRING PAIRS: (5/7) (8/33) (5/10) (4/33) (3/5) (8/32)

FORMULAE:

((14 + 14) - 3 = 25))

(5 + 3 + 9 + 2 + 9 + 4 = 32)

((35 - (5 x 3) - 9 = 2 + 9))

(7 - 5 + 17 + 1 = 20)

((26 - 17) + 5 = 2 x 7))

(5 + 2 = 7) (9 + 9 = 17 + 1)

Figure 24

Biases

The occurrences began with a supernatural occurrence and also a hot number. The (30) occurred three times in a row in column one at rows one through three. The first occurrence of the (30) was also a part of an instance of Kismet. Precisely twenty spins after the first occurrence of the (30) in the first column, this number again occurred in the second column at row one. This in turn was part of a strong bias in favor of numbers ending in (0). The first number in all three columns was (30/30/00), respectively, thereby comprising a formula: *(30 – 30 = 0)*. The others follow.

The first column then experienced a marked low bias. Beginning at row four and continuing through row twelve, all of the occurrences were low numbers (below (19)): (11/17/12/11/14/6/3/8).

The first column also demonstrated a noticeable column bias. Half of the numbers, or 50% of these occurrences were in the middle column: (11/17/11/14/8/26/17/20/23/11).

There were two hot digits in these sixty occurrences. The numbers ending in (0) were fifteen: (30/30/30/00/20/10/30/20/00/0/20/20/00/0/30). The (1) was also a hot digit, occurring nine times in the following numbers: (11/11/11/1/21/31/11/11/31).

In addition to the aforementioned (30), there were also two other hot numbers. The (11) occurred five times, or 8.3% of the time. In the third column, the (25) occurred three times in eleven spins, comprising 27.2% of the occurrences with that range.

Column two also experienced a marked even bias. Beginning at the ninth row and continuing to row eighteen, with one exception all of the numbers in this range of ten, or 90%, were even: (24/20/20/32/14/8/22/18/6).

The third column experienced a marked digit bias in favor of the (5). Of all the numbers in this column, five, or 25%, ended in (5): (5/35/25/25/25).

Also in the third column, there was a noticeable high bias. From row twelve through row twenty, with one exception all of the nine numbers in this range, or 88.8%, were high (above (18)): (30/28/25/29/25/31/27/29).

Note that there was a consecutive bias in all three columns at row sixteen. Three consecutive even integers occurred, though not in the usual order: (18/20/22).

Lastly, observe that all of the numbers in the twentieth row were black, odd numbers in the second column of the board.

Kismet

In addition to the aforementioned (30), there were two other examples of Kismet. In the first column at row six, the (00) occurred. This number recurred again precisely twenty spins later in column two. Further, in the second column at row twenty, the (29) occurred. This number recurred precisely twenty spins later at the bottom of column three.

Recurring Pairs & Trios

The recurring pairs were first the (11/20), first occurring at a precise twenty spin interval of one another in columns one and two at row four. This pair then recurred in the same manner in columns two and three at row eleven, though reversed.

Then the (30/30) recurred as a pair by first occurring back-to-back in column one at rows one and two. This number then recurred precisely twenty spins later in column two at row one.

The (11/30) then remarkably occurred back-to-back in column one at rows three and four. This pair then recurred in the same manner, back-to-back at row twenty of column one and then again at row one of column two. Quite remarkably this pair also recurred a second time, also back-to-back in column three at rows eleven and twelve.

The (25/31) also behaved remarkably by first occurring back-to-back in column three at rows seven and eight. Remarkably this pair recurred in precisely the same fashion, back-to-back in the same column shortly thereafter, at rows seventeen and eighteen.

The (0/35) then emulated its cousins above by also occurring back-to-back in column two at rows seven and eight. Remarkably this pair recurred in exactly the same fashion in column three at rows three and four. Note also that each pair was followed by a black, even number.

The last of the pairs to recur was the (18/22) which first occurred back-to-back in column two at rows sixteen and seventeen. Upon the appearance of an (18) in column three at row sixteen, opposite the aforementioned (22), this pair then recurred.

Standard Pairs & Drought

Remarkably, no standard pairs were observed. There was accordingly a standard pair drought.

Formulae

In addition to that previously mentioned, there were several formulae observed, indicating a strong presence of "The Powers-That-Be." First they state that

(19 + 11 = 30). Then they inform us that *(35 – 0 – 2 = 33)*. Next they state unequivocally that *(14 + 6 = 20)* and also that *(15 + 20 = 35)*. Then they remind us, however redundantly, that *(6 + 21 = 27)*. They remind us also that *(6 = 31 – 25)* and that

(35 – 0 – 24 = 11). Lastly they reiterate the universal truth that *(30 + 0 + 5 = 35)*. It would be difficult for Pythagoras to contradict these assertions.

FIGURE 24

			NON-OCCURS				
**30*	**30*	OO*	4	1	1	19	1
30*	12	5*	7	2	1	20	4
30*	15*	35*	9	3	1	21	1
11*	20*	0*	13	4		22	1
17	36	2*	34	5	1	23	1
**OO	**OO	33*		6	2	24	1
12	35*	25*		7		25	3
11	0*	31*		8	2	26	1
14*	24*	11*		9		27	1
6*	20*	28		10	1	28	2
3	20*	11*		11	5	29	3
8	32	30*		12	2	30	5
26	14	28		13		31	2
17	1	25		14	2	32	1
16	8	29		15	1	33	1
20	22*	18*		16	1	34	
10	18*	25*		17	2	35	2
23	6*	31*		18	2	36	1
19*	21*	27*		0	2	OO	3
11*	**29	**29				MODE:	

**Kismet
*Superna tural Occurrence

RECURRING PAIRS: (11/20) (30/30) (11/30) (25/31) (0/35)

(18/22)

FORMULAE: $(30 - 30 = 0)$ $(19 + 11 = 30)$

$(14 + 6 = 20)$ $(15 + 20 = 35)$ $(6 + 21 = 27)$

$(6 = 31 - 25)$ $(35 - 0 - 24 = 11)$

$(30 + 0 + 5 = 35)$ $(35 - 0 - 2 = 33)$

Figure 25

Biases

These numbers began with an obvious divisible bias which lasted from rows one through three in column one. Each of the first three numbers are divisible by (7): (7/14/28). Note also that these three numbers are in perfect sequence and that they show a steady upward progression. Numbers two and three are doubled from that previous.

Also in these eighty observances one can see two instances of wheel bias. These occurred at rows five and eleven. What is quite remarkable is the fact that both of these instances of bias pertain to one small section of the wheel. At row five one can see that all of the four numbers in that row, (13/24/36/36), are in one small area of the wheel. In the eleventh row also one can see this same wheel bias, where three of the four numbers in that row are also contained in the same area of the wheel as that already mentioned:

(3/34/15). It appears therefore that "The Gods" favored that section of the wheel at regular intervals.

Other biases which can be seen here are in column two from rows one through four. Here one can see that all of these numbers are not only located in the first column of the board, but also that all of these numbers are black. One can therefore observe a pronounced first black bias.

Further, one can also see in this range a pronounced color bias in favor of black numbers. In addition to the aforementioned four numbers, the two numbers immediately following were also black: (4/10/31/28/24/33).

Shortly thereafter the aforementioned pattern reversed itself. Beginning at row eleven in column two, all of the following six numbers were red, revealing a pronounced color bias in favor of red numbers: (34/23/7/36/16/36). However, this is merely part of a remarkable string of red bias. Note that with one exception all of the numbers from row eleven through row twenty, or 90%, were red: (34/23/7/36/16/36/18/18/25).

Further, in column four from rows one through six one can see a marked high bias. All of the first six numbers in this column were high (above (18)): (28/35/35/30/36/22). This pattern then immediately reversed itself and became a pronounced low bias. All of the next nine numbers from row seven through row fifteen were low (below (19)): (13/17/1/7/4/17/15/11/18).

Recurring Pairs & Trios

The pairs which recurred here began with the (4/7) which can be seen at row one of columns one and two, when these two numbers occurred at a precise twenty spin interval of one another. They then reappeared back-to-back in column four at rows ten and eleven.

The (3/34) then emulated its cousins above when these two numbers first occurred opposite and precisely within twenty spins of one another in columns one and two at row eight. What is quite extraordinary however is the fact that these two numbers duplicated this feat in the same two columns at row eleven. Then they reappeared again back-to-back at rows nineteen and twenty in column one, thereby forming a second recurring pair.

It was then the turn of the (11/23) which first occurred back-to-back in column one at rows seventeen and eighteen. This pair then duplicated this feat at rows nine and ten in column three when they recurred back-to-back.

Then the (18/34) first occurred directly opposite one another at a precise twenty spin interval in columns one and two at row nineteen. This pair then recurred when they duplicated this feat, recurring at the same twenty spin interval of one another in columns three and four, at row fifteen, though reversed.

The (10/31) became a recurring pair and a standard pair when these two numbers first occurred back-to-back in column two at rows two and three. This pair then recurred upon the reappearance of another (31) in column three at row two, directly opposite the aforementioned (10).

Then the (13/36) showed a remarkable affinity for one another, first occurring opposite one another at a precise twenty spin interval in columns one and two at row sixteen. This pair then recurred back-to-back in column three at rows four and five. Note also that these two numbers occurred at a precise forty spin interval of one another in columns one and three at row five, though this fails to count as a recurring pair. Further note that only one number, a (22), separated these two numbers in column four where they occurred at rows five and seven.

Also, the (28/31) recurred as a pair when they first occurred opposite one another at a precise twenty spin interval in columns one and two at row three. This pair then recurred upon the reappearance of another (28) immediately following the aforementioned (31) in column two at rows three and four.

The (19/31) then emulated its cousins immediately preceding when these two numbers first occurred opposite one another at a precise twenty spin interval in columns two and three at row three. Upon the reappearance of another (31) immediately preceding the aforementioned (19), this pair then recurred. Note also that these two numbers are adjacent to one another on the wheel.

The (0/28) also emulated its cousins immediately preceding when these two numbers first occurred back-to-back in column one at rows three and four. Upon the reappearance of another (28) opposite the aforementioned (0) in column two at row four, this pair then recurred.

Then the (11/15) had its turn to recur as a pair when these two numbers first occurred back-to-back in column three at rows ten and eleven. These two numbers then duplicated this feat when they recurred back-to-back in column four at rows thirteen and fourteen.

The (14/34) then emulated its cousins above when they first occurred back-to-back in column two at rows seven and eight. This pair then duplicated this feat and recurred in the same precise manner in column three at rows fourteen and fifteen.

The (8/27) then emulated some of its cousins above when these two numbers occurred opposite one another at a precise twenty spin interval at row twenty in columns three and four. Upon the reappearance of another (8) in column four, back-to-back with the aforementioned (27), this pair then recurred.

Then the (00/8) further emulated its cousins above when these two numbers first occurred back-to-back in column three at rows nineteen and twenty. Upon the reappearance of another (8) in column four at row nineteen, this pair then recurred.

The last pair which the author observed to have recurred, actually did so twice. The (18/33) first occurred back-to-back in column one at rows six and seven. Upon the reappearance of another (33) opposite the aforementioned (18) in column two at row six, this pair then recurred. In addition, this pair recurred a second time when these two numbers again occurred back-to-back in column two at rows seventeen and eighteen.

Sandwiches

One sandwich was observed, albeit a fat one with rather thin "bread." In column two at rows eight through eleven the sequence was: (34/2/2/34).

Formulae

"The Gods" were up to their usual antics when they not-so-subtly reminded us that *(7 + 4 = 11)*. Then they call to our attention the fact that *(16 = 34 – 18)*, and that

(3 = 21 / 7). Further, they point out the fact that *(23 + 11 = 34)*. "The Gods" then become quite mischievous when they cleverly tell us that *((23 – 7) + 36 – 16 = 36))*. They then utter a statement of equal complexity when they inform us that *((36 – (5 + 8 + 0) = 23))*. Pythagoras' disciples would have to bow to these dictates.

Drought

In addition to the fact that these eighty numbers reveal a substantial standard pair drought, the last phenomenon which one can see here is the fact that all of the numbers which failed to occur, (6/20/26/32), were even. Note also that three of these numbers were in the middle column. Two of these numbers, the (20) and the (32) were adjacent to one another on the wheel.

FIGURE 25
NON-OCCURS

	Aug 28			NON-OCCURS
7*	4*	11*	28	6
14	10*	31*	35	20
28*	31*	19*	35	26
0*	28*	13*	30	32
13	24	**36*	**36	
18*	33*	5	22	
33*	14*	8	13	
3*	34*	0	17	
9	2	23*	1	
**11	2	**11*	7*	
3*	34*	15*	4*	
21*	23	24	17	
**7	**7	3	15*	
17	36	14*	11*	
12	16	34*	18*	
13*	36*	12	27	
23*	33	28	36	
11*	18	23	29	
34*	18*	OO*	8*	
3*	25	8*	27*	

1	1	19	1
2	2	20	
3	4	21	1
4	2	22	1
5	1	23	4
6		24	2
7	4	25	1
8	3	26	
9	1	27	2
10	1	28	4
11	5	29	1
12	2	30	1
13	4	31	2
14	3	32	
15	2	33	3
16	1	34	4
17	3	35	2
18	4	36	5
0	2	OO	1
		MODE:	

**Kismet
*Superna tural Occurrence

RECURRING PAIRS: (4/7) (3/34) (11/23) (18/34) (10/31) (13/36) (28/31)

(19/31) (0/28) (11/15) (14/34) (8/27) (00/8) (18/33)

SANDWICH: (34/2/2/34)

FORMULAE: (7 + 4 = 11) (16 = 34 - 18) (23 + 11 = 34)

((23 - 7) + 36 - 16 = 36)) ((36 - (5 + 8) + 0 = 23))

(3 = 21 / 7)

Figure 26

These numbers are offered to demonstrate the relationship between the two numbers contained in the standard pair (00/26). Accordingly, the numbers of The Black Pentacle were not highlighted. Only the two numbers of this Standard Pair are shown in **bold**. Note that this is an abbreviated set of occurrences with only forty numbers. The frequency of occurrence of the two numbers in question over a short interval is what makes this set of occurrences special.

Biases

The wheel demonstrated a marked bias towards the (00) and (26). Nine of the forty numbers which occurred were of this pair, or 22.5% of the total. Put another way, 12.5% of the total of forty numbers were (26), and 10% were the (00). The standard pair (00/26) is also a recurring pair in this instance. As such it can be seen three times, first at rows one and two, and then again at rows five through seven in column two. This pair can also be seen at row fourteen in both columns. As such, this pair occurred and then recurred thrice.

Of the overall total of forty numbers, one can also observe a pronounced column bias beginning at the third row of the first column. The numbers (26/26/23/29) are all not only in the middle column, but they are also in a small section of the column, and they are contiguous.

At rows seven through thirteen in the first column, one can observe a marked color bias. Seven consecutive numbers were red: (18/36/12/16/30/34/9). One can also see a pronounced even bias within the aforementioned string of numbers. The first six of these numbers were even.

Color bias can further be seen in the second column at rows eight through thirteen. All of these six numbers were red: (34/9/7/30/34/21). Astute observers will note that even though these occurrences were charted on the first day of the first month, the (1) failed to occur. "The Gods" obviously disfavored the (1).

Standard Pairs

Another standard pair, (18/36) can be observed at rows seven and eight in column one. The final standard pair can be seen at row six: (26/29).

Recurring Pairs & Trios

There were two additional recurring pairs. In addition to the (00/26) previously mentioned. One can observe the (30/34) which first occurred at rows eleven and twelve of the first column. This pair recurred precisely twenty spins later in the second column at the same two rows. Further, the pair (0/24) occurred at row sixteen. This pair recurred at row eighteen.

Kismet

Three examples of Kismet can be observed. These are at rows eleven, twelve and nineteen where one can see the (30), (34) and (7) recurring at precise twenty spin intervals, respectively.

Formulae

Lastly, formulae were sparse. However, the "Powers-That-Be" were their usual mischievous selves when they informed us that *(0 = 7 – 7)*. Further, their cleverness at making a point can also be seen when they tell us that *((3 x 26) – 26 – 23 = 29))*. Even Pythagoras would likely be loathe to disagree with these statements.

FIGURE 26
NON-
OCCURS

1-Jan		NON-OCCURS				
4	**26***	1	**1**		**19**	
3	**OO***	5	**2**	1	**20**	1
26*	14	8	**3**	1	**21**	1
26*	33	11	**4**	1	**22**	
23*	**OO***	13	**5**		**23**	1
29*	**26***	15	**6**	1	**24**	2
18*	**OO***	17	**7**	3	**25**	
36*	34	19	**8**		**26**	5
12	9	22	**9**	2	**27**	1
16	7	25	**10**	1	**28**	
**30*	**30*	28	**11**		**29**	1
**34*	**34*	31	**12**	1	**30**	2
9	21	32	**13**		**31**	
26*	**OO***		**14**	1	**32**	
10	20		**15**		**33**	1
24*	0*		**16**	1	**34**	3
2	27		**17**		**35**	1
0*	24*		**18**	1	**36**	1
**7	**7		**0**	2	**OO**	4
6	35		**MODE:**	26		

**Kismet
*Supernat ural
 Occurrence
**RECURRING
PAIRS:**   (00/26) (30/34) (0/24)

FORMULAE: (0 = 7 - 7)

                  ((3 x 26) - 26 - 23 = 29))

Figure 27

These numbers are offered to demonstrate that a time lapse between occurrences does not necessarily mean that this lapse would influence the numbers. Or put another way, any pattern which was meant to occur would likely have occurred anyway.

Recording of numbers began as usual and then it halted in the second column at row four when the (16) occurred. Then followed a lapse of approximately fifteen minutes. The occurrences then resumed. What is noteworthy is two things. First, when the play resumed, the first number to occur was identical to that which had occurred when the play halted. That is, the (16) repeated. What is most astounding however is the fact that when the second (16) occurred, this caused a number to repeat at the precise interval at which another number had repeated. That is, at the fourth and fifth rows in each column, a number repeated. This caused the recurring pair (16/23) with both numbers in precise relation to one another. The reader will also note that the (16) and (23) are nearly adjacent to one another on the wheel.

Recurring Pairs & Trios

In addition to the recurring pair discussed previously, the (8/21) occurred at the top of columns two and three. This pair recurred in the third column at rows eleven and twelve. Another pair which recurred was the (6/20) which first occurred at rows eleven and twelve in column one. This pair recurred in the third column at rows nine and ten, though not in the same order.

The fourth recurring pair can be observed in the first column when the (19/24) occurred back-to-back at rows thirteen and fourteen. This pair recurred in the last row of columns two and three.

In addition the (7/16) occurred in the second and third columns at row four. This pair recurred in the second column at rows ten and eleven.

Remarkably there was one recurring trio, (5/16/21) which can be seen in columns one and two at rows seventeen and eighteen. This trio recurred in the second column at rows seventeen through nineteen.

Further, the (0/21) occurred together at precise twenty spin intervals at row twelve. This pair recurred in inverse order at row nineteen in the same columns. The final pair which occurred and then recurred in inverse order was the (16) and the (24). These first occurred at a precise twenty spin interval of one another at row fourteen in columns one and two. This pair then recurred in inverse order at row eighteen in columns two and three.

Sandwiches

Other noteworthy phenomena are that this set of occurrences began with a sandwich. The (22) occurred and then repeated at rows one and two of column one. Then followed the (18), which was followed by a (23) which repeated. The sequence was therefore (22/22/18/23/23).

In the third column at rows three and four, and then again at rows seven and eight, the (7) and (28) produced what some might call a sandwich. The (10) and (27) were sandwiched between a (28) and (7) which recurred in the precise order in which they had previously occurred. It is further worth noting that the (10) and (27) are adjacent to one another on the wheel.

Formulae

The first of "The Gods'" handiwork states that *(17 + 19 = 36)*. Then they inform us that *(19 + 8 + 1 = 28)*. Further they tell us that *(27 = 28 – 7 + 6)* and that *((22 + 6) x 1 = 28)*. At a right angle they tell us that *(24 + 16 = 1 + 10 + 21 + 8)*. Matter-of-factly they inform us mortals that *((29 – 16) + 14 = 22 + 5))* and also that *(5 + 16 = 21)*. Becoming more mischievous they tell us at two right angles that *(11 + 29 = 21 + 19)*. Even Pythagoras would have to concede these universal truths.

FIGURE 27
NON-OCCURS

4-Dec

			NON-OCCURS				
22*	21*	8*	3	**1**	2	**19**	3
22*	**6***	1*	12	**2**	1	**20**	2
18*	15	28*	13	**3**		**21**	4
23*	16*	7*	25	**4**	1	**22**	3
23*	16*	**10**	30	**5**	1	**23**	3
9	8	27*	31	**6**	3	**24**	3
17*	29	28*	34	**7**	3	**25**	
19*	27	7*	35	**8**	3	**26**	1
36*	0	**6***	OO	**9**	1	**27**	3
26	16*	20*		**10**	2	**28**	2
20*	7*	8*		**11**	1	**29**	3
6*	0*	21*		**12**		**30**	
19*	29*	**10***		**13**		**31**	
24*	16*	1*		**14**	1	**32**	1
32	14*	27		**15**	1	**33**	1
23	22*	4		**16**	5	**34**	
21*	5*	33		**17**	1	**35**	
11*	16*	24*		**18**	1	**36**	1
29*	21*	0*		**0**	3	**OO**	
2	19*	24*		**MODE:**	16		

RECURRING PAIRS: (8/21) (16/23) (6/20) (19/24) (7/16) (7/28)

(0/21) (16/24)

RECURRING TRIO: (5/16/21)

SANDWICH: (22/22/18/23/23)

FORMULAE: (17 + 19 = 36) (19 + 8 + 1 = 28)

(27 = 28 - 7 + 6) ((22 + 6) x 1 = 28))

(24 + 16 = 1 + 10 + 21 + 8)

((29 - 16) + 14 = 22 + 5)) (5 + 16 = 21)

(11 + 29 = 21 + 19)

173

Figure 28

These numbers are offered to demonstrate the frequency of incidence of "Kismet." Accordingly, the five numbers of The Black Pentacle are not highlighted. Only the numbers which reveal the prevalence of Kismet are shown in **bold**. Note also that this set of occurrences differs from most of the other figures of this type in that one hundred occurrences are shown.

Kismet

The first incidence of Kismet occurred at row sixteen in columns two and three when the (11) first occurred and then recurred precisely twenty spins later. This number repeated its behavior at row six in columns four and five when it occurred in column four and then recurred precisely twenty spins later.

The (2) acted similarly in that it occurred at row fourteen in column three and then recurred precisely twenty spins later in the fourth column.

In addition, the (23) emulated its siblings. This number occurred at row three of the fourth column and then recurred at the same row precisely twenty spins later in column five.

The final incidence of Kismet began at row twelve of the fourth column when the (5) occurred. This number then recurred at the same row in the fifth column precisely twenty spins later.

The reader will note what should be obvious: that all of these five incidences of Kismet occurred in the second column.

Biases

With respect to biases, one can first observe a marked wheel bias at the first row in columns one through four. All of the numbers (21/16/18/33) are located within one small section of the wheel. One can also observe a marked wheel bias at rows eighteen through twenty in column four where the sequence was: (3/34/36). Each of these numbers is in a small section of the wheel, and are evenly spaced from one another.

Further, one can observe a marked consecutive bias at rows seven through nine in column one where three consecutive numbers occurred: (34/33/35), though not in the usual order. A second consecutive bias can be observed at row six in columns two through five where the sequence was (9/10/11/11).

One can further observe a marked color bias beginning at the end of column one and extending through row ten of column two. All of the numbers in question except one, the (13), were red: (23/16/19/21/3/9/5/21/23/1).

Recurring Pairs & Trios

The other noteworthy phenomena were that there were ten incidences of recurring pairs. First the (2) and (21) occurred at the first two rows of the first column. This pair recurred at row eight in columns two and three, and then recurred again at rows eighteen and nineteen in column two.

Further, at row twelve of the first and second columns the (18) and (20) occurred. These numbers were again paired when they occurred back-to-back at rows fifteen and sixteen in the fifth column.

Further, at row sixteen the (11) and the (16) occurred at precise twenty spin intervals of one another in columns one and two. These numbers were paired again when they recurred back-to-back at rows five and six in the fourth column.

In addition, with respect to recurring pairs, the (14) and (23) were paired at the twentieth row of columns one and two, respectively. These two numbers were again paired back-to-back at rows two and three of the fourth column.

At row four of columns one and two the (3) and (7) first occurred at precise twenty spin intervals of one another. This pair recurred in the exact manner at row eighteen in columns three and four.

At row eighteen the (5) and the (21) occurred at precise twenty spin intervals of one another in columns one and two, respectively. This pair recurred at rows seven and eight in the second column.

In the third column at rows seventeen and eighteen the (7) and the (26) occurred back-to-back. This pair recurred in the precise same order in column four at rows nine and ten.

In the last row of columns three and four, the (13) and the (36) occurred precisely within twenty spins of one another. This pair recurred at rows four and five of the fifth column.

At the top of columns four and five the (28) and the (33) occurred precisely within twenty spins of one another. The occurrence of the

(33) immediately following the (28) at rows one and two of the fifth column caused this pair to recur.

The (5) and the (34) occurred at row seven in columns one and two, precisely within twenty spins of one another. This pair recurred in precisely the same manner at row nineteen in columns four and five.

The (5) and the (33) occurred at row fifteen in columns three and four. This pair recurred back-to-back at rows twelve and thirteen in column four.

Here one can also observe one recurring trio. The (17), (13) and the (8) occurred within twenty spins of one another at the fifth row in columns one, two and three, respectively. This trio recurred at precise intervals of one another at the fourth row in columns three through five, though not in the original order.

Formulae

With respect to prevalent formulae, one can observe that *(16 + 8 = 24)*, that

(20 = 4 x 5), and that *(21 = 7 x 3)*. The mathematical logic therein cannot be questioned, even by Pythagoras.

Standard Pairs

Standard pairs were first the (16/19) at rows one and two in column two. Then there was the (13/33) at rows twenty and one of the third and fourth columns, respectively. Next there was the (0/00) at row fifteen in columns one and two. Lastly there was the (26/00) at row eight in columns four and five.

FIGURE 28

			9-Mar		NON-OCCURS				
21*	16	18	33*	28*	12	**1**	2	**19**	3
2*	19	15	14*	33*	31	**2**	5	**20**	2
1	21	36	**23*	**23	32	**3**	3	**21**	4
7*	3*	8*	17*	13*		**4**	2	**22**	1
17*	13*	8*	16*	36*		**5**	6	**23**	5
24	9*	10*	**11*	**11		**6**	2	**24**	4
34*	5*	23	24	30		**7**	5	**25**	2
33*	21*	2*	26	OO		**8**	3	**26**	3
35*	23	19	26*	16*		**9**	1	**27**	1
6	1	29	7*	8*		**10**	1	**28**	1
14	11	29	OO	24*		**11**	6	**29**	4
18*	20*	4*	**5*	**5		**12**		**30**	1
7	24	27	33*	11		**13**	3	**31**	
22	6	**2	**2	25		**14**	3	**32**	
0	OO	5*	33*	20*		**15**	2	**33**	5
16*	**11*	**11	3	18*		**16**	5	**34**	2
16	25	26*	19	4		**17**	2	**35**	1
5*	21*	7*	3*	15		**18**	3	**36**	3
29	2*	7	34*	5*		**0**	1	**OO**	3
23*	14*	13*	36*	29				**MODE:**	

**Kismet
*Supernatural Occurrence

RECURRING PAIRS: (2/21) (18/20) (11/16) (14/23) (3/7)

(5/21) (7/26) (13/36) (28/33) (5/34) (5/33)

RECURRING TRIO: (8/13/17)

FORMULAE: (16 + 8 = 24) (20 = 4 x 5) (21 = 7 x 3)

177

Figure 29

These numbers are presented in order to demonstrate the frequency of incidence of the numbers of *The Black Pentacle*: (6/10/17/26/31). Recall above in *The Numerology Of Roulette/The Black Pentacle* that the author asserted that these numbers have a special relationship with one another. Here portrayed is a set of eighty occurrences where these five numbers permeate the total number of observations. As such, the author is compelled to use this set of eighty observations to demonstrate how to implement the five number generic system found in Figure 42. Refer also to Figure 43. Here one can see how much, betting only the five numbers in question with a specified starting wager, one would have won.

Biases

This set of eighty numbers also demonstrated a marked wheel bias which can be seen at row five. Here one can see that at precise twenty spin intervals in columns two through four all three numbers were in a small section of the wheel: (15/36/24).

While it is not immediately apparent, if one observes this group of numbers closely then one can see quite an unusual phenomenon: no number ending in (9) occurred. That is, nowhere can one observe a (9), (19) or a (29). "The Gods" frowned on the (9) this date and accordingly declared a digit drought. In this vein, one can also see that the only number ending in (1) which occurred was the (31).

Lastly, "The Gods" also seemed to have looked upon odd numbers with displeasure. With one exception, all of the numbers which failed to occur were odd. In other words, this set of eighty numbers experienced a marked even bias. Also, note that fifty-three of the eighty occurrences, or 66%, were even.

Recurring Pairs & Trios

The recurring pairs which are prevalent begin with the (17/35) which can be seen at row nine in columns one and two. This pair recurred twice in the second column, first at rows nine and ten, and then again at rows twelve and thirteen. The last two occurrences of this pair are part of a sandwich: (35/17/20/35/17).

One can also observe the (12/36) occur first at rows four and five in the third column. This pair recurred in the same column at rows fourteen and fifteen, and then again in the fourth column at rows twelve through fourteen.

The entire set of occurrences began with the pair (6/28). This pair recurred in the same column at rows fifteen and sixteen, though not in the original order.

The first two columns began with the (6/14) paired. This pair recurred in precisely the same manner at row sixteen in the same columns. This pair again recurred in the first column at rows eighteen and nineteen.

One can also observe the (10/31) occur at rows three and four of the fourth column, and then recur at rows seven and eight in the same column. Note that this is also a standard pair.

Likewise one can observe the (6/17) occur in column one at rows eight and nine. This pair recurred at rows two and three in the third column.

Further, one can see the (6/7) first occur in columns one and two at row eight. This pair then recurred back-to-back at rows sixteen and seventeen in column three.

Further, one can observe the (18/32) first occur back-to-back in the third column at rows ten and eleven. This pair recurred in the fourth column at rows eighteen and nineteen.

Also, one can see the (15/28) first occur precisely at twenty spins of one another in columns three and four at row nine. This pair recurred in the fourth column when the (28) again occurred immediately after the (15) at rows nine and ten.

In the second column at rows eleven and twelve one can see the (20/35) occur back-to-back at rows six and seven. This pair recurred in the same column at rows nineteen and twenty.

At the third row in columns two and three one can see the (6/25) occur within twenty spins of one another. This pair recurred when these two numbers occurred back-to-back at rows sixteen and seventeen in the fourth column.

The (6/30) first occurred back-to-back in column one at rows sixteen and seventeen. This pair again recurred in the same order in the third column at rows seventeen and eighteen.

Further, one can see the (18/28) occur back-to-back in the third column at rows nine ant ten. This pair recurred when the (28) again occurred in the fourth column at row ten, occurring precisely twenty spins after the (18).

Then one can observe the (12/31) occur precisely within twenty spins of one another in columns two and three at row fifteen. This pair recurred in columns three and four at row four.

The (17/34) which is by the way a standard pair, occurred precisely within twenty spins of one another in columns one and two at row thirteen. When the (34) recurred in the second column at row fourteen, then this constituted a recurring pair.

Lastly with respect to recurring pairs, note that the (0/10) first occurred in the first and second columns at row seven. This pair recurred in the fourth column when these two numbers again appeared back-to-back at rows six and seven.

Standard Pairs

There were six standard pairs. The first occurred in column two at rows thirteen and fourteen when the (17/34) occurred. Next occurred was the (32/23) in the third column at rows eleven and twelve. Then occurred the (10/31) twice in close proximity in the fourth column at rows three and four, and then again at rows seven and eight. Next occurred the (18/36) in column four at rows nineteen and twenty. Lastly the (34/17) again occurred at precise twenty spin intervals of one another at row thirteen in columns one and two.

Formulae

One can observe multiple formulae. First the "Powers That Be" have decreed the universal truth that *(30 = 18 + 6 + 6)*. "The Gods" have further affirmed that *(20 – 2 = 18)*. In addition "The Gods" have affirmed that *(16 + 3 + 12 = 31)*. Next at a right angle they obtusely inform us that *(2 x 18 = 36)*. Then they blandly inform us that *(23 + 25 = 36 + 12)*. In a quadrangle they cleverly tell us that *(6 + 12 + 7 = 25)*. Then they matter-of-factly tell us that *(35 – 23 = 12)*. Lastly in a right angle they tell us that *(35 = 17 + 18)*. These axioms could not be disputed, even by Pythagoras.

Sandwiches

The Gods have also prepared two sandwiches. The preparation of the first was begun in column two at row nine and it continued through row thirteen. One can observe therein the sequence: (35/17/20/35/17). The preparation of the second sandwich began in column three at row eighteen and it was completed at row one in column four. One can observe the sequence: (30/2/2/30).

Kismet

There were two instances of Kismet, both of which were numbers of The Black Pentacle. At the seventh row of column one, the (10) occurred. Precisely sixty spins later, this number again occurred at the same row in column four. Also, at row seventeen, the (6) occurred in column three and then it again occurred precisely twenty spins later at the same row in column four.

FIGURE 29

				NON-OCCURS				
6*	14*	31	30*	1	1		19	
28*	23*	17*	24	4	2	3	20	2
24	25*	6*	10*	5	3	1	21	
16	3	12*	31*	9	4		22	1
OO	15	36*	24	11	5		23	3
12	26	8	0*	19	6	8	24	4
**10*	0*	13	**10*	21	7	2	25	3
6*	7*	16	31*	27	8	1	26	3
17*	35*	28*	15*	29	9		27	
2	17*	18*	28*		10	3	28	4
23	20*	32*	33		11		29	
22	35*	23*	12*		12	5	30	3
34*	17*	25*	36*		13	1	31	4
26	34*	36*	12*		14	3	32	2
28*	31*	12*	6*		15	2	33	1
6*	14	7*	25*		16	2	34	2
30*	18*	**6*	**6*		17	4	35	3
14*	26	30*	32*		18	3	36	4
6*	20*	2*	18*		0	2	OO	1
24	35*	2*	36*			MODE:	6	

**Kismet
*Supernatural Occurrence

RECURRING PAIRS: (17/35) (12/36) (6/28) (6/14) (10/31) (6/17) (6/7) (18/32)

(15/28) (20/35) (6/25) (18/28) (12/31) (17/34) (0/10)

(6/30)

SANDWICHES: (30/2/2/30) (35/17/20/35/17)

FORMULAE: (30 = 18 + 6 + 6) (20 - 2 = 18) (16 + 3 + 12 = 31)

(2 x 18 = 36) (23 + 25 = 36 + 12) (6 + 12 + 7 = 25)

(35 - 23 = 12) (35 = 17 + 18)

Figure 30

These numbers are offered to demonstrate the prevalence of recurring pairs. Recall that a recurring pair is two numbers which do not normally occur together. However, for a given interval which is known only to the "Powers-That-Be," they tend to occur together often. Here the two numbers which the Powers-That-Be have decreed should be paired most often are the (14) and the (36). Note that these two numbers are not a Standard Pair.

(Note that in order to emphasize the two numbers in question, the five numbers of The Black Pentacle are not shown in **bold.** Only the two numbers in question are so highlighted).

Recurring Pairs & Trios

The (14/36) first occurred at rows nineteen and twenty in column one. The pair then recurred at row twelve in columns two and three, at precise twenty spin intervals of one another. This pair then recurred in column three at rows eleven and twelve. The fourth pairing of these numbers was in the fourth column at rows ten and eleven. This last back-to-back pairing of the two also constituted a fifth coupling because the (14) at row eleven was precisely twenty spins after the (36) had previously occurred.

Also, note that the (14/36) were nearly paired a sixth time in column two when only two spins at rows thirteen and fourteen separated them. Lastly, it must be emphasized that this is the most prominent instance of recurring pairs which the author has observed.

Recurring pairs other than the above were eight. First there was the (23/25), which pair first occurred in columns two and three at the second row. These two numbers then recurred in the same two columns at row twenty, though not in the same order.

The next recurring pair was the (15/34). These two numbers first occurred back-to-back in column one at rows nine and ten. This pair then recurred in the same column at rows seventeen and eighteen.

The (8/00) occurred within perfect relation to one another, first at row five of columns two and three. This pair then recurred in precise relation to one another at row four of columns three and four. The fact that the (8) occurred back-to-back in the first pairing and then also the second pairing is all the more noteworthy.

In addition, the (4/23) occurred within twenty spins of one another at row two of columns one and two. This pair then recurred back-to-back at row twenty of column three and row one of the fourth column.

The (8/11) alternated positions at the nineteenth row of columns two through four, constituting another recurring pair.

The (25/33) were paired first at row thirteen of rows two and three. This pair recurred again in the precise same manner at row two of columns three and four.

The (36) of the previous recurring pair (14/36) was also paired with the (25), first directly opposite one another at row twenty in columns one and two. This pair (25/36) then recurred back-to-back in the second column at rows twelve and thirteen.

The last pair to recur was the (22/33), which two numbers occurred precisely in relation to one another at row sixteen in columns three and four. When the (33) occurred back-to-back with the (22) at rows sixteen and seventeen in column four, then this constituted a recurring pair.

Biases

Other noteworthy phenomena were the occurrence of four black, even numbers at the first row of all four columns, which constituted a color bias (black) and an even bias: (22/26/28/4). Note also that all of the numbers in the seventh row are numbers divisible by three, which constitutes a divisible bias, and also a column bias (third column): (3/9/24/6).

Note also that all of the numbers in the eighth row are even, which constitutes an even bias: (24/34/4/6).

A column bias and a board bias can further be observed in the nineteenth row. All of the numbers (14/11/8/11) are not only all in the second column. They are also located in a small section of the board because they are consecutive on the board.

Lastly, one can observe an extraordinary example of even bias in the fourth column at rows five through fourteen where there were ten consecutive occurrences of even numbers: (2/32/6/6/36/36/14/26/34/6).

Formulae

Several formulae can be seen. First "The Gods" reaffirm once again that $(25 + 9 = 34)$. Then they reaffirm that $(6 \times 6 = 36)$. Becoming more clever, they tell us that $(14 + 26 - 34 = 6)$. They become mischievous when they tell us that $((7 \times 8) - 8 = 24 + 24))$. Sarcastically they convey that $(24 = 34 - 4 - 6)$. Then they tell us that $((14 = (11 - 8) + 11))$. Haughtily they tell us that $(10 + 1 = 33 - 22)$. Lastly they become more witty when they inform us that $((10 \times 5) - 36 = 14))$. To these universal truths Pythagoras would likely concur.

Kismet

Incidences of Kismet were two. The first can be seen at row ten of columns one and two where the (34) occurred precisely within twenty spins of one another. The second incidence can be seen at row nineteen where the (11) occurred in the second column. This number again occurred precisely forty spins later in column four. The fact that the number which separated the two occurrences of the (11) was the (8) in the third column is all the more remarkable because the (8/11) is a standard pair.

Standard Pairs

Other standard pairs to be observed here are the (10/31) in column one at rows fifteen and sixteen, and the (6/36) in the fourth column at rows eight and nine.

Unusual Phenomena

A most rare and interesting phenomena is the occurrence of two sets of consecutive repeats. These can be seen first in the third column at rows four through seven where the sequence was: (8/8/24/24). Then one can observe a second consecutive repeat in the fourth column at rows seven through ten: (6/6/36/36). Note also that all of the numbers involved are even, and that three of these are in the third column.

FIGURE 30

24-Feb				NON-OCCURS				
22	26	28	4*	18	1	3	19	
4*	23*	25*	33*	19	2	2	20	2
16	35	7*	24	21	3	1	21	
12	1	8*	OO*	30	4	3	22	3
25	OO*	8*	2		5	1	23	2
17	25*	24*	32		6	3	24	4
3	9*	24*	6*		7	1	25	5
24*	34*	4*	6*		8	3	26	3
15*	20	10*	36*		9	1	27	2
**34*	**34*	5*	36*		10	3	28	1
12	27	36*	14*		11	3	29	2
29	36*	14*	26*		12	2	30	
0	25*	33*	34*		13	1	31	1
22	20	11	6*		14	4	32	1
31	14	10	17		15	2	33	4
10	1	33*	22*		16	1	34	5
15*	26	2	33*		17	2	35	1
34*	13	29	27		18		36	5
14*	**11*	8*	**11*		0	1	OO	2
36*	25*	23*	1				MODE:	

**Kismet
*Superna tural Occurrence

**RECURRING
PAIRS:**   (23/25) (15/34) (14/36) (8/00) (4/23)(8/11) (25/33) (25/36) (22/33)

FORMULAE: (25 + 9 = 34) (6 x 6 = 36) ((14 + 26) - 34 = 6))

((7 x 8) - 8 = 24 + 24)) (24 = 34 - 4 - 6)

((14 = (11 - 8) + 11)) (10 + 1 = 33 - 22)

((10 x 5) - 36 = 14))

Figure 31

These numbers are offered to demonstrate the prevalence of a standard pair over a given interval. In other words, the "Powers That Be" have decreed that two numbers should be regularly paired over this interval. Refer to Figure 40. The pair (13/33) is listed therein. Note that the numbers of The Black Pentacle are not highlighted here. Only the two numbers of this Standard Pair (13/33) are shown in **bold**. Also note that this is a departure from the usual display of sixty numbers. Eighty numbers are provided here in order to demonstrate the prevalence of the pair in question.

Biases

Note that the incidence of these two numbers (13) and (33) are ten, or 12.5% of the total of eighty numbers. This is indicative of a number bias in favor of these two numbers. Note also that the mode is (33), which is one-half of this pair.

Other indicators that the wheel was biased in favor of the two numbers in question are first, that of the two incidences of Kismet, the mode, (33) at row four of columns one and four constitutes one of these incidences. The only other incidence of Kismet is the occurrence of the (32) at row ten in columns two and four.

Also, note that of the only two numbers to repeat, the (33) was one of these, both of which were in the fourth column at rows four and five, and then again at rows seventeen and eighteen. The other was the (32), also in the fourth column, at rows ten and eleven.

With respect to the (13), it was obviously a hot number in column three, occurring three times in eight spins at rows one, five and eight, or 37.5% of the time. The (33) was also fairly "hot" in the fourth column, occurring four times in fifteen spins, or 26.6% of the time within that range.

Other noteworthy phenomena are first the obvious consecutive bias at the top of column four at rows one through three where the sequence was: (15/16/17). This phenomenon is repeated in the same column at rows twelve through fourteen where the sequence was: (4/2/6). These numbers which constitute a consecutive even bias, are consecutive even integers, though not in the usual order.

A pronounced even bias can be observed in the second column at rows three through ten where the sequence was: (8/4/32/28/6/20/22/32). An even bias can further be seen in column four at rows six through fourteen. The sequence in this range was: (20/22/12/16/32/32/4/2/6). Three additional even biases can be seen at rows ten, fourteen and twenty, in which the sequences were, respectively, (16/32/10/32), (18/34/28/6), and (32/6/10/24). One odd bias can be seen at row fifteen where the sequence is: (33/23/17/29).

Lastly, observant readers will already have detected that this set of eighty observances shows a marked digit or number bias. None of these eighty numbers ends in (1). Put another way, none of the numbers (1/11/21/31) occurred. These were apparently looked on with much disfavor by "The Gods."

Recurring Pairs & Trios

Note that of the eleven pairs which recurred in these eighty numbers, three of the recurring pairs included the (33): (33/33) at rows four and five and then again at rows seventeen and eighteen in column four, (33/25) at row eleven in columns one and two, and then again in columns three and four at row four, and (33/23) first at row fifteen in columns one and two, and then again back-to-back at rows sixteen and seventeen in column four. Further, in the one sandwich which is prevalent, it included the (13), twice: (13/25/0/25/13). In addition, one of the formulae which can be observed computes to 33: *(16 + 17 = 33).*

In addition to those referenced above, other pairs which recurred were the (25/27) first occurring back-to-back at rows five and six in row one. This pair then recurred at row two in columns two and three.

Also, the (16/32) first occurred at row ten in columns one and two. This pair then recurred back-to-back at rows nine and ten in column four.

Further, the (10/19) occurred first back-to-back at rows two and three in column one. This pair then recurred precisely within twenty spins of one another at row twelve in columns one and two.

In addition, the (18/34) first occurred back-to-back at rows thirteen and fourteen in column one. A second appearance of the (34) in column two at row fourteen caused this pair to recur.

Further, the (6/28) first occurred back-to-back in column two at rows six and seven. This pair then recurred at precise twenty spin intervals of one another in columns three and four at row fourteen.

Also, the (3/30) first occurred back-to-back in column two at rows sixteen and seventeen. This pair then recurred with a second appearance of the (30) in column three at row seventeen.

In addition, the (5/36) first occurred at row one in columns one and two. This pair then recurred back-to-back in the third column at rows twelve and thirteen.

Also with respect to recurring pairs, the (15/16) first occurred back-to-back in the first column at rows nine and ten. This pair then recurred at rows one and two in the fourth column.

Lastly with respect to recurring pairs, the (4/32) first occurred back-to-back in column two at rows four and five. This pair then recurred in column four at rows eleven and twelve.

Standard Pairs

With respect to standard pairs, the first can be observed in the first column at rows sixteen and seventeen where the (24) and (22) occurred back-to-back. Then the (16) and the (32) occurred in column four at rows nine and ten.

Sandwiches

To reiterate, the only sandwich which "The Gods" prepared can be seen at the top of column three in rows one through five: (13/25/0/25/13).

Formulae

Six formulae can be observed. "The Gods" have again reaffirmed in column two at rows seventeen through nineteen that *(3 + 5 = 8)*; in column four at rows two through four that *(16 + 17 = 33)*; also in column four at rows twelve through fourteen that *(4 + 2 = 6)*; in column four again at rows fourteen through sixteen that *(6 = 29 − 23)*; at row fourteen in columns two through four that *(34 − 28 = 6)*; and lastly in column two at rows three through five that *(8 x 4 = 32)*. Disciples of Pythagoras might be compelled to concede these universal truths.

The System Is The Key

FIGURE 31

Jan 24

				NON-OCCURS
36*	5*	**13***	15*	1
19*	27*	25*	16*	11
10*	8*	0*	17*	21
**33	4*	25*	**33*	31
27*	32*	**13***	33	35
25*	28*	30	20	
16	6*	29	22	
23	20	**13**	12	
15*	22	4	16*	
16*	**32	10	**32*	
33*	25*	OO	32*	
19*	10*	5*	4*	
34*	7	36*	2*	
18*	34*	28*	6*	
33*	23*	17	29*	
24	30*	14	23*	
22	3*	30*	**33*	
9	5*	2	**33**	
26	8*	17	34	
32	6	10	24	

Number	Count		Number	Count
1	1		**19**	2
2	2		**20**	2
3	1		**21**	
4	3		**22**	3
5	3		**23**	3
6	3		**24**	2
7	1		**25**	4
8	2		**26**	1
9	1		**27**	2
10	4		**28**	2
11			**29**	2
12	1		**30**	3
13	3		**31**	
14	1		**32**	5
15	2		**33**	7
16	4		**34**	3
17	3		**35**	
18	1		**36**	2
0	1		**OO**	1
			MODE:	33

** Kismet
* Supernatural Occurrence

RECURRING PAIRS: (33/33) (25/27) (25/33) (16/32) (10/19) (18/34) (6/28)

(23/33) (3/30) (5/36) (15/16) (4/32)

SANDWICH: (13/25/0/25/13)

FORMULAE: $(3 + 5 = 8)$ $(16 + 17 = 33)$ $(4 + 2 = 6)$ $(6 = 29 - 23)$

$(34 - 28 = 6)$ $(8 \times 4 = 32)$

Figure 32

These numbers are offered to demonstrate how the wheel can be biased in favor of one number, or in other words, how a pronounced number bias can manifest itself. In these eighty observances one can see a marked bias in favor of the (6). Accordingly, in order to highlight this phenomenon the numbers of The Black Pentacle are not highlighted. Only the occurrences of the (6) are shown in **bold**.

Biases

The wheel favored the (6) seven times or 8.7% of the time during the eighty occurrences. This number bias is not unusual. What is unusual is the pattern of the bias. Such bias is quite pronounced during a certain interval and it is obviously what caused this number to be the mode.

Two occurrences of the (6) were isolated in column two at row eight, and again in column three at row four. All of the other occurrences of the (6) were confined to the last three rows of column three and also to the last row of columns two through four. As such, these five occurrences exhibit a distinctive, obvious pattern. This contiguous pattern is something which the author has never observed before or since, and as such it is nothing short of astounding. The author accordingly declares this pattern as proof conclusive of the influence of "The Supernatural" in the game of roulette.

Further, these clustered sixes have formed what the author has only observed twice: the repetition of a trio, that is, a set of three identical numbers repeating in the same order: (6/6/6) and (6/6/6). The trio at row twenty of columns two through four is one of the most striking examples of Kismet the author has ever observed. This is not the only instance however, in which he has observed the same number occur and then recur at precise forty and then sixty spin intervals. Another example of this phenomenon can be seen in Figure 37, at wheel two. Note also that this occurrence of three sixes back-to-back in column three is one of The Terrible Trios listed in Figure 40.

Further, this astounding run of three sixes back-to-back at the end of the third column is part of a quite amazing run of even bias. Beginning at row sixteen in column three, all of the numbers continuing to row seven of column four were even numbers: (2/14/6/6/6/14/12/12/32/26/30/28).

Inasmuch as this set of eighty observances contains four columns, one can observe quite a pronounced bias in many of the rows because each row contains four numbers. At row two one can see that all of the four numbers therein show an even bias: (28/14/8/12). This even bias can also be seen at rows four and twenty, where the respective sequence at each row was: (36/18/6/32) and (22/6/6/6).

Conversely, one can see a marked odd bias at rows fourteen and fifteen, where the respective sequences were: (5/1/15/23) and (13/31/15/7).

Further, at row seven one can see three biases. In addition to the fact that this row shows a number bias in favor of the (28), one can also see a pronounced color bias (black) and also a high bias. All of these four numbers are above (18).

At row eleven, one can see an unusual example of wheel bias. All of the four numbers therein occurred in one small section of the wheel: (3/36/3/13).

Lastly, the most perceptive reader will have observed what by now should have been quite obvious: that four numbers repeated in this sample of eighty observances. Each of these repeating numbers, (6/12/15/18) are in the third column of the board and are divisible by three. This indicates a pronounced column bias and a divisible or multiple bias.

Sandwiches

The reader will also note that the three consecutive sixes are part of the only sandwich one can see in this set of observances. This can be observed beginning at row seventeen in column three and continuing to row one in column four. The sequence there is: (14/6/6/6/14). If one desires to stretch the point, note that this sandwich is enclosed by two numbers which both end in (2): (2/14/6/6/6/14/12).

Recurring Pairs & Trios

The recurring pairs here are six. First there is the (28/31) which first occurred at a precise twenty spin interval of one another at row twelve in columns one and two. This pair then recurred in the same manner at row seven in columns two and three. This pair then recurred a second time with the reappearance of the (28) at row seven in column four.

The (28/30) occurred back-to-back in column two at rows twelve and thirteen. This pair then recurred back-to-back in column four, though not in the same order, at rows six and seven.

In addition, the (14/24) occurred within twenty spins of one another at row seventeen in columns three and four. With the reappearance of the (14) immediately after the (24) at row eighteen in column four, this pair recurred.

Another pair which recurred was the (6/25) which first occurred back-to-back at rows nineteen and twenty in column two. With the reappearance of the (6) again at row nineteen in column three, this pair then recurred.

An additional recurring pair, (6/18) can be seen when the (18) first occurred at row eight in column one. Its mate, the (6) occurred twenty spins later in column two at the same row. Then in column two the (18) occurred again at row four. In perfect symmetry with the original coupling, the (6) occurred again twenty spins later in column three at row four. This second coupling constitutes a recurring pair.

The last pair to recur was the (6/14) which occurred in column three at rows seventeen and eighteen. This pair then recurred upon the appearance of a (14) in column four at row eighteen. Note that this second pairing is distinct from the coupling of these two numbers in the aforementioned sandwich. As such, it constitutes an additional recurrence of this pair.

Standard Pairs

Standard pairs which prevailed here are, first the (18) and the (36) at precise twenty spin intervals of one another at row four of columns one and two. These were immediately followed in both columns at row five by the (10) and the (31). Six spins later the last standard pair was followed in both columns at row eleven by the (3) and the (36). Then at row fifteen in columns one and two the (13) and the (31) occurred. Then in columns two and three one can see the (6) and the (36) occur precisely within twenty spins of one another at row eight. Three spins later at row eleven one can again see the (3) and the (36) occur in the same two columns. At row nine in columns three and four one can see the (23) and the (32) occur precisely within twenty spins of one another.

Formulae

Six formulae can be observed in which "The Gods" have reaffirmed that numbers always add precisely. It will be observed in the second column at rows thirteen through fifteen that *(30 + 1 = 31)*; in the same column at rows fourteen through sixteen that *(1 + 31 = 32)*; in the third column at rows thirteen through fifteen that *(0 = 15 – 15)*, and in column one at rows two through four that *(28 + 8 = 36)*. "The Gods'" power at making computations can truly be observed at row eleven where one can observe their decree that ((3 + 36) / 3 = 13)). Lastly, "The Gods" have revealed the complexity of their logic in the last formula which they have decreed. Beginning at row eleven in column three and continuing through row seventeen, they have decreed that: *((3 + 34 + 0 –15) – 15) x 2 = 14))*. These are universal truths all, from which truths Pythagoras could not dissent.

FIGURE 32

		Dec. 23		NON-OCCURS				
10	33	30	14*	0	1	2	19	3
28*	14	8	12	11	2	1	20	
8*	18	3*	12	16	3	3	21	1
36*	18*	6*	32	20	4	1	22	1
31	10	9*	26	29	5	2	23	2
OO	17	35	30*		6	7	24	2
**28	**28	31*	**28*		7	1	25	2
18	6	36	5		8	2	26	1
13	21	23*	32*		9	1	27	1
1	35	OO	4		10	2	28	5
**3*	36*	**3*	13*		11		29	
31*	28*	34*	19		12	2	30	3
34	30*	OO*	13		13	5	31	4
5	1*	15*	23		14	4	32	3
13	31*	15*	7		15	2	33	1
25	32*	2*	19		16		34	2
19	17	14*	24*		17	2	35	3
35	24	6*	14*		18	3	36	3
27	25*	6*	13		0		OO	3
22	**6*	**6*	**6*			MODE:	6	

**Kismet
*Supernatural
Occurrence

RECURRING PAIRS: (28/31) (28/30) (14/24) (6/14) (6/18) (6/25)

RECURRING TRIOS: (6/6/6) (6/6/6)

FORMULAE: (30 + 1 = 31) (1 + 31 = 32)   ((3 + 36) / 3 = 13))

(0 = 15 - 15)   (28 + 8 = 36)

((3 + 34 + 0 - 15) - 15) x 2 = 14))

SANDWICH: (14/6/6/6/14)

195

Figure 33

These numbers are provided in order to demonstrate a most unusual phenomenon: a triple bias which can be seen on the wheel and also on the board. This is also another form of number bias. However, in this instance the bias is in favor of four numbers. Further, it is quite unusual for a small group of numbers which have a common attribute to be so favored. In this set of eighty observances however, one can detect a pronounced bias in favor of the third black numbers. That is, these four black numbers in the third column of the board prevail often here: (6/15/24/33). Accordingly, because the purpose here is to emphasize the prevalence of the four numbers in question, the numbers of The Black Pentacle are not highlighted.

Refer to the effigy of a standard U. S. roulette wheel provided. One can observe thereon that these four numbers are grouped in two distinct clusters in different sections of the wheel, and also in one column of the board. Further note also that each group of numbers is separated by one red number on the wheel, and by two red numbers on the board. The symmetry of this game is therefore manifested. For these reasons the numbers in question have demonstrated three biases: (1) wheel, (2) number and (3) board.

Biases

The third black occurred 21.2% of the time in this set of eighty occurrences. This means that these four numbers occurred approximately twice as often as they should have. Inasmuch as they are only four numbers of the total possibilities of thirty-eight, they should have occurred only 10.5% of the time. Note also that the mode is (33).

The first column is that in which this third black bias is most apparent. Note that nine of the numbers in this column are our four numbers. That is, 45% of the first column is third black. If one considers only the first seventeen rows of column one, then this bias is commensurately more pronounced. The third black occurred within this range 52.9% of the time. The range where the third black is also quite apparent is in the third column, where four of the twenty occurrences, or 20% were of this attribute. It is also noteworthy that of the four numbers in question, only the (15) occurred in the fourth column. The (15) was therefore a hot number within this range, occurring three times in sixteen spins, or 18.7% of the time.

Other noteworthy phenomena are that in the second column one can see quite a pronounced low bias. Beginning at row ten and extending through row eighteen, all of these numbers are low (below (18)): (2/10/7/16/9/3/4/8).

Recurring Pairs & Trios

There were seven recurring pairs. The first of these was the occurrence of the (20/30) at the top of both columns three and four. With the occurrence of the (20) again at row two of the fourth column, this constituted a recurring pair.

The next pair to recur was the (32/33). This pair first occurred within a twenty spin interval of one another at row three of columns one and two. This pair then recurred back-to-back in the third column at rows eleven and twelve. With the appearance of another (33) at row thirteen in column three, this pair then recurred a second time.

Further, the (9/12) first occurred back-to-back in the fourth column at rows six and seven. This pair then recurred within twenty spins of one another at row nineteen of columns three and four.

Next the (9/28) first occurred within a twenty spin interval of one another at row seven in columns three and four. This pair then repeated the same pattern and recurred within twenty spins of one another at row nineteen in columns two and three.

Further, the (3/33) first occurred back-to-back in column one at rows seven and eight. When the (3) again appeared at row eight in column two, this caused the pair to recur.

Also, the (10/33) first occurred within a twenty spin interval of one another at row eleven in columns two and three. This pair then recurred at row thirteen in columns three and four.

The last pair to recur was the (20/29) which first occurred back-to-back at rows one and two in column three. Upon the reappearance of the (20) at row two in column four, this caused the pair to recur.

There was one occurrence of a recurring trio. The (9/11/14) first occurred back-to-back in column three at rows eighteen through twenty. Remarkably this trio recurred back-to-back in column four at rows seven through nine, though reversed. Further remarkably this trio recurred a second time upon the appearance of a (14) in column four at row twenty opposite the aforementioned (11) in column three at row twenty.

Formulae

Four formulae materialized. Here "The Gods" again confirmed the universal truth that $(16 = 0 + 9 + 3 + 4)$. In addition, they reiterated the fact that $(18 + 12 = 30)$. Must they remind us that $(25 = 15 + 10)$? Lastly they restate that $(18 - 15 + 11 = 14)$. Pythagoras himself could not dissent from these axioms.

FIGURE 33

	17-Dec			NON-OCCURS				
15	OO*	20*	30*	17	**1**	2	**19**	2
6	4	29*	20*	21	**2**	1	**20**	3
33*	32*	22	**15**	31	**3**	3	**21**	
1	25	18*	27	35	**4**	2	**22**	1
6	13	12*	27	36	**5**	2	**23**	1
OO*	32	30*	12*		**6**	4	**24**	2
3*	26	28*	9*		**7**	4	**25**	4
33*	3*	23	11*		**8**	1	**26**	2
11	25	**24**	14*		**9**	3	**27**	2
6	2	7	13		**10**	2	**28**	2
24	10	**33***	25*		**11**	3	**29**	1
34	7	32*	**15***		**12**	4	**30**	2
1	16*	**33***	10*		**13**	2	**31**	
12	0*	**6**	19		**14**	3	**32**	3
33	9*	5	20		**15**	5	**33**	6
19	3*	18	7		**16**	1	**34**	1
33	4*	25	26		**17**		**35**	
5	8	14	**15**		**18**	3	**36**	
7	28*	9*	12*		**0**	1	**OO**	2
18	**15**	11*	14*			**MODE:**	33	

*Supernatural Occurrence

RECURRING PAIRS: (20/30) (33/32) (9/12) (9/28) (3/33) (20/29)

RECURRING TRIO: (9/11/14)

FORMULAE: $(16 = 0 + 9 + 3 + 4)$ $(18 + 12 = 30)$ $(25 = 15 + 10)$

$(16 - 0 - 9 - 3 = 4)$ $(18 - 15 + 11 = 14)$

Figure 34

This was a special set of observances, in that the numbers on two adjacent wheels were simultaneously observed. As such, this set of sixty occurrences should be considered with those in Figure 35. The numbers which occurred simultaneously on both wheels were: (18), (22), (1), a recurrence of (1), and (10). They are marked with a "+."

These numbers should be conclusive proof of the influence of the "Supernatural" on the numbers in this game. The "Powers That Be" are indeed strong when they can make numbers occur simultaneously on two wheels with relative frequency. These formidable powers are even more greatly manifest when they can cause two numbers on separate wheels to occur back-to-back simultaneously. These are the (22) and the (1). Note also that one number, (1), experienced virtual simultaneous recurrence on the two wheels within a short time frame. All of these five simultaneous occurrences are detailed below.

Note also that each of these Figures 34 and 35 contain different amounts of numbers. The reason for this is of course that the "action" on one wheel was greater than that on the other. This in turn caused more numbers to be observed in Figure 35 than are provided here. Further, note that only the numbers of The Black Pentacle are marked in **bold**.

Simultaneous Occurrences

At row seventeen in column one the (18) occurred. Simultaneously it occurred on the wheel adjacent. At the top of the second column the (22) and (1) occurred back-to-back in rows one and two. Quite extraordinarily the same two numbers occurred back-to-back simultaneously on the wheel adjacent. The (1) then recurred at row ten in column two. Simultaneous with this occurrence the (1) occurred on the wheel adjacent. Lastly, the (10) occurred at row six in column three. This number simultaneously occurred on the adjacent wheel.

Biases

Many of the rows in these eighty numbers demonstrate some form of bias. The first row shows a marked black bias. All of the numbers in this row are black: (8/22/29/20). Conversely, the second row shows a red bias. All of the numbers in this row are red: (19/1/14). At rows five, twelve and sixteen one can also observe even bias. The sequences in these rows are (32/20/2/22), (2/16/20/26) and (34/6/32) respectively.

A marked red bias can be seen at rows nine through eleven. The respective sequences in these rows are (30/3/9/5), (5/1/16/30) and (7/34/14/21). Note that three of the numbers in this last string signify a pronounced divisible bias, in that the (7), (14) and (21) are divisible by (7).

One can further see not only a pronounced high bias but also a top dozen bias at row fifteen where the sequence is (30/29/36/30).

There is also bias in the columns, which began with an unusual divisible bias in column one at rows seven through ten. All of the consecutive numbers in these rows are divisible by (5): (15/35/30/5).

At rows nine, ten, eleven and thirteen in column two, one can see an unusual example of a double bias. The numbers in this range are biased in favor of red numbers in the first column: (1/34/16/25).

An even bias can be seen again in the third column at rows three through eight where the sequence is: (30/2/2/10/14/6). Omitting the (9) at row nine, the even bias continued for eleven occurrences. That is, ten of these eleven numbers from row three through row thirteen, or 90.9%, were even: (30/2/2/10/14/6/16/14/20/18).

Recurring Pairs & Trios

There were eleven instances of recurring pairs. First there was the (4/4) which occurred at a precise twenty spin interval of one another in columns one and two at row eighteen. Upon the occurrence of a (4) in column two at row seventeen, immediately preceding the aforementioned (4), this pair then recurred.

Then the (29/30) appeared in the same manner in columns one and two directly opposite one another at row fifteen. This pair then recurred with appearance of this duo back-to-back at row twenty in column two and at row one of column three.

Further, the (19/30) first occurred back-to-back at rows nineteen and twenty in column two. With the reappearance of the (19) at row twenty in column three, this pair then recurred.

Also, the (19/35) behaved in a most unusual manner when these two numbers occurred directly opposite one another in column two and three at row nineteen. This pair then recurred with the reappearance of the (19) at row twenty in column three. Quite extraordinarily, this pair then recurred again when the (35) reappeared at row twenty in the fourth column.

Next the (6/14) first occurred back-to-back in column three at rows seven and eight. With the reappearance of the (14) at row eight in the fourth column, this pair then recurred.

Further, one can see a (14/31) which occurred at a precise twenty spin interval of one another in columns three and four at row seven. Upon the appearance of a (14) in column four at row eight, immediately following the aforementioned (31), this pair then recurred.

Then the (2/10) first occurred directly opposite one another in columns two and three at row six. When the (2) then reappeared before the (10) at rows five and six in column three, this pair then recurred.

Further, the (5/30) first occurred back-to-back at rows nine and ten in column one. This pair then recurred when they reappeared at the same two rows in reverse order in column four.

Then the (28/35) first occurred directly opposite one another at row nineteen in columns three and four. When the (35) reappeared at row twenty in column four, this pair then recurred.

Further, one can see in column two at rows five and six the (2/20) occur back-to-back. When the (2) again occurred in column three at row five, opposite the (20), this pair then recurred.

Lastly with respect to recurring pairs, we have an example of one which is also a standard pair. The (4/18) occurred first back-to-back in column one at rows seventeen and eighteen. With the reappearance of the (4) in column two at row seventeen, this standard pair then recurred. Note that this is one of the standard pairs listed in Figure 40.

The only trio which recurred has produced a phenomenon which again proves the capacity of the numbers in this game to astound. In column one at rows thirteen through fifteen, one can see that the (17), (8) and (30) occurred back-to-back. Then in column four these three numbers recurred back-to-back in precisely the same order. This phenomenon might best be labeled Triple Kismet. Note also that each trio is followed by a large, red even number.

Standard Pairs

In addition to the standard pair referenced above, there is the (13/31) in column four at rows six and seven.

Kismet

The above double occurrence of the (17), (8) and (30) at precise sixty spin intervals are merely three examples of Kismet. One can also see in the first and second columns at row eight the occurrence of the (35) at precise twenty spin intervals. There is also the (25) which occurred at row fourteen in column two and then recurred precisely twenty spins later. This is part of the sandwich described below.

The Final two examples of Kismet are highly unusual but they reaffirm the power of "The Supernatural" to influence numbers. Here two small, black numbers, the (4) and the (11) repeated themselves at the eighteenth row in columns one through four at precise twenty spin intervals. The power of the Supernatural to create symmetry, which is one of the unique attributes of this game, is again made manifest.

Sandwiches

Further, the only sandwich to occur should also astound the reader. The two occurrences of (25) directly opposite one another in columns two and three at row fourteen were sandwiched between two occurrences of an (8) at the same row in columns one and four. The sequence of this Kismet Sandwich was therefore (8/25/25/8).

Formulae

The formulae which materialized have once again revealed the mischievous nature of the "Powers-That-Be." First, they have reaffirmed in columns two, three and four at row four that *(25 + 2 = 27)*. Then we are reassured at row five in columns two through four that *(20 + 2 = 22)*. It is further confirmed by "The Gods" in column one at rows ten through twelve that *(5 = 7 – 2)*. Also in the same column we are shown at rows eight through ten that *(35 = 30 + 5)*. At rows seven through nine in column two we are confronted with the fact that *(32 = 35 – 3)*. In column three at rows four through seven we are informed once again by the "Powers-That-Be" that *(2 + 2 + 10 = 14)*. Then at rows nine through twelve in column four they tell us that *((30 = (21 + 26) – 17))*. "The Gods" then become quite mischievous when they cleverly state in column one at rows eleven through fourteen that *(7 + 2) = (17 – 8)*. Pythagoras would have to submit to their dictates.

FIGURE 34

	Dec. 17		(left)	NON-OCCURS				
8	22+	29*	20	12	**1**	2	**19**	4
19	1+	0	14	23	**2**	4	**20**	4
34	20	30	**17**	24	**3**	1	**21**	1
4	25*	2*	27*		**4**	4	**22**	2
32	20*	2*	22*		**5**	3	**23**	
OO	2*	**10+***	13		**6**	2	**24**	
15	32*	14*	**31**		**7**	1	**25**	3
**35*	**35*	**6***	14*		**8**	3	**26**	1
30*	3*	9	5*		**9**	1	**27**	2
5*	1+	16	30*		**10**	1	**28**	1
7*	34	14	21*		**11**	2	**29**	2
2*	16	20	**26***		**12**		**30**	6
**17*	OO	18	**17*		**13**	1	**31**	1
**8*	**25*	**25*	**8*		**14**	4	**32**	3
**30*	29*	36	**30*		**15**	1	**33**	1
34	**6**	0	32		**16**	2	**34**	3
18*+	4*	19	5		**17**	3	**35**	4
**4*	**4*	**11	**11		**18**	2	**36**	1
27	19*	35*	28		**0**	2	**OO**	2
33	30*	19*	35*			**MODE:**	30	

**Kismet
*Supernatural Occurrence
 + Signifies simultaneous occurrence on the opposite wheel

**RECURRING
PAIRS:** (4/4) (29/30) (19/30) (19/35) (6/14) (2/10) (5/30)

(28/35) (4/18) (14/31) (2/20)

**RECURRING
TRIO:** (8/17/30)

SANDWICH: (8/25/25/8)

FORMULAE: (25 + 2 = 27) (20 + 2 = 22) (5 = 7 - 2)

((7 + 2) = (17 - 8)) (2 + 2 + 10 = 14)

(32 = 35 - 3) (35 = 30 + 5)

((30 = (21 + 26) - 17))

Figure 35

This was a special set of observances, in that the numbers on two adjacent wheels were simultaneously observed. As such, this set of occurrences should be considered with those in Figure 34. The numbers which occurred simultaneously on both wheels were: (18), (22), (1), a recurrence of (1), and (10). They are marked with a "**+**."

These numbers should be conclusive proof of the influence of the "Supernatural" on the numbers in this game. The "Powers That Be" are indeed strong when they can make numbers occur simultaneously on two wheels with relative frequency. These formidable powers are even more greatly manifest when they can cause two numbers on separate wheels to occur back-to-back simultaneously. These are the (22) and the (1). Note also that one number, (1), experienced virtual simultaneous recurrence on the two wheels within a short time frame. All of these five simultaneous occurrences are detailed below.

Note also that each of these Figures 34 and 35 contain different amounts of numbers. The reason for this is of course that the "action" on one wheel was greater than that on the other. This in turn caused more numbers to be observed here than were provided in the preceding Figure.

Note also that here one can see the author's usual practice of highlighting the numbers of The Black Pentacle in **bold**. However, in a slight departure from this norm the author was compelled to also highlight a most unusual phenomenon of the occurrence of consecutive numbers which show quite a pronounced consecutive bias. These numbers from (28) to (32) are also shown in **bold** in order to again demonstrate the power of "The Supernatural" to influence numbers. They are further detailed below. Note that in column two at rows fourteen and fifteen, and again in column three from rows fourteen through seventeen, these numbers are shown in **bold** and also in ***italics***.

Simultaneous Occurrences

At row three in column two the (18) occurred. Simultaneously it occurred on the wheel adjacent. In the same column the (22) and (1) occurred back-to-back at rows seven and eight. Quite extraordinarily the same two numbers occurred back-to-back simultaneously on the wheel adjacent. The (1) then recurred at row thirteen in column two. Simultaneous with this occurrence the (1) occurred on the wheel adjacent. Lastly the (10) occurred, coincidentally, at row ten in column three. This number simultaneously occurred on the adjacent wheel.

Biases

One phenomenon which will be emphasized here, but which should be obvious is that of these one hundred twenty occurrences, three numbers failed to occur: (7), (14) and (15). In view of the large number of occurrences, this constitutes a pronounced number bias against these numbers. "The Gods" had apparently decreed that this was not the day for these three numbers to occur in one hundred twenty occurrences.

Hot numbers which materialized were, first the (11) which occurred three times in four spins in the first column from rows two through five, or 75% of the time. The (12) was also hot in column one occurring three times in seven spins from rows fourteen through twenty. Further, the (29) was fairly hot also, occurring three times in fourteen spins from rows one through fourteen, or 21.4% of the time within this range in column two.

Further, one can observe a most pronounced wheel bias in column three from rows four through seven. These four numbers (17), (22), (5) and (34) are in one small section of the wheel and are contiguous.

In addition, the (32) was "red" hot in the third and fourth columns from row sixteen in column three to row one in column four, occurring within that range three times in six spins, or 50% of the time. Then it was the turn of the (27) to become "red" hot in column four when it likewise occurred three times in five spins from row five to row nine, or 60% of the time within this range.

Next it was the turn of the (30) to radiate heat, occurring three times in fifteen spins in column five from rows five through nineteen, or 20% of the time.

A number of other biases can be seen also. In column six from rows six through eight, these three numbers (31), (18) and (19) revealed a wheel bias, in that these numbers are adjacent to one another on the wheel. In addition, the ninth row in columns two through four indicated that the wheel was biased at precise intervals in favor of the

(29), (25) and the (27) which are situated in one small section of the wheel.

A situation similar to that described above materialized at row twelve in columns four through six where all three numbers in this row, (8), (5) and (2) revealed a board bias. Each of these numbers are confined to one small section of the board. It is even more remarkable that the numbers are in perfect descending order.

Further, the fact that each of the numbers at row sixteen are even is quite remarkable, indicating a bias in favor of even numbers at precise intervals: (24/32/16/6/4).

The next bias observed here should astound the reader as much as it did the author. Note that all of the numbers in row thirteen show a bias for numbers confined to a very limited section of the wheel: (00/1/10/36/27/10). With only one exception they are contiguous.

The final bias should further astound the reader. In a part of the chart which extends from column two to column three one can observe the consecutive numbers twenty-eight to thirty-two, first at rows fourteen and fifteen in column two. The phenomenon extends to rows fourteen through seventeen in column three. One can therefore see all of the numbers twenty-eight through thirty-two clustered within one contained segment of the chart. These are highlighted in *italics* and in **bold.**

Recurring Pairs & Trios

A secondary purpose of these charted numbers is to further demonstrate the propensity of pairs to recur. Note that these occurrences contain thirty-four recurring pairs. In all of the charts which the author prepared in this book, this is the highest percentage which the author observed of the occurrence of recurring pairs relative to the total number of occurrences. The ratio of recurring pairs to total occurrences is therefore 34:120 or 28%.

The first of the pairs to recur here was the (16/28) which numbers first appeared back-to-back in column one at rows eleven and twelve. This pair then recurred in column two at rows nineteen and twenty.

Then the (12/29) appeared back-to-back at row twenty in column one and row one of column two respectively. When the (29) reappeared at row fourteen in column two directly opposite the aforementioned (12), this pair then recurred.

The next pair to recur was the (2/29) which first appeared back-to-back at rows one and two in column two. This pair recurred when they reappeared in columns five and six at row fifteen precisely twenty spins from one another.

Then the (10/11) occurred directly opposite one another at row four in columns one and two. This pair then recurred in the same precise manner in columns two and three at row ten.

The (13/16) occurred in precisely the same manner as the preceding pair. These two numbers occurred directly opposite one another, that is, within twenty spins of one another at row four in columns five and six. This pair then recurred in precisely the same manner in the same two columns at row twenty.

The same can be said for the (27/30) which first appeared opposite one another in columns four and five at row five. This pair then recurred in the same manner in the same two columns at row nine.

The (00/32) occurred in the same manner, first appearing opposite one another at row sixteen in columns two and three. This pair then recurred opposite one another in columns four and five, at row one.

The (16/22) emulated the above four pairs, first occurring opposite one another in columns two and three at row five. This pair then repeated this pattern and recurred at row four in columns four and five, although in reverse order.

The (9/29) emulated the above five pairs, and then some, first occurring opposite one another at row one in columns two and three. This pair then recurred in this same manner at row two in columns five and six. In addition, this pair then recurred a second time when they appeared back-to-back at rows two and three in column six.

Further, the (31/34) first occurred opposite one another at row six in columns five and six. When the (34) appeared again at row five before the (31) in column six, this pair then recurred.

Then the (16/30) occurred back-to-back in column five at rows four and five, and also at rows nineteen and twenty. The second appearance constituted a recurring pair.

The (18/30) emulated the preceding pair in the same column, first occurring back-to-back at rows nine and ten, and then repeating at rows eighteen and nineteen. The second appearance constituted a recurring pair, though in reverse order.

Then the (32/35) occurred opposite one another at row seventeen in columns two and three. This pair then recurred when the (35) again occurred immediately after the (32) at rows seventeen and eighteen in column three.

In columns three and six the (10/20) occurred back-to-back at rows ten and eleven, and at rows thirteen and fourteen, respectively. The second appearance constituted a recurring pair.

The (20/33) first occurred back-to-back at rows eleven and twelve in column three. Upon the reappearance of the (33) at row eleven in column four, directly opposite the aforementioned (20), this constituted a recurring pair.

The (22/27) first occurred opposite one another at row five in columns three and four. When the (22) reappeared in column four, preceding the aforementioned (27), this pair then recurred.

The (16/23) occurred opposite one another in columns one and two at row twelve. Then this pair recurred back-to-back at rows five and six in column two.

The (00/24) emulated the preceding pair when these two numbers first occurred opposite one another in columns one and two at row sixteen. This pair then recurred back-to-back at row twenty in column four and at row one in column five.

Further, the (9/16) first occurred back-to-back at row twenty in column two and at row one of column three. Upon the reappearance of the (9) at row twenty in column three, directly opposite the aforementioned (16), then this constituted a recurring pair.

Then the (27/34) occurred opposite one another in columns four and five at row six. This pair then recurred back-to-back in column four at rows eight and nine.

The (27) then approximated its behavior in the preceding pair when it occurred back-to-back with the (35) in column two at rows seventeen and eighteen. When the (35) reappeared in column three at row eighteen, directly opposite the aforementioned (27), this pair then recurred.

Uniquely, the (11/34) occurred opposite one another in columns three, four and five at row seven, alternating between the numbers. Upon the reappearance of the (34) in column four at row eight, this constitutes a recurring pair.

Further, the (34/36) first occurred back-to-back in column three at rows seven and eight. Upon the reappearance of the (34) in column four at row eight, directly opposite the aforementioned (36), then this constitutes a recurring pair.

At opposite ends of the charted numbers one can see the (20/29) occurring opposite one another in columns one and two, at row nine. Many spins later this pair recurred when they reappeared back-to-back in column six at rows fourteen and fifteen.

Similarly, the (13/29) emulated the preceding pair when they first occurred opposite one another at row two in columns four and five. This pair then *recurred* when they reappeared back-to-back in column six at rows three and four.

Further, the (8/33) first occurred opposite one another in columns three and four at row twelve. This pair then recurred upon the reappearance of the (33) in column four at row eleven, preceding the aforementioned (8).

The (8/34) emulated the preceding pair when these two numbers first occurred opposite one another in columns four and five at row eight. Upon the reappearance of the (34) in column five at row seven, repeating itself, then this caused this pair to recur.

Also, the (17/22) first occurred back-to-back in the third column at the fourth and fifth rows. This pair recurred when the (22) reappeared in the fourth column at row four, directly opposite the aforementioned (17).

Then the (5/28) occurred directly opposite one another in columns one and two at row eleven, that is, precisely within twenty spins of one another. When the (28) reappeared in column five, constituting Kismet, with the (5) following at row twelve, this pair then recurred.

It was then the turn for the (2/11) to behave similarly as those preceding when these two numbers occurred precisely within twenty spins of one another in columns one and two at row two. This pair then reappeared together in column four at rows fourteen and fifteen when they occurred back-to-back. This second pairing constitutes a recurring pair.

In column two the (1/29) demonstrated "The Gods'" penchant for symmetry when they occurred back-to-back in column two at rows eight and nine. When these numbers repeated themselves in the same precise manner shortly thereafter at rows thirteen and fourteen, this pair then recurred.

It was then the turn of the (5/27) to occur precisely within twenty spins of one another, and then to recur in a pair. They did this in columns three and four at row six, and then in column five at rows twelve and thirteen.

Further, the (30/34) occurred back-to-back in column five at rows five and six. The reappearance of the (34) in column six at row five, directly opposite the aforementioned (30), constituted a recurring pair.

Lastly, the (4/29) emulated some of its cousins above when they occurred back-to-back in column five at rows two and three. This pair then recurred when the (29) reappeared in column six at row three, directly opposite the aforementioned (4). This pair then recurred a second time when they occurred again back-to-back in column six at rows fifteen and sixteen.

One trio recurred in a most unusual manner. The (9), (16) and the (24) occurred directly opposite one another at row twenty in columns two through four. These three numbers then recurred when the (16) and the (24) reappeared back-to-back in column four at rows sixteen and seventeen. With the reappearance of the (9) in column five at row seventeen, this trio then recurred. Note that these three numbers were contiguous in both the first occurrence and also in the first recurrence. Remarkably there was a second recurrence of this trio at row twenty in columns two through four.

Standard Pairs

Standard pairs which materialized here were, first the (10/31) which occurred back-to-back in column three at rows thirteen and fourteen. The (4/18) then occurred precisely within twenty spins of one another in columns one and two at row three.

The next standard pair to occur was the (16/32) in columns three and four at row sixteen, occurring precisely within twenty spins of one another.

Then the standard pair (27/30) occurred in the same manner as that preceding when these numbers occurred precisely within twenty spins of one another in columns four and five at row five. This pair then repeated its antics when it occurred again in the precise same manner at row nine in the same two columns.

Kismet

Incidences of Kismet were quite prolific. At row three in column one the (4) occurred. It recurred precisely eighty spins later at the same row in column five. At row six in column one the (23) occurred and then recurred precisely twenty spins later at the same row in column two. Then the (34) occurred at row seven in column three, recurring precisely forty spins later in column five at the same row. Next the (36) first occurred at row eight in column one. Its recurrence came precisely forty spins later at the same row in column three. Further, the (28) appeared in column one at row eleven. As did the aforementioned (4), it recurred precisely eighty spins later at the same row in column five. Astute observers can see the symmetry of these two black, even numbers in the first column. Then the (10), also a black, even number in the first column occurred at row thirteen in column three. Precisely sixty spins later it recurred at the same row in column six. Then the (2) occurred and then recurred at a precise twenty spin interval of one another at row fifteen in columns four and five, respectively. Lastly, the (16) emulated its cousins above when it occurred at row twenty in column two. Precisely sixty spins later it recurred at the same row in column five. It is remarkable that five of these incidences of Kismet were even and in the first column.

Formulae

With respect to formulae which prevailed in this set of one hundred twenty numbers, "The Powers-That-Be" again demonstrated their penchant for creating complexities. First they reiterated the fact that $(12 + 12 = 24)$. Reiteration of the fact that $(28 - 16 + 9 = 21)$ followed. Then they declared that $(17 + 22 - 5 = 34)$. They then mischievously informed us that $((13 + 20) - 22 + 27 - 27 = 11))$. Then they reasserted the fact that $(28 = 30 - 2)$. Their mischief is again apparent when they assert that

$((34 + 27 + 0) - 33 + 8 = 36))$. The "Powers-That-Be further display their antics when they assert that $((1 + 31) - 2 = (10 + 20))$. Need they also remind us that $(23 - 22 = 1)$, and that $(1 = 29 - 28)$?

"The Gods" then cleverly declare that $((27 + 3) / 2) - 6 + 9 = 18))$.

They ease up a bit when they inform us that *(36 x 1 = 36)*. However, they revert to their mischief in the final two formulae which they convey: *((18 + 30 – 16) – 23 = 9))*, and then that

((19– 11) + 10 + 0 = 18)). Pythagoras himself would be confounded but compliant with these truths.

FIGURE 35

		17-Dec				NON-OCCURS				
35	29*	9*	32*	OO*	23*	7	**1**	3	**19**	2
11*	2*	21*	13*	29*	9*	14	**2**	4	**20**	4
**4	18+	21	20*	**4	29*	15	**3**	2	**21**	3
11*	**10***	**17***	22*	16*	13*		**4**	3	**22**	3
11	16*	22*	27*	30*	34*		**5**	3	**23**	4
**23	**23*	5*	27*	34*	31*		**6**	1	**24**	3
25	22*+	**34*	11*	**34	18		**7**		**25**	3
**36*	1*+	**36*	34*	8*	19		**8**	2	**26**	1
20*	29*	25	27*	30*	13		**9**	4	**27**	5
19*	11*	**10*+**	0*	18*	1*		**10**	4	**28**	4
**28*	5*	20*	33*	**28*	31*		**11**	6	**29**	6
16*	23*	33*	8*	5*	2*		**12**	4	**30**	4
OO	1*+	**10	36*	27*	**10*		**13**	4	**31**	3
12*	*29**	*31**	11*	3*	20*		**14**		**32**	3
12*	*28**	*30**	**2*	**2*	29*		**15**		**33**	2
24*	OO*	*32**	16*	6*	4		**16**	6	**34**	6
21	35*	*32**	24*	9*	3		**17**	2	**35**	3
OO	27*	35*	12	18*	25		**18**	4	**36**	3
34	28*	**26**	**17**	30*	0		**0**	2	**OO**	4
12*	**16*	9*	24*	**16*	13*				**MODE:**	

**Kismet
*Supernatural Occurrence
+ Signifies simultaneous occurrence on the opposite wheel

RECURRING PAIRS: (16/28) (12/29) (2/29) (10/11) (13/16) (27/30) (31/34) (16/30) (18/30)

(32/35) (10/20) (20/33) (22/27) (16/23) (00/24) (00/32) (9/16) (27/34)

(27/35) (16/22) (11/34) (34/36) (9/29) (20/29) (13/29) (8/33) (8/34)

(17/22) (5/28) (2/11) (1/29) (5/27) (30/34) (4/29)

RECURRING TRIO: (9/16/24)

FORMULAE: $(12 + 12 = 24)$ $((28 - 16) + 9 = 21))$ $((17 + 22) - 5 = 34))$

$((13 + 20) - 22 + 27 - 27 = 11))$ $((34 + 27 + 0) - 33 + 8 = 36))$

$(28 = 30 - 2)$ $((27 + 3) / 2) - 6 + 9 = 18))$ $(36 \times 1 = 36)$

$((18 + 30 - 16) - 23 = 9))$ $((19 - 11) + 10 + 0 = 18))$

$((1 + 31) - 2 = 10 + 20))$ $(23 = 22 + 1)$ $(1 = 29 - 28)$

Figure 36

These numbers are provided in order to demonstrate at least one instance in which all of the thirty-eight possibilities on the wheel can occur within a certain timeframe. That is, the contention of the author above under The System Approach/Primary Considerations For Workable Systems, that all numbers will materialize on any wheel eventually over a given interval, is hereby proven. Note in the corresponding chart that there were no "Non-Occurs."

Biases

Noteworthy phenomena to be observed here are first the biases in some of the rows. Note that all of the numbers in row five are even: (30/8/20/34). Note also that each of the three numbers in columns one, two and three at row fourteen reveal a wheel bias. These numbers are confined to a small section thereon: (36/13/3). Further, one can also observe a marked odd bias at row sixteen where all of the numbers in each of the six columns are odd: (9/15/27/25/7/21).

Lastly concerning the biases to be observed in the rows, at row eight one can see two pronounced biases therein. Note that all of the numbers in this row are even: (22/22/12/22/30/32). Further, what is most remarkable is the fact that five of the numbers therein, four of which are consecutive from row one through row four, end in (2). This is a pronounced digit bias.

Other biases which can be seen are a pronounced color bias in column one at rows nine through fourteen. Each of the six numbers in this string are red: (30/32/19/36/12/36). Conversely, each of the seven numbers in column three from rows one through seven are black: (35/8/8/2/20/33/8). The same pattern, or bias, can be seen in column four from rows ten through sixteen. All of the numbers in this range show a marked bias towards red numbers: (32/27/18/23/14/25/25). To a slightly lesser extent this color bias can also be seen in column six from rows eight through twelve. All of the five numbers in this string are red: (32/16/21/12/32).

Lastly with respect to biases which can be seen here, one can observe a pronounced even bias in column six from rows eight through seventeen. With two exceptions, all of the numbers in this string of ten numbers, or 80%, are even: (32/16/12/32/4/26/6/2). Further, one can see a marked consecutive bias in column five at rows one through three. All of these numbers, (6/4/5) are consecutive, though not in the usual order.

Recurring Pairs & Trios

The pairs which began first recurred with the (7/11) which initially occurred back-to-back at rows fourteen through sixteen in column five. Then these two numbers occurred precisely within twenty spins of one another at row eighteen in columns five and six, occurring directly opposite one another.

The (18/23) behaved similarly as the pair preceding when they first occurred precisely within twenty spins of one another at row ten in columns two and three. They then recurred as a pair when they occurred back-to-back in column four at rows twelve and thirteen.

Next, the (22/26) behaved quite remarkably back-to-back in column one at rows seven and eight. What is remarkable is that they duplicated this feat in the same manner precisely sixty spins later at the same rows in column four. This unusual phenomenon of this pair recurring might best be labeled Double Kismet. The (22/26) occurred back-to-back at a precise sixty spin interval of one another at rows seven and eight. The influence of the "Supernatural" in roulette is thereby strongly reaffirmed.

The (11/23) behaved similarly with those preceding when they occurred at precise twenty spin intervals of one another in columns one and two at row nineteen. They then duplicated this feat when they occurred in the same manner at row nine in columns four and five becoming a recurring pair.

Further, the (16/23) occurred back-to-back in column five at rows nine and ten. Upon the reappearance of the (16) in column six at row nine directly opposite the aforementioned (23), this pair then recurred.

Next it was the turn of the (35/36) to recur as a pair. They first occurred back-to-back at row twenty of column two and also at row one of column three. They then duplicated this feat when they recurred in the exact same manner in column four at the last two rows.

Then the (8/8) behaved similarly as its cousins above when they first occurred back-to-back in column three at rows two and three.

They then occurred precisely within twenty spins of one another in columns three and four at row two, becoming a recurring twin pair. Note also that Kismet has occurred in columns three and four at row two.

The (15/23) then emulated the aforementioned (8) when these two numbers first occurred back-to-back in column two at rows eighteen and nineteen. Upon the reappearance of the (15) in column three at row nineteen, directly opposite the aforementioned (23), this pair then recurred.

Next it was the turn of the (19/36) to recur as a pair when they first occurred back-to-back in column one at rows eleven and twelve. When they again occurred directly opposite one another at a precise twenty spin interval in columns four and five at row nineteen, this pair then recurred.

Then the (16/32) copied its cousins immediately preceding when these two numbers first occurred directly opposite one another at row ten in columns four and five. They then recurred as a pair when they occurred back-to-back in column six at rows eight and nine.

Next it was the turn of the (18/27) to emulate its cousins immediately preceding when they first occurred back-to-back in column four at rows eleven and twelve. They then recurred as a pair when the (18) reappeared in column five directly opposite the aforementioned (27) at row eleven.

Then it was the turn of the (8/35) to copy the antics of the preceding numbers when this pair first occurred directly opposite one another at a precise twenty spin interval in columns two and three at row two. This pair recurred upon the reappearance of the (35) immediately preceding the aforementioned (8) at row one in column three.

The (22/30) then occurred back-to-back in column one at rows eight and nine. These two numbers met up again in columns four and five at a precise twenty spin interval and directly opposite one another at row eight, becoming a recurring pair.

The (8/36) also first occurred directly opposite one another in columns three and four at row three. Upon the reappearance of the (8) which occurred immediately preceding the aforementioned (36), this pair then recurred. Note also that the (8) trebled itself in this quadrangle.

Next it was the turn of the (15/27) to emulate its cousins immediately preceding when they first occurred back-to-back in column two at rows fifteen and sixteen. Upon the reappearance of the (27) at row sixteen in column three, this pair then recurred.

The last of the pairs to recur was the (8/20) which first occurred back-to-back in column two at rows four and five. With the reappearance of another (20) in column three at row five, directly opposite the aforementioned (8), this pair then recurred.

Another excellent example of the capacity of the "Supernatural" to influence roulette numbers is the occurrence of the first recurring trio, (22/30/32) in column one at rows eight through ten. This trio quite remarkably recurred in an unusual manner at row eight in columns four through six, in the exact same sequence as that in which they initially occurred. Note also that each (22) is part of a remarkable phenomenon of Triple Kismet in columns one, two and four at row eight.

The only other trio to recur here was the (22/25/27) which occurred in columns two through four at row fifteen. This trio recurred upon the appearance of a (27) in column three at row sixteen, and a (25) in column four also at row sixteen, immediately following the aforementioned (25).

Kismet

The occurrences of Kismet other than those referenced above were, first the (32) in columns one and four which occurred at a precise sixty spin interval of one another at row ten. Next, there was the (18) in columns two and four which occurred at a precise forty spin interval of one another at row twelve.

Standard Pairs

The standard pairs which can be seen are first, one of the "Opposite Twins," the (13/31) which occurred in column three at rows twelve and thirteen. Further, the (0/00) occurred also in column five at rows twelve and thirteen. Then the (16/32) occurred in column six at rows eight and nine. This was immediately followed by the (12/21) at the next two rows in column six. These are the last of the standard pairs to occur here back-to-back.

The standard pairs which occurred opposite one another precisely twenty spins apart began with the (18/36) which occurred in columns one and two at row twelve. Then another of the "Opposite Twins," a (23/32) occurred in columns three and four at row ten. The (32) was part of the next standard pair to occur which, quite coincidentally occurred precisely twenty spins after the last. In columns four and five one can see the (16/32) at row ten.

Formulae

The formulae which can be seen here began with "The Gods" proclaiming again that *(18 = 0 + 0 + 7 + 11)*. Then they remind us that *(18 = 5 + 13)*. We are then reminded that *((32 – 27) + 18 = 23))*. Further, they reaffirm the fact that

((27 = (18 + 23) – 14)). "The Gods'" antics ease up a bit when they declare that

(4 = 5 – 1), and that *(2 x 7 = 14)*. Our Supernatural Hosts then revert to their antics when they cleverly remind us that *((31 – 15) – 0 + 2 = 11 + 7))*. With these universal truths, Pythagoras would be loathe to disagree.

FIGURE 36

		18-Nov				NON-OCCURS				
13	7	35*	**31**	**6**	33	NONE	**1**	4	**19**	3
9	35*	**8*	**8*	4*	23		**2**	3	**20**	2
28	24	8*	36	5*	27		**3**	1	**21**	2
OO	20	2	4	1*	24		**4**	4	**22**	4
30	8	20	0	34	OO		**5**	2	**23**	6
19	**17**	33	1	8	18		**6**	3	**24**	2
**26*	12	8	**26*	28	**31**		**7**	4	**25**	2
**22*	**22*	12	**22*	30*	32*		**8**	6	**26**	4
30*	35	0	11*	23*	16*		**9**	3	**27**	4
**32*	18*	23*	**32*	16*	21		**10**	1	**28**	2
19*	**6**	1	27*	18*	12		**11**	4	**29**	1
36*	**18*	13	**18*	0	32		**12**	5	**30**	3
12	5	**31**	23*	OO	4		**13**	3	**31**	4
36	13	3	14*	7*	**26**		**14**	2	**32**	4
29	27	22*	25*	11*	**6**		**15**	3	**33**	2
9	15	27*	25*	7*	21		**16**	2	**34**	2
23	**17**	1	**10**	**26**	2*		**17**	2	**35**	4
31*	15*	0*	2*	11*	7*		**18**	5	**36**	5
11*	23*	15*	36*	19*	14*		**0**	4	**OO**	3
34	36*	4	35*	12	9				**MODE:**	

**Kismet
*Supernatural Occurrence

RECURRING PAIRS: (7/11) (23/18) (26/22) (11/23) (16/23) (36/35) (8/8) (15/23) (19/36)

(16/32) (18/27) (8/35) (22/30) (8/36) (15/27) (8/20)

RECURRING TRIOS: (22/30/32)   (22/25/27)

FORMULAE: (18 = 0 + 0 + 7 + 11) (18 - 5 = 13) ((32 - 27) + 18 = 23))

((27 = (18 + 23) - 14)) (4 = 5 - 1) (2 x 7 = 14)

((31 - 15) - 0 + 2 = 11 + 7))

Figure 37

This final group of observances should not fail to astound the reader as much as it astounded the author. Here the "Powers-That-Be" have reaffirmed in the highest degree the influence which they have over numbers. After examining these occurrences, there should be no doubt that roulette numbers or any numbers in games where numbers are supposed to be random are not always so, and that they are continuously subjected to supernatural influences.

Note in Figure 37 that these observances are a distinct departure from all of the Figures preceding. Here the author recorded the numbers on two wheels simultaneously and then prepared one summary for both wheels. This is the primary reason why this set of numbers should not fail to astound. As one can see, and what the author will examine below, is that quite often pairs of numbers will recur on two wheels which are situated opposite one another. Note also in the corresponding Figure that eleven pairs of numbers occurred on both wheels. Another reason why these numbers should intrigue is that they demonstrate a marked bias in favor of the middle column of the board. Forty-five percent (45%) of the occurrences here are in that column. In all of the charts which the author prepared for this book, this is the most profound example of board bias which the author has observed.

Further, this is the most profound example of repeating numbers which the author has ever observed. To reiterate, it is not unusual for numbers to repeat (occur twice in a row). This phenomenon occurs quite often. However, the author has never before observed an instance where three numbers repeated *consecutively*. Note in the observances on wheel two in column three from rows five through ten, three numbers in a row repeated themselves: (32), (14) and (20). Note also that each of these numbers is in the middle column of the board.

This Figure is also a distinct departure from the author's usual practice of highlighting the numbers of The Black Pentacle in **bold.** In order to highlight the aforementioned bias in favor of the middle column numbers of the board, all of the numbers which occurred in this column only are shown in **bold.**

Biases

Observe in the aforementioned string of numbers (32), (14) and (20) that they are part of a prolonged bias in favor of middle column numbers. From row four through row fourteen in column three on wheel two, all of the numbers are in this column: (35/32/32/14/14/2 0/20/29/23/26/23). Observe also that fourteen of the twenty numbers in this column of the chart are in the middle column of the board: (35/32/32/14/14/20/20/29/23/26/23/23/35/11). Further, an astute observer will notice that there was a pronounced bias against the smallest numbers in the middle column. All of the aforementioned numbers form an unbroken string comprising the larger numbers in that column. In other words, there was an abject bias against the (2), (5) and the (8).

With respect to biases, one additional observation is in order here. Note that four numbers failed to occur on both wheels in one-hundred eighteen occurrences: (1), (16), (19) and (30). All of these numbers are red. Note also that three of these numbers are located in the first column of the board. One can only assume that "The Gods" had decreed that this was not the day for these numbers to occur. Or put another way, they looked with disfavor on half of the red numbers in the first column.

Recurring Pairs & Trios

The recurring pairs on Wheel One are first the (5/29) which occurred both ways: at a precise twenty spin interval, opposite one another in both columns at row seventeen, and also back-to-back in column two at rows six and seven.

Then the (5/28) occurred first back-to-back on Wheel One in column two at rows twelve and thirteen. Very soon after this pair recurred in the same column at rows sixteen and seventeen, though not in the same order. The phenomenon might best be labeled a recurring hot pair.

Then it was the turn of the (17/17) to recur as a pair when this number first occurred directly opposite itself at a precise twenty spin interval in both columns on Wheel One at row ten. This pair became another "recurring twin" upon the reappearance of itself back-to-back in column two at rows ten and eleven. Note also that the (17) occurring at a precise twenty spin interval of itself at row ten is Kismet.

On Wheel Two the recurring pairs began with the (29/33) which first occurred back-to-back in column one at rows nineteen and twenty. Then this pair recurred at a precise twenty spin interval, occurring directly opposite one another in columns three and four at row eleven.

Then the (20/29) first occurred on Wheel Two back-to-back in column three at rows ten and eleven. Upon the reappearance of a (29) directly opposite a (20) in columns three and four at row nine, this pair then recurred. Note also that each pair is distinct from the other.

Also on Wheel Two, the (11/20) first occurred at a precise twenty spin interval of one another in columns one and two at row five. This pair then recurred in the same manner in columns two and three at row ten, albeit in reverse order.

Further on Wheel Two, the (7/13) first occurred back-to-back in column one at rows seven and eight. This pair then duplicated this feat and recurred back-to-back in column three at rows two and three, although in reverse order.

Then the (7/35) first occurred at a precise twenty spin interval of one another on Wheel Two in columns one and two at row seven. This pair then recurred back-to-back in column three at rows three and four.

The last of the pairs to recur on Wheel Two alone was the (9/24) which first occurred back-to-back in column one at rows fifteen and sixteen. This pair then recurred at a precise twenty spin interval, directly opposite one another in columns three and four at row sixteen.

To reiterate, the fact that the following pairs recurred on both wheels, that is, occurred on one wheel and then recurred on the other, should astound any fan of numerology. The first of these was the (20/28) which occurred on Wheel One in columns one and two at row four at a precise twenty spin interval of one another. This pair then recurred on Wheel Two in column one, back-to-back at rows five and six.

Then the (24/29) first occurred on Wheel One at row six, directly opposite one another at a precise twenty spin interval. This pair then recurred on Wheel Two in column one, back-to-back, at rows twelve and thirteen.

Next, the (11/15) first occurred on Wheel One back-to-back in column one at rows two and three. On Wheel Two these two numbers recurred as a pair when they occurred at a precise twenty spin interval of one another and also opposite one another in columns two and three at row twenty.

Further, the (13/17) first occurred back-to-back on Wheel One in column one at rows ten and eleven. On Wheel Two this pair recurred in the precise manner in which it occurred on Wheel One, back-to-back in column one at rows one and two.

The (9/23) duplicated the feat of its cousins immediately preceding when this pair first occurred back-to-back in column one on Wheel One at rows fourteen and fifteen. On Wheel Two this pair recurred in the precise manner in which it occurred on Wheel One when it occurred back-to-back in column four at rows sixteen and seventeen.

A recurring pair materialized when the (24) occurred back-to-back in column one at rows five and six on Wheel One. This number was reincarnated as triplets when it recurred as a trio on Wheel Two at row sixteen in the first three columns at precise twenty and forty spin intervals after first occurring. Note also that this double recurrence of (24) at precise twenty and forty spin intervals after first occurring is a most remarkable example of Double Kismet.

The (11/32) first occurred on Wheel One at rows one and two in column one. This pair recurred and also spawned two identical sets of twins when it recurred on Wheel Two, twice, in precisely the same manner. These occurrences were at row five in columns two and three, and again at row six in columns three and four. Note that each set of numbers is distinct on Wheel Two. That is, these two additional sets are not a "Siamese Twin."

Next it was the turn of the (17/36) to emulate its cousins above when these two numbers first occurred back-to-back on Wheel One in column one at rows nine and ten. This pair recurred and in the process duplicated this feat when these two numbers again occurred back-to-back on Wheel Two at rows fourteen and fifteen in column two.

The (9/11) also showed a penchant for recurring precisely as a pair when these two numbers first occurred at a precise twenty spin interval of one another and also directly opposite one another on Wheel One at row fourteen. These two numbers duplicated this feat on Wheel Two when they recurred in the same precise manner, at a precise twenty spin interval and opposite one another at row twenty in columns three and four.

Next the (28/29) first occurred opposite one another at a twenty spin interval on Wheel One at row thirteen. On Wheel Two these two numbers then recurred as a pair when they occurred back-to-back in column four at rows eight and nine.

The last of the pairs to recur on both wheels was the (15/24) which first occurred back-to-back in column one at rows six through eight on Wheel One. When the (24) reappeared at row eight, this was the first recurrence. This pair then recurred again on Wheel Two when these two numbers appeared opposite one another at a precise twenty spin interval in columns one and two at row thirteen.

Standard Pairs

There were three standard pairs, all of which occurred on Wheel Two in column four at rows three and four, five and six, and lastly at rows twelve and thirteen. These were (22/24), (8/11) and (12/21), respectively. What is remarkable is that two of them occurred back-to-back. Further, all three pairs occurred in close proximity.

Sandwiches

There was only one sandwich which also materialized on Wheel Two. In column two at rows one through four, one can see a rather thick sandwich, albeit with rather thin "bread": (12/18/18/12).

Formulae

Here "The Gods" were on the case as usual as they have prepared formulae for our amazement/amusement. They have reaffirmed on Wheel One that *(17 – 13 = 4)*. Then on Wheel Two they remind us that *(14 + 21 = 35)*. Observe that all of these numbers are multiples of (7). They further remind us that *(33 = 21 + 12)*, and also that

(8 + 6 + 9 = 23). Observe that all of the numbers in the former set are multiples of (3), and that they are all in the third column. Lastly, "The Gods" again demonstrate their usual antics when they declare that *((20 + 29) – 23 = 26))*. Observe that all of these numbers are high, being above (18). Also observe that these four numbers are contiguous on the board. Pythagoras would again have to concede these universal truths.

FIGURE 37

21-Dec

WHEEL 1		WHEEL 2				NON-OCCURS
32*	20	17*	12*	22	6	1
11*	3+	**13*	18*	**13*	27	16
15*	31	28	18*	7*	24	19
28*	20*	9	12*	35*	22	30
24*	8	20*	11*	32*	8	
24*	29*	28*	25	32*	11*	
15*	5*	7*	35*	14*	11	
24*	11*	**13*	**13	14*	28*	
36*	4*	34	36+	20*	29*	
**17*	**17*	10	11*	20*	25	
13*	17*	5*	21	29*	33*	
4*	5	29*	13	23*	21	
29*	28*	24*	15*	26*	12*	
9*	11*	OO	36*	23	8*	
23+*	2	9*	17*	18	6*	
OO	28	**24*	**24*	**24*	9*	
29	5	36*	14	**23	**23*	
31	14	32+	21	0	5	BOARD
4		29*	**35	**35	5	MIDDLE
12		33*	15*	11*	9*	COLUMN
						TOTALS
6	13	6	6	14	8	53
						45%

					MODE:		
1	1		19				
2	2	1	20	5			
3	3	1	21	3			
4	4	3	22	2			
5	5	6	23	5			
6	6	2	24	8			
7	7	2	25	2			
8	8	3	26	1			
9	9	5	27	1			
10	10	1	28	6			
11	11	8	29	7			
12	12	4	30				
13	13	6	31	2			
14	14	4	32	4			
15	15	4	33	2			
16	16		34	1			
17	17	5	35	4			
18	18	3	36	4			
0	0	1	OO	2			

** Kismet

* Supernatural Occurrence

+signifies simultaneous occurrence of Standard Pair on both wheels

RECURRING PAIRS: Wheel 1: (5/29) (5/28) (13/17) (17/17) (9/24)

Wheel 1 & Wheel 2:   (20/28) (24/29) (11/15) (13/17) (9/23) (24/24)

(11/32) (17/36) (9/11) (28/29) (15/24)

Wheel 2:   (29/33) (20/29) (11/20) (7/13) (7/35)

SANDWICH: Wheel 2: (12/18/18/12)

FORMULAE: Wheel 1: (17 - 13 = 4) ((29 - 5) - 11 + 4 = 17))

Wheel 2: (14 + 21 = 35) (33 = 21 + 12) (8 + 6 + 9 = 23)

(5 = 29 - 24) ((12 + 8) - 6 + 9 = 23))

((20 + 29) - 23 = 26))

AFTERWORD

The audience therefore has the benefit of having reviewed the results of the 2,379 observations which the author documented in order to make his case. After having reviewed the above, the audience should thereby be conditioned to seek and also to discern the unusual phenomena which occur in roulette. The audience should further be convinced that numbers in games of chance are not always random, as they are purported to be. Aspiring players and regular practitioners of this game should also have come to understand that in playing this game, one is more creative than one had previously imagined. One is indeed only limited by his own imagination in devising systems to beat "The House." Further, in pursuing this game one should come to understand, as the author has, that a new system can always be found to make this game more interesting.

The audience should now be satisfied that the author has made his case that there is an element of the occult in roulette. The author has proven that the supernatural element which causes roulette numbers to behave in abnormal manner is always prevalent. The author has accordingly unified the occult with standard number theory. The standard theory of numbers, especially as it pertains to gaming in general, is hereby rendered obsolete.

With that accomplished, the author hereby offers guarantees and also suggests certain rules to game by:

A. Guarantees

The author offers herein two guarantees:

(1) That by following the guidelines herein, the player will become conditioned to seeking and therefore discerning number patterns; and

(2) That after having become conditioned to seek and to discern number patterns, the numbers in roulette will never fail to fascinate.

B. Cardinal Rules

There are certain "Cardinal Rules" which one might be well advised to follow for successful gaming. They are:

o   Always place an equal amount on each number;

o   Bet consistently, over as many spins as possible;

o   Never approach the game with a preconceived notion about which numbers one intends to bet. Only bet numbers which one has observed occurring that day;

o   Record the numbers which one observes in a chart with twenty rows and then examine the chart in order to detect patterns;

o   When utilizing a system such as those detailed in Figures 42 through 44,
     do not skip spins;

o   Always bet so that one can recover what has already been sacrificed;

o   Always allow one's self more than one chance to hit a number. Conversely, one might be well advised to *never* bet all of one's money at once;

o   Keep one's eyes on one's bets in order to ensure that the bets may not have been   moved;

o   Upon winning, recover the winning bet unless one wants to duplicate that wager;

o   Count one's winning chips.

C. How To Beat "The House"

Beating "The House" should be therefore as easy as 1- 2- 3. In light of the above, one should therefore only have to:

1. "clock" the wheel
2. bet accordingly
3. win

In a homage to the French who are generally acknowledged to have perfected the modern game of roulette, the author hereby admonishes players to: (1) *faites vos jeux*, (2) *bonne chance, et* (3) *laissez les bontemps roullez*!

FIGURE 38
VITAL STATISTICS

	RANKING	NUMBER	FREQUENCY	RELATIVE FREQUENCY	PROBABLE FREQUENCY
MODE	1	11	3.45%	82/2379	38/2379
	2	30	3.24%	77/2379	**
	3	22	3.03%	72/2379	**
	4	36	2.98%	71/2379	**
	5*	6	2.94%	70/2379	**
	5*	7	2.94%	70/2379	**
	6*	9	2.90%	69/2379	**
	6*	12	2.90%	69/2379	**
	6*	14	2.90%	69/2379	**
	7*	20	2.82%	67/2379	**
	7*	23	2.82%	67/2379	**
	8	27	2.77%	66/2379	**
	9	34	2.73%	65/2379	**
	10*	5	2.69%	64/2379	**
	10*	29	2.69%	64/2379	**
	11*	4	2.65%	63/2379	**
	11*	8	2.65%	63/2379	**
	11*	17	2.65%	63/2379	**
	11*	18	2.65%	63/2379	**
	11*	25	2.65%	63/2379	**
	12*	10	2.61%	62/2379	**
	12*	24	2.61%	62/2379	**
	12*	28	2.61%	62/2379	**
	13*	2	2.56%	61/2379	**
	13*	15	2.56%	61/2379	**
	14	OO	2.52%	60/2379	**
	15*	13	2.44%	58/2379	**
	15*	16	2.44%	58/2379	**
	15*	32	2.44%	58/2379	**
	15*	33	2.44%	58/2379	**
	16*	1	2.40%	57/2379	**
	16*	19	2.40%	57/2379	**
	17	35	2.35%	56/2379	**
	18*	26	2.19%	52/2379	**
	18*	0	2.19%	52/2379	**
	19	21	2.14%	51/2379	**
	20	31	2.06%	49/2379	**
	21	3	2.02%	48/2379	**
ALL NUMBERS:					2.63%

*Tie

FIGURE 38B
VITAL STATISTICS (continued)

	FREQUENCY	RELATIVE FREQUENCY	PROBABLE FREQUENCY
FIRST DOZEN (1 - 12):	778	34.32%	33.00%
SECOND DOZEN (13 - 24):	748	33.00%	33.00%
THIRD DOZEN (25 - 36):	741	32.69%	33.00%
FIRST COLUMN (1 - 34):	736	32.47%	33.00%
SECOND COLUMN (2 - 35):	766	33.79%	33.00%
THIRD COLUMN (3 - 36):	765	33.75%	33.00%
1 - 18 (LOW):	1150	50.73%	50.00%
19 - 36 (HIGH):	1117	49.27%	50.00%
RED:	1142	50.37%	50.00%
BLACK:	1125	49.63%	50.00%
EVEN:	1164	51.35%	50.00%
ODD:	1103	48.65%	50.00%
ALL ZEROS:	112	4.71%	5.26%
ZERO:	52	2.19%	2.63%
DOUBLE ZERO:	60	2.52%	2.63%
THE BLACK PENTACLE:	296	13.06%	13.16%

NOTE: Red and black numbers are only compared with one another. The computed frequencies accordingly do not include the zeros.

NOTE: Even and odd numbers are only compared with one another. The computed frequencies accordingly do not include the zeros.

NOTE: The numbers of The Black Pentacle are compared with all numbers including both zeros.

FIGURE 39

The Contiguous Black Pentacle			The Extreme Supernatural	
13	25	**17**	**23-Apr**	**16-May**
32	**16	**16	**16***	**16***
36	*10**	7	21	27
1	*31**	**17**	36	0
26	*17**	20	25	22
35	*26**	14	32	17
34	*6**	15	**18***	**18***
1	16	32	8	23
3	4	**31**	18	30
13	0	OO	27	5
6	0	3	13	20
5	**31**	25	OO	21
22	16	1	**5***	**5***
9	12	14	0	13
1	8	3	9	1
25	7	**10**	0	2
14	21	12	35	26
24	21	**10**	6	27
10	23	25	**3***	**3***
15	**26**	3	6	4
			25	21

**Kismet
*Supernatural Occurrence

Outside Bet Progression
Wageing Even Numbers
($1.00 chips)

Spin	Number	Bet	Won
1	14	5	10
2	6	10	20
3	6	20	40
4	18	40	80
5	24	80	160
6	26	160	320
7	12	320	640
8	20	640	1280
9	22	1280	**2560**

FIGURE 40

Standard Pairs

0/OO	8/11	13/31	18/36	26/29
3/36	10/31	16/19	22/24	27/30
4/18	13/33	16/32	23/32	
6/36	12/21	17/34	26/OO	

The Terrible Trios
Those numbers which the author has seen occur thrice in a row:

4	7	15	24	31
5	10	19	27	34
6	13	23	30	OO

Dice Rolls

	Sep. 28					Sep. 30		
4	7	6	7		6	7	**11**	9
5	9	4	9		5	7	7	5
4	9	8	9		6+	7	9	7
10	7	10	8		4	9	11	9
4+	9	11	9		4+	9	9	11
7	6	3	7		6+	7	9	5
6	5	5	9		8	6	5	7
9	4+	**8**	**8**		**11**	9	6+	7
9	5	9	6		10	6	9	11
8	9	7	7		6	9	8	9
9	10+	4	7		10	8	5	8
8+	**8**	**8**	**8**		3	9	4	4+
8	**8**	10	10		6	7	4	7
7	5	9	4+		9	9	7	6
6	5	7	4+		7	5	8	4+
7	8	5	9		9	6+	8	8
7	7	8	5		4+	3	8+	4
6	7	7	12		2	4	6+	7
3	6	5	2		6	12	12	7
3	3	12	9		6	7	11	7

+ indicates that the number was a "hard" number

FIGURE 41
NUMBER SEQUENCE
This chart facilitates the use of the "Radar Bet".

9	28	**0**	2	14
10	27	**OO**	1	13
27	OO	**1**	13	36
28	0	**2**	14	35
36	24	**3**	15	34
35	23	**4**	16	33
34	22	**5**	17	32
33	21	**6**	18	31
32	20	**7**	11	30
31	19	**8**	12	29
30	26	**9**	28	0
29	25	**10**	27	OO
20	7	**11**	30	26
19	8	**12**	29	25
OO	1	**13**	36	24
0	2	**14**	35	23
24	3	**15**	34	22
23	4	**16**	33	21
22	5	**17**	32	20
21	6	**18**	31	19
18	31	**19**	8	12
17	32	**20**	7	11
16	33	**21**	6	18
15	34	**22**	5	17
14	35	**23**	4	16
13	36	**24**	3	15
12	29	**25**	10	27
11	30	**26**	9	28
25	10	**27**	OO	1
26	9	**28**	0	2
8	12	**29**	25	10
7	11	**30**	26	9
6	18	**31**	19	8
5	17	**32**	20	7
4	16	**33**	21	6
3	15	**34**	22	5
2	14	**35**	23	4
1	13	**36**	24	3

FIGURE   42
Five Number/Sixteen Spin System
($1.00 chips)

	Spin	Bet	Cum. Bet	Poss. Win	Net Win	Cum. Num. Bet	Bet Type
	1	5	5	36	31	5	straight
	2	5	10	36	26	10	*
	3	5	15	36	21	15	*
	4	5	20	36	16	20	*
	5	5	25	36	11	25	*
	6	5	30	36	6	30	*
	7	5	35	36	1	35	*
raise	8	10	45	72	27	40	*
	9	10	55	72	17	45	*
	10	10	65	72	7	50	*
raise	11	15	80	108	28	55	*
	12	15	95	108	13	60	*
raise	13	20	115	144	29	65	*
	14	20	135	144	9	70	*
raise	15	25	160	180	20	75	*
raise	16	30	190	216	26	80	*

190
Total
Wager

FIGURE 43
Sample Five-Number System
($1.00 chips)
Wagering the numbers of *The Black Pentacle*
in Figure 29

Round	Spin	Number Hit	Bet	Cum. Bet	Poss. Win	Net Win	Total Net Win
1	1+	6	5	5	36	31	31
2	1		5	5	36		
	2		5	10	36		
	3		5	15	36		
	4		5	20	36		
	5		5	25	36		
	6+	10	5	30	36	6	37
3	1+	6	5	5	36		
4	1+	17	5	5	36		
5	1		5	5	36		
	2		5	10	36		
	3		5	15	36		
	4		5	20	36		
	5+	26	5	25	36	11	48
6	1		5	5	36		
	2+	6	5	10	36	26	74
7	1		5	5	36		
	2		5	10	36		
	3+	6	5	15	36	21	95
8	1		5	5	36		
	2		5	10	36		
	3		5	15	36		
	4		5	20	36		
	5		5	25	36		
	6		5	30	36		
	7+	26	5	35	36	1	96
9	1		5	5	36		
	2		5	10	36		
	3		5	15	36		
	4+	17	5	20	36	16	112
10	1		5	5	36		
	2		5	10	36		
	3+	17	5	15	36	21	133
11	1		5	5	36		
	2+	31	5	10	36	26	159
12	1		5	5	36		
	2		5	10	36		
	3+	26	5	15	36	21	180

+ signifies a "hit"

FIG. 43 (cont'd)
Sample Five-Number System
($1.00 chips)

Round	Spin	Number Hit	Bet	Cum. Bet	Poss. Win	Net Win	Total Net Winnings
13	1		5	5	36		
	2		5	10	36		
	3+	31	5	15	36	21	201
14	1+	17	5	5	36	31	232
15	1+	6	5	5	36	31	263
16	1		5	5	36		
	2		5	10	36		
	3		5	15	36		
	4		5	20	36		
	5		5	25	36		
	6		5	30	36		
	7		5	35	36		
	8		10	45	72		
	9		10	55	72		
	10		10	65	72		
	11		15	80	108		
	12		15	95	108		
	13		20	115	144		
	14+	6	20	135	144	9	272
17	1		5	5	36		
	2		5	10	36		
	3		5	15	36		
	4		5	20	36		
	5		5	25	36		
	6+	10	5	30	36	6	278
18	1+	31	5	5	36	31	309
19	1		5	5	36		
	2		5	10	36		
	3+	10	5	15	36	21	330
20	1+	31	5	5	36	31	361
21	1		5	5	36		
	2		5	10	36		
	3		5	15	36		
	4		5	20	36		
	5		5	25	36		
	6		5	30	36		
	7+	6	5	35	36	1	362
22	1		5	5	36		
	2+	6	5	10	36	26	388

+ signifies a "hit"

Total Winnings

FIGURE 44
Sample Five-Number System
(\$1.00 chips)
Wagering the numbers *divisible By '7'*
as detailed in Figure 11

Round	Spin	Number Hit	Bet	Cum. Bet	Poss. Win	Net Win	Total Net Win
1	1		5	5	36		
	2		5	10	36		
	3+	35	5	15	36	21	21
2	1		5	5	36		
	2		5	10	36		
	3		5	15	36		
	4		5	20	36		
	5+	28	5	25	36	11	32
3	1		5	5	36		
	2		5	10	36		
	3		5	15	36		
	4		5	20	36		
	5		5	25	36		
	6		5	30	36		
	7+	14	5	35	36	1	33
4	1		5	5	36		
	2		5	10	36		
	3		5	15	36		
	4		5	20	36		
	5		5	25	36		
	6+	14	5	30	36	6	39
5	1		5	5	36		
	2+	35	5	10	36	26	65
6	1+	7	5	5	36	31	96
7	1+	14	5	5	36	31	127
8	1		5	5	36		
	2		5	10	36		
	3		5	15	36		
	4		5	20	36		
	5		5	25	36		
	6		5	30	36		
	7		5	35	36		
	8		10	45	72		
	9		10	55	72		
	10		10	65	72		
	11		15	80	108		
	12		15	95	108		
	13		20	115	144		

+ signifies a "hit"

FIG. 44   (cont'd)
Sample Five-Number System
($1.00 chips)
Wagering the numbers divisible *by* '7'
as detailed in Figure 11

Round	Spin	Number Hit	Bet	Cum. Bet	Poss. Win	Net Win	Total Net Win
8	14		20	135	144		
	15+	**14**	5	160	180	20	**147**
9	1+	**28**	5	5	36	31	**178**
10	1		5	5	36		
	2		5	10	36		
	3+	**21**	5	15	36	21	**199**
11	1		5	5	36		
	2+	**7**	5	10	36	26	**225**
12	1		5	5	36		
	2		5	10	36		
	3		5	15	36		
	4		5	20	36		
	5+	**35**	5	25	36	11	**236**
13	1+	**14**	5	5	36	31	**267**
	1		5	5	36		
	2		5	10	36		
	3+	**28**	5	15	36	21	**288**
14	1		5	5	36		
	2		5	10	36		
	3+	**7**	5	15	36	21	**309**

Total
Winnings

+ signifies a "hit"

GLOSSARY

Basket - a three number bet consisting of the numbers 0-00-2 on which the payoff is 11:1. This wager is synonymous with a Street Bet (see Street Bet).

Bias - a numerical pattern which indicates that multiple occurrences have a common attribute, or a lack thereof, over a given interval
- color
- column
- consecutive
- digit
- divisible
- dozen
- even
- line
- multiple
- number
- odd

Black Pentacle - the numbers 6, 10, 17, 26 and 31 which have a special relationship and which are demonstrative of the supernatural influence in roulette

Board Section System - concentrating one's bets on a particular area of the gaming board on which one places a bet

Casino Chip - one which can be used at any table and at any game. The counterpart is the table chip which must be used at the table where it is purchased. (See Table Chip).

Clocking - observing the numbers on a roulette wheel over a certain interval in order to detect patterns among the numbers

Color Bias - multiple occurrences of numbers of like color.

Colored Nickel - a five dollar chip which can be used only at the roulette table where it was purchased. (See Nickel)

Colored Quarter - a twenty-five dollar chip which can be used only at the roulette table where it was purchased. (See Quarter)

Column - any one of three horizontal sets of numbers on a roulette board with twelve numbers each, from 1 – 34, 2 – 35 and 3 - 36. The odds of winning a bet of this type is 2:1.

Column Bet - betting one of the columns 1 – 34, 2 – 35 or 3 – 36, on which the payoff is 2:1. This is an outside bet. (See Outside Bet).

Column Bias - numbers occurring consecutively in the same column, or substantially so, within one of the three columns of the board.

Consecutive Bias - multiple occurrences of consecutive numbers, either in normal order or in any order which indicates a logical progression or regression. At least three numbers must have occurred in some logical order for this phenomenon to be observed.

Corner Bet - betting four contiguous numbers on the board. This is the only means to bet four numbers with one chip. The payoff is 8:1.

Digit Bias - numbers with a common last digit occurring frequently over a extended period. An example is 30/20/10/00.

Dirty Stack - a stack of table chips which contains more than one color of chips. This indicates that the dealer who sold the chips mistakenly mixed the colors.

Divisible Bias - numbers which are divisible by a certain number occurring often over an extended interval. An example is 14/7/35/21. All are divisible by 7. This is identical to Multiple Bias (See Multiple Bias).

Dozen - one of the three groups of twelve numbers when viewing the board vertically: 1 – 12, 13 – 24 and 25 – 36.

Dozen Bet - betting one of the dozens 1 – 12, 13 – 24 or 25 – 36, on which the payoff is 2:1. This is an outside bet. (See Outside Bet).

Dozen Bias - numbers occurring substantially within one of the three dozens of the board, over a prolonged interval

Drought - numbers with a certain attribute not occurring over an extended interval

En Prison - another term for the European practice of "Surrender", or the U. S. practice known as the "Reimbursement Rule" whereby the bettor surrenders half of his losing, even money bet on the red or the black when one of the green (0 or 00) occurs. (See Reimbursement Rule and Surrender).

Equation Search Puzzles - These are counterparts to the word search puzzles which are published in many periodicals in which readers are given a grid of letters. Readers are then invited to find words therein. The charts contained herein can be construed as Equation Search Puzzles in which the reader is given a grid of numbers and is invited to find pronounced mathematical equations. The presence of these mathematical equations demonstrate that the numbers which occur in roulette are influenced by supernatural forces.

Even Bias - a prolonged string of numbers which are divisible by 2

Hedging - diluting one's bet by spreading the bet over a greater amount of numbers than one otherwise would. This practice increases one's probability of winning but it also reduces one's payoff in direct proportion to the degree to which the bet is hedged.

High Bias - multiple occurrences which indicate that the wheel is biased in favor of numbers above 18. This is the counterpart to Low Bias.(See Low Bias).

Hit - winning a bet on a number. This precludes any bet on which the odds of winning are less than 5:1. The counterpart is the occurrence in which a number merely occurs without any money being wagered. (See Occurrence).

Hot Digit - a common attribute of any given amount of frequently occurring numbers

Hot Number - frequent occurrences of a number over an interval of any duration

House - the gaming establishment which one intends to beat

Inside Bet - betting a specific number or a specific group of numbers, on which the payoff is at least 5:1. These therefore preclude any bet on a color (1:1), high/low bets (1:1), even/odd bets (1:1), dozen bets (2:1), or column bets (2:1).

Kismet - a word which originated in the Middle East which means "fate" or "destiny." For the purpose of this book, the term means the recurrence of a number at intervals of twenty, or forty, etc., after it was initially observed. (See Rule Of Twenty).

Line Bet - betting six contiguous numbers on which the payoff is 5:1. There is one exception: The line containing the five numbers 0-00-1-2-3 pays 6:1 and is sometimes referred to as the "Top Line." (See Top Line).

Line Bias - a prolonged interval in which the numbers show a tendency to occur along any one of the twelve lines on the gaming board which divides numbers in groups of three

Low Bias - multiple occurrences which indicate that the wheel is biased towards numbers below 19. This is the counterpart to High Bias. (See High Bias).

Mode - the most common occurrence of a group of numbers. According to the standard rules of mathematics, there can only be one mode.

Multiple Bias - repetition of numbers which are a multiple of a certain number over an extended interval. An example is 4/8/12/16. All are multiples of 4. This is the counterpart to Divisible Bias. (See Divisible Bias).

Nickel/Red Nickel - a five dollar chip which is can be used at any gaming table. (See Colored Nickel).

Number Bias - the propensity of occurring numbers to favor any given number. When this phenomenon occurs over an interval of short duration, this means that the number in question is a Hot Number. (See Hot Number).

Numerology - a subset of occultism by which the meaning of numbers is interpreted. (See Occult/Occultism).

Occult/Occultism - the philosophy of hidden matters; attempting to uncover what has heretofore been hidden. This is an element of numerology (See Numerology).

Occurrence - any number which materializes on a wheel. If one has money on the number, then one has a Hit. See Hit).

Odd Bias - the propensity of numbers to lean towards those which are odd, i. e., not divisible by 2

Outside Bet - one on which the odds of winning are less than 5:1. These include any bet on a color (1:1), high/low (1:1), even/odd (1:1), dozen (2:1), and column (2:1). These therefore preclude straight bets (35:1), split bets (17:1), street bets (11:1),

corner bets (8:1), Top Line bets (6:1) and line bets (5:1).

Pythagoras - Greek mathematician, philosopher and an early advocate of numerology, from the 6th century, B. C.

Quarter/Green Quarter - a twenty-five dollar chip which can be used at any gaming table. (See Colored Quarter).

Radar Bet - centering one's bet around one number on the wheel and also betting the numbers on either side

Recurring Pair - two numbers occurring back-to-back at least twice, or within a precise interval of one another, though not necessarily in the same order. This pair occurs in such manner only for a limited period and is not normally observed in this game. The limited interval of their occurrence is what sets these apart from Standard Pairs. (See Standard Pair). This phenomenon can also occur for a trio of numbers. (See Recurring Trio).

Recurring Trio - three numbers occurring back-to-back at least twice, or within a precise interval of one another, though not necessarily in the same order. This phenomenon can also occur for a pair of numbers. (See Recurring Pair).

Reimbursement Rule - the U. S. counterpart to The Surrender Rule in European casinos, also known as *En Prison*, by which one is "reimbursed" one-half of one's losing, even-money bet on the red or the black when one of the green,(0) or (00) occurs. (See *En Prison* and Surrender).

Roullez - French (infinitive) word meaning "to roll"

Round - a designated number of spins which one allocates to hitting a number. The system which one uses determines the duration. Hitting the desired number signifies the end of the round. (See Hit).

Rule Of Twenty or **Rule Of Multiples Of Twenty** - the propensity of numbers to repeat themselves at precise intervals of twenty, or of forty, etc. (See Kismet).

Sandwich - a number surrounded by two other identical numbers, which are in turn surrounded by two other identical numbers. There are a myriad of variations, however. The guiding principle is symmetry. This is a pronounced instance of symmetry and is an example of a Supernatural Occurrence. (See Supernatural Occurrence).

Slat - The device which divides each number on the wheel. These vary in dimension depending on the manufacturer.

Split Bet - dividing a bet between two numbers. This is "hedging" in its least basic form.

Standard Pair - a pair of numbers which recurs commonly, either together or within precise intervals of one another. What sets these apart from Recurring Pairs is that they are often observed together in this game. (See Recurring Pair).

Straight Bet - betting one number, on which the payoff is 35:1. This is the only bet which is not hedged.

Street - any one of the twelve horizontal sets of numbers in the board with three numbers each, from 1 – 3, 4 – 6, 7 – 9, 10 – 12, 13 – 15, 16 – 18, 19 – 21, 22 – 24, 25 – 27, 28 – 30, 31 – 33, and 34 – 36. The odds of winning on a street is 11:1.

Supernatural - a power which cannot be seen but which causes phenomena which can be observed

Supernatural Occurrence - numbers behaving in a manner which is out of the ordinary, apparently caused by a power which cannot be seen, but which seems to influence numbers.

Surrender - the European counterpart to the Reimbursement Rule in U. S. casinos, by which one surrenders half of one's losing, even money bet on the red or on the black when one of the green (0 or 00) occurs. This is also called *En Prison* in Europe. (See *En Prison* and Reimbursement Rule).

Table Chip - one which must be used at the roulette table where purchased. The value can be what the player desires, according to the House rules. This chip has no value at any table other than where it was purchased. As such, this type of chip is unique to roulette. The counterpart is the casino chip which can be used at any table anywhere in the casino where chips are bet. (See Casino Chip).

Top Line – the five numbers at the "top" of the board, 0-00-1-2-3. (See Line Bet).

Wheel Section System - concentrating one's bets on a particular area of the wheel. The counterpart is the Board Section System.(See Board Section System).

BIBLIOGRAPHY

Allen, J. Edward, *The Basics Of Winning Roulette*, New York, NY, Cardoza Publishing, 1985

Cardoza, Avery, *How To Win At Gambling*, New York, NY, Cardoza Publishing

The Diagram Group, *The Book Of Gambling Games*, New York, NY, Main Street, 2004, c1996

Glazer, Andrew N. S., *Casino Gambling The Smart Way: How To Have More Fun And Win More Money*, Franklin Lakes, NJ, Career Press, c1999

Grochowski, John, *Winning Tips For Casino Games*, Lincolnwood, IL, Publications International, Ltd. c1995

Jensen, Marten, *Secrets Of Winning Roulette*, New York, NY, Cardoza Publishing, 1998

Patrick, John, *John Patrick's Roulette: A Pro's Guide To Managing Your Money and Beating The Wheel*, Seacaucus, NJ, Carol Publishing Group, 1998

John Patrick Productions, *The Casino Survival Kit* (video recording), Short Hills, NJ, 1990

Root, Wayne Allyn, *The King Of Vegas' Guide To Gambling*, New York, New York, The Penguin Group, 2004

Scoblete, Frank, *Spin Roulette Gold: Secrets Of Beating The Wheel*, Chicago, IL, Bonus Books, Inc., 1997

Scoblete, Frank, *Guerilla Gambling: How To Beat Casinos At Their Own Games*, Chicago, IL, Bonus Books, Inc., 1993

Thomason, **Walter** *The Experts' Guide To Casino Games: Expert Gamblers Offer Their_Winning Formulas*, Seacaucus, NJ, Carol Publishing Group, c1997

INDEX